Guide to the Chess Openings

Guide to the Chess Openings

Leonard Barden and Tim Harding

David McKay Company, Inc.
New York

GUIDE TO THE CHESS OPENINGS

Published in Great Britain as *The Batsford Guide to Chess Openings*

First American Edition, 1977

Library of Congress Catalog Card Number: 76-19118

ISBN: 0-679-13052-7

Printed in Great Britain

CONTENTS

SYMBOLS

+ Check

= Balanced position

! Good move

!! Excellent move

? Bad move

?? Losing move

!? Interesting move

?! Doubtful move

Ch Championship

corres Correspondence game

simul Simultaneous display

W or *B* at the side of each diagram indicates which side is to move.

In the text a number in brackets refers to the relevant diagram number.

PREFACE

This book is intended to be a guide and not an encyclopaedia. We have therefore not attempted to cover openings which can be advantageously avoided or which are hardly ever employed in match and tournament play. In addition, where reasonable, we have avoided duplicating material given in other of our books.

Leonard Barden's *A Guide to Chess Openings* was published in 1957 (by Routledge and Kegan Paul). Nearly two decades have passed, and many of the examples given in that book have been superseded by improvements in the master tournament arena, while fashion has brought some openings (e.g. the Pirc and Modern Benoni defences) into favour, at the expense of others which were popular in the fifties (like the Open Lopez and the Queen's Gambit Slav). This new book takes full account of these changes, but retains the most typical features of the earlier work—the explanatory material based on discussion of typical positions, and the illustrative games.

The choice of opening variations making up the opening repertoires for White and Black was made by the authors jointly. Leonard Barden also made numerous specific suggestions. Additional research and preparation of the book for publication was done by Tim Harding. We should also like to acknowledge the advice and help of our editors, Bob Wade and Kevin O'Connell, to whom all errors in spelling should be attributed! Les Blackstock helped with chapter nine, and various other people also made helpful suggestions. The proofs were read by Harry Zirngibl.

LWB
TDH
London, January 1976

1 INTRODUCTION: HOW TO STUDY THE OPENINGS

This book is written to help two categories of chess players. Primarily, it is written for the moderate player whose chess is confined to club, tournament, or games by correspondence and telephone, and who, with limited time for chess, finds great difficulty in keeping up with and assimilating the mass of information given in chess magazines. This type of player needs to find a repertoire of openings, in which the basic ideas are easily understandable, and the number of variations which have to be kept in mind is not too great.

The second category of player who should be able to gain considerably from this book is the improving player who wishes to do well in weekend tournaments, or to merit a higher board in his club or county team. A junior who is starting to play for his school team or who is competing in local or national tournaments should find the basic approach of value. Those who then wish to go deeper into any specific opening, having mastered the treatment in this volume, should find what they require in the monographs comprising the Batsford Contemporary Chess Openings series, together with a subscription to a magazine giving the latest games from international tournaments.

In this guide, we indicate how a player can satisfactorily confine himself to one or two defences against 1 P–K4 and 1 P–Q4. With White, there are various systems which are particularly dangerous when handled by a player whose style is suited to the particular opening. We have tried to show, for instance, how various lines on the white side of the popular King's Indian and Sicilian Defences can be formidable weapons for the combinative or positional player.

Aims of the Opening

The fundamental conflict in all openings is between the attempt by White to gain the advantage through utilizing the initiative conferred by the first move, and Black's corresponding endeavour to reach a clear equality, or to create a complicated situation in which both sides have attacking chances. In practice, this conflict often takes a set strategical form. White hopes to obtain one of the three diagrammed ideal pawn structures, the first arising

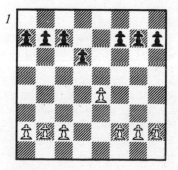

1

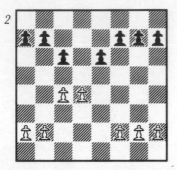

from KP and the second from QP openings; the third, a more emphasized form known as the Maroczy Bind, can arise from a number of different openings.

In each of these positions, White possesses a slight advantage in space, since his centre pawns are on the fourth rank whilst Black's are only on the third. We give some examples of these advantageous formations, showing how White naturally strengthens his position still further.

Kashdan-Reshevsky, match 1942: 1 P–K4 P–K4 2 N–KB3 N–QB3 3 B–N5 P–QR3 4 B–R4 P–Q3 5 P–B4 B–Q2 (Better is 5 . . . B–N5.) 6 N–B3 N–B3 7 P–Q4 P×P 8 N×P N×N 9 B×B+ Q×B 10 Q×N B–K2 11 0–0 0–0 12 P–QN3 KR–K1 13 B–N2 B–B1(4).

In what follows, we can see how White is able to utilize his extra space to build up a K-side attack, whereas Black finds only insufficient counterplay: 14 QR–Q1 R–K3 15 KR–K1 QR–K1 16 P–B3 K–R1 17 N–K2 Q–B1 18 Q–B2 N–Q2 19 N–Q4 R.K3–K2 20 Q–N3 P–KB3 21 N–B5 R–K3 22 P–KR4 P–QN4 23 P×P P×P 24 P–R5 Q–R3 25 P–R3 P–B4 26 R–Q5 N–K4 27 KR–Q1 N–B2 28 Q–R4 N–K4 29 P–B4 N–B2 30 P–R6 P–N3 31 B×P+ K–N1 32 N–N3 B×P 33 B–N2 B–N2 34 P–B5 B×B 35 P×R R×P 36 Q–N4 and White won with his material advantage.

Our next illustration shows how a devastating K-side attack can be built up from the typical space advantage resulting from 1 P–Q4 (compare diagram 2).

Szabo-Bisguier, Buenos Aires 1955: 1 P–Q4 P–Q4 2 P–QB4 P–QB3 3 N–KB3 N–B3 4 N–B3 P–K3 5 P–K3 QN–Q2 6 B–Q3 B–Q3 7 P–K4 P×KP 8 N×P N×N 9 B×N N–B3 (The correct freeing

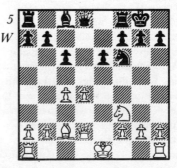

move is *9 . . . P–K4.*) 10 B–B2 B–N5+ 11 B–Q2 B×B+ 12 Q×B 0–0(*5*).

Szabo now continued energetically with 13 N–K5 Q–B2 14 0–0–0 and rapidly obtained a winning attack: 14 . . . P–B4 15 Q–K3 P–QN3 16 P×P P×P 17 P–KN4 R–N1 18 KR–N1 Q–N3 19 P–N3 R–N2 20 P–N5 N–K1 21 B×P+ K×B 22 Q–R3+ K–N1 23 R–N4 Black resigned: if 23 . . . P B3 24 P–N6.

In the next example, White exploits his advantage by positional means: his disinclination for K-side attack in this case is due to the strong defensive formation which Black inaugurated with the fianchetto of his KB.

Bogoljubow–Gilg, Bad Pyrmont 1949: 1 P–K4 P–QB4 2 N–KB3 P–Q3 3 P–Q4 N–KB3 4 B–N5+ B–Q2 5 B×B+ Q×B 6 N–B3 P×P 7 N×P P–KN3 8 0–0 B–N2 9 N–Q5! (A tactical finesse: if now *9 . . . N×KP* there comes *10 R–K1*.) 9 . . . 0–0 10 B–N5 N×N 11 P×N P–KR3 12 B–K3 N–R3 13 Q–Q2 K–R2 14 P–QB4(*6*).

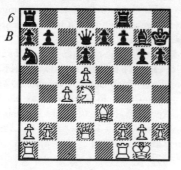

6
B

A typical middle game advantage resulting from the plus in space: White has a Q-side majority of pawns, and the black KP is backward on an open file. In the sequel, White is able to improve the placing of his pieces more easily than Black: 14 . . . N–B4 15 QR–Q1

P–R3 16 P–QN3 P–QN4 17 N–B6 N–K5 18 Q–B2 N–B3 19 P–KR3 KR–B1 20 B–Q4 Now White threatens to besiege the KP by doubling rooks on the K-file: Black avoids this, only to concede to his opponent the decisive advantage of two united passed pawns. 20 . . . P–K4 21 B–K3 N–N1 22 P–B4 P–B4 23 P×KP P×KP 24 B–B2 R–K1 25 KR–K1 QR–B1 26 P–B5 P–K5 27 N–R5 N–K2 28 P–B6 Q–Q1 and now White could have decided the game at once by 29 N–N7 Q–B2 30 P–Q6 Q×BP 31 Q×Q R×Q 32 P–Q7.

Black has two methods – one simple, one complicated – of nullifying the dangers of a space disadvantage. The simple method is to bring about a freeing advance of a centre pawn: in openings with 1 P–K4 P–K4, the freeing move is . . . P–Q4; in 1 P–Q4 P–Q4 openings, it is . . . P–K4. In openings with 1 P–QB4, it can be either move! Here are a few illustrations of Black 'liberation movements':

Scotch Game: 1 P–K4 P–K4 2 N–KB3 N–QB3 3 P–Q4 P×P 4 N×P N–B3 5 N–QB3 B–N5 6 N×N NP×N 7 B–Q3 P–Q4 8 P×P P×P.

Italian Game: 1 P–K4 P–K4 2 N–KB3 N–QB3 3 B–B4 B–B4 4 P–B3 N–B3 5 P–Q4 P×P 6 P×P B–N5+ 7 B–Q2 B×B+ 8 QN×B P–Q4.

Ruy Lopez: 1 P–K4 P–K4 2 N–KB3 N–QB3 3 B–N5 P–QR3 4 B–R4 N–B3 5 0–0 B–K2 6 R–K1 P–QN4 7 B–N3 P–Q3 8 P–B3 N–QR4 9 B–B2 P–B4 10 P–KR3 Q–B2 11 P–Q4 0–0 12 QN–Q2 BP×P 13 P×P B–N2 14 N–B1 P–Q4.

Queen's Gambit Declined: 1 P–Q4 P–Q4 2 P–QB4 P–K3 3 N–QB3 N–KB3 4 B–N5 QN–Q2 5 P–K3 P–B3 6 N–B3 B–K2 7 R–B1 0–0 8 B–Q3 P×P 9 B×P N–Q4 10 B×B Q×B 11 0–0 N×N 12 R×N P–K4.

Nimzo-Indian Defence: 1 P–Q4 N–KB3 2 P–QB4 P–K3 3 N–QB3 B–N5 4 P–K3 P–B4 5 B–Q3 0–0 6 N–B3 P–Q4 7 0–0 N–B3 8 P–QR3 B×N 9 P×B QP×P 10 B×P Q–B2 11 B–Q3 P–K4.

English: 1 P–QB4 P–QB4 2 N–QB3 N–QB3 3 P–KN3 P–KN3 4 B–N2 B–N2 5 P–K3 P–K3 6 KN–K2 KN–K2 7 0–0 0–0 8 P–Q4 P×P 9 N×P P–Q4 10 P×P N×P.

Of course, playing ... P–Q4 or ... P–K4 does not in itself guarantee equality; cramped positions must be freed slowly and (as in the Ruy Lopez example) the crucial advance must be prepared, and timed accurately. An example of a premature 'freeing move' comes from the Ponziani: after 1 P–K4 P–K4 2 N–KB3 N–QB3 3 P–B3 P–Q4!? 4 Q–R4!, with threats like 5 N×P, and with B–N5 or P–Q4 in reserve, Black must either surrender a pawn or return to the defensive.

The more complicated possibility for Black is to allow White to obtain a pawn centre of a pawn on Q4 plus another on QB4 and/or K4, in the expectation of being able to obtain play against the slight weakness on black squares which a fianchettoed KB can press against. White may have to put more pawns on white squares to guard his QBP and KP, thus increasing the scope of Black's KB and reducing that of his own. Black can then advance his centre pawns or bishops' pawns to demolish the white centre: the rationale behind modern counter-attacking 'defences' like the King's Indian, Modern Benoni and Pirc. In the following game, note how all Black's play is devoted to hammering away at these black-square weaknesses.

P a c h m a n - B r o n s t e i n ,

Moscow–Prague 1946: 1 P–Q4 N–KB3 2 P–QB4 P–Q3 3 N–QB3 P–K4 4 N–B3 QN–Q2 5 P–KN3 P–KN3 6 B–N2 B–N2 7 0–0 0–0 8 P–N3 R–K1 9 P–K4 P×P 10 N×P N–B4 11 R–K1 P–QR4 12 B–N2 P–R5 13 R–QB1 P–B3 14 B–QR1 P×P 15 P×P Q–N3 16 P–R3 N3–Q2 17 R–N1 N–B1 18 K–R2 P–R4 19 R–K2 P–R5 20 R–Q2 R×B 21 R×R B×N 22 R×B N×NP 23 R×P Q×P 24 R–R2 Q×P+ 25 K–R1 Q×N 26 R–R3 B×P 27 R×N B×B+ 28 K×B Q×P 29 R–Q4 Q–K3 30 R×P R–R1 31 Q–K2 P–R6+ White resigned.

A general classification of types of opening advantage would reveal that those due to significant strengths or weaknesses in the pawn formation are the most important. Before the principles of sound development and the importance of the centre were thoroughly understood, advantages based on mobility (of which control of the centre – which necessarily involves more freedom for the player dominating it – is a special case), and on the relative security of the two kings, were more common than they are today.

Nevertheless, it would be wrong to over-emphasize the static features in a position, which derive from the pawn formation, and to imagine that pawn weaknesses are necessarily virtually equivalent to the loss of the game. The mistake was especially common in the 1920s and 1930s, an exaggeration due mainly to the fact that the successes of the great strategical masters, Capablanca, Rubinstein, Fine, Euwe and Reshevsky, seemed to show that victory was normally to be had in this way. Alekhine, whose outstanding results stemmed much more from his rich use of combinatorial art, was thought to be exceptional – but on the masters of the post-war era, Alekhine is clearly the major influence! The games of the Soviet grandmasters, especially, show new facets of the importance of mobility and combinatorial play: the 'dynamics' of chess. In the victories of Botvinnik, Spassky, Tal and Korchnoi, one frequently sees unusual or what would once have been called anti-positional types of pawn formation adopted, just to allow a free functioning of the pieces. Yet the balance should not be swung too far in the other direction, for some great Soviet masters, above all Petrosian and Smyslov, depend largely for their success on the same means as Capablanca and Rubinstein.

The Isolated QP

Understanding openings depends not only on being acquainted with typical kinds of advantages: we can also progress by consideration of positions where there are various strong and weak factors for each side. An outstanding example of this is the isolated queen's pawn (IQP), whose advantages and drawbacks have been the subject of dispute for several decades. Its importance stems from the fact that it can arise from a number of well-known openings, with examples as diverse as the Caro-Kann Defence, Queen's Gambit Accepted and the Nimzo-Indian Defence, as well as less obvious variations like the Italian Game.

Diagram 7 shows a typical IQP situation, which arises from the sequence 1 P–Q4 N–KB3 2 P–QB4 P–K3 3 N–QB3 B–N5 4 P–K3 P–B4 5 B–Q3 0–0 6 N–B3 P–Q4 7 0–0 QP×P 8 B×BP N–B3 9 B–Q3 P×P 10 P×P B–K2. The pros and cons of this

position can be summarized in tabular form.

Advantages of the Isolated Pawn
1) Outposts for knights at K5 and QB5;
2) chances of K-side attack, by Q–Q3 and B–R2–N1, supported by the outposts;
3) Chance of a break-through in the centre by P–Q5;
4) Strengthening of black squares;
5) Difficulty in development of Black's QB.

Disadvantages of the IQP
1) Strong square for a black knight at Q4;
2) Isolated pawn must be defended by pieces, as there are no adjacent pawns;
3) Endgame is unfavourable to White, as static features then gain in importance;
4) Black's QB may be effectively posted on the diagonal QR1–KR8;
5) Good play for Black on the white squares.

There is no final answer to the question: Is the IQP strong or weak? For when, as in diagram 7, the balance between the two sides is very delicately poised, success or failure can depend on small, sometimes chance, factors. White

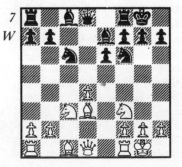

7
W

can gain a certain strengthening of his attacking possibilities from the situation of his QRP at R3, which facilitates the setting up of the Q+B mating battery on the QN1–KR7 diagonal. Were the QRP instead at R2, White might have to be satisfied with the formation queen at Q3 and bishop at QB2 (instead of QN1), when there is the constant danger of destruction of the battery by . . . N–QN5.

We now give some illustrations of both success and failure of the IQP. In the last resort, preference for one side or the other is a matter of style. The attacking player will normally think of the IQP in terms of the possibilities it gives him for middle game attack: the positional player will consider it, rather, as a potential target in the ending.

Success of the IQP

Barden-G. S. Brown, Oxford 1953: 1 P–Q4 P–Q4 2 N–KB3 P–B4 3 P–K3 N–KB3 4 P–B4 BP×P 5 KP×P P×P 6 B×P P–K3 7 0–0 B–K2 8 N–B3 QN–Q2 9 B–KN5 N–N3 10 B–Q3 0–0 11 R–B1 B–Q2 12 B–N1 B–B3 13 Q–Q3 P–N3 14 N–K5 R–B1 15 QR–Q1 B–Q4 16 Q–R3 N.B3–Q2 17 B–KR6 R–K1 18 P–B4 B–KB3 19 B–KN5 B×B 20 N×BP K×N 21 Q×RP+ Black resigned.

Petrosian-Balashov, Moscow 1974: 1 P–QB4 N–KB3 2 N–QB3 P–K3 3 P–Q4 B–N5 4 P–K3 P–B4 5 B–Q3 P–Q4 6 N–B3 0–0 7 0–0 QP×P 8 B×BP N–B3 9 B–Q3 P×P 10 P×P B–K2 (diagram 7!) 11 R–K1 P–QN3 12 P–QR3 B–N2 13 B–B2 R–B1 14 Q–Q3 R–K1? (*14 . . . P–N3 is necessary, though 15 B–R6 R–K1 16 QR–Q1 is better for White.*) 15 P–Q5! P×P 16 B–N5 N–K5 (*16 . . . P–N3? 17 R×B! Q×R 18 N×P*) 17 N×N P×N 18 Q×P

P–N3 19 Q–KR4 Q–B2 (*19 . . . P–KR4 20 B–N3!*) 20 B–N3 P–KR4 (*20 . . . B–B1 21 B–KB4*) 21 Q–K4 K–N2 22 B×P! K×B 23 B–R6 Q–Q3 (*23 . . . B–Q3 24 N–N5+ K–B3 25 N–R7+!*) 24 Q–QB4+ K–B3 25 QR–Q1 N–Q5 26 Q×N+ Q×Q 27 R×Q R–B4 28 P–KR4 Black resigned. The pin after B–KN5 will be too strong.

Failure of the IQP

Regedzinsky-Rubinstein, Lodz 1917: 1 P–Q4 P–Q4 2 N–KB3 N–KB3 3 P–B4 P–K3 4 B–N5 QN–Q2 5 N–B3 B–K2 6 P–K3 0–0 7 B–Q3 P×P 8 B×P P–QR3 9 0–0 P–QN4 10 B–Q3 B–N2 11 Q–K2 P–B4 12 QR–Q1 P×P 13 P×P N–N3 14 N–K4 N×N 15 B×B Q×B 16 B×N KR–Q1 17 R–Q3 B×B 18 Q×B QR–B1 19 KR–Q1 N–Q4 20 R3–Q2 N–B3 21 Q–K3 Q–N2 22 P–KR3 P–R3 23 R–K2 Q–Q4 24 P–QN3 Q–Q3 25 R–QB1 N–Q4 26 Q–Q2 Q–B5 27 R–B2 Q×Q 28 R.K2×Q R×R 29 R×R N–N5 30 R–N2 R–QB1 31 K–B1 R–B8+ 32 K–K2 R–QR8 33 K–Q2 R×P 34 R×R N×R 35 N–K5 N–N5 36 N–Q7 P–B3 37 P–N3 K–B2 38 N–N6 K–K2 39 K–B3 P–QR4 White resigned.

Spassky-Korchnoi, 30th USSR Ch 1962: 1 P–Q4 N–KB3 2 P–QB4 P–K3 3 N–KB3 P–Q4 4 N–B3 P–B4 5 BP×P N×P 6 P–K3 N–QB3 7 B–B4 P×P 8 P×P B–K2 9 0–0 0–0 10 R–K1 P–QR3 11 B–Q3 N–B3 12 B–KN5 P–QN4 13 R–QB1 B–N2 14 B–N1 R–B1 15 P–QR3 N–QR4 16 Q–Q3 P–N3 17 B–R6 R–K1 18 N–K5 N–B5 19 N×N P×N 20 Q–Q2 Q–N3 21 B–B4 KR–Q1 22 B–K5 N–N5 23 Q–K2 N×B 24 P×N R–Q5 25 B–K4 QR–Q1 26 B×B Q×B 27 N–K4 Q–N4 28 N–B3 Q–N1 29 R–QB2 R–Q6 30 P–KN3 R1–Q5 31 N–Q1 Q–N6 32 N–K3 B–N4 33 N–B1

P–QR4 34 P–B4 B–K2 35 KR–B1 B–B4
36 K–R1 Q–N2+ 37 Q–N2 Q–Q4 38
P–QR4 R–KB6 39 N–Q2 R–B7 40
Q×Q P×Q 41 N–B1 R–Q6 42 R–B3
R×R 43 P×R P–Q5 44 P×P B×P
White resigned.

History of Openings

We have seen how strategic ideas come
into being, in essence from the pawn
formation, and how they may be
modified through a more aggressive
placing of the pieces of the player with
the inferior pawn formation. The same
idea could be presented in an historical
form, by comparing the same openings
as played several decades ago with their
treatment by present-day masters. Here
are some examples which illustrate the
wide difference of outlook that the years
have made to the Ruy Lopez and the
Queen's Gambit Declined.

A Ruy Lopez of 80 Years Ago
Steinitz-Chigorin, 2nd match game
1892

1	P–K4	P–K4
2	N–KB3	N–QB3
3	B–N5	N–B3
4	P–Q3	

A slow and solid development which
is not seen today, because masters
realize that if Black is given time to
develop peacefully he can always
obtain an adequate foothold in the
centre. So 4 P–Q4 or 4 0–0 would be
played nowadays.

4	...	P–Q3
5	P–B3	P–KN3

A present-day master would approve
of this!

6 QN–Q2

Perhaps this move shows that masters
have lost as well as gained in the last 80
years. We can recall few master games

since 1945 in which White has castled
Q-side in the Ruy Lopez. The one
outstanding exception is a variation of
the Steinitz Defence Deferred: 1 P–K4
P–K4 2 N–KB3 N–QB3 3 B–N5
P–QR3 4 B–R4 P–Q3 5 B×N+ P×B 6
P–Q4 P–B3 7 B–K3 N–K2 8 N–B3
N–N3 9 Q–Q2 B–K2 10 0–0–0! The
idea is, that although it is generally
more dangerous to castle long because
the area of the king's field to be
defended is greater, this is compensated
for by the exposed position of the black
knight on KN3: White can attack it by
P–KR4–5 and thus gain an extra tempo
for his own K-side attack.

In the present position, the modern
master might well play 6 0–0 without
much thought. Steinitz does not:
flexibility of thinking is one of the
constitutents of a world champion.

6	...	B–N2
7	N–B1	0–0
8	B–R4	

8 N–K3 was more accurate.

8 ...   N–Q2

Here the obvious and simple move
was 8 ... P–Q4, but Chigorin was fond
of manoeuvring his knights behind his
defensive lines.

9 N–K3

9 N–N3 is more appropriate, as will
be seen two moves later.

9	...	N–B4
10	B–B2	N–K3
11	P–KR4	

Not a present-day move, for the
modern master would have seen and
been worrying about the coming ...
P–KB4 several moves ago. If the knight
was at KN3 instead of K3, then 11
P–KR4 would make 11 ... P–B4 12
P×P P×P 13 N–R5 B–R1 14 B–R6 very
dangerous for Black.

11 ...   N–K2?(*8*)

Overdoing the mysterious knight moves. The direct 11 . . . P–KB4 was very strong, e.g. 12 N–Q5 P–B5 followed by . . . N–K2 and . . . P–B3. It would then be dangerous for White to castle on either side, and his attack would be slowed down because of Black's strong KBP.

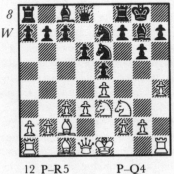

| 12 P–R5 | P–Q4 |
| 13 RP×P | BP×P? |

Better 13 . . . RP×P; Chigorin underestimates the danger from this opening of a diagonal. with his queen and king on it, and an enemy bishop in the offing.

| 14 P×P | N×P |
| 15 N×N | Q×N |

16 B–N3 Q–B3 17 Q–K2. (The consequences of Black's incorrect strategy are now obvious. White has pressure on the weak KP, open lines for his bishops, and the KR-file. This would add up to a win today, and we shall see that it did also in 1892!) 17 . . . B–Q2 18 B–K3 K–R1 19 O–O–O QR–K1 (with the idea of . . . N–Q5.) 20 Q–B1 P–QR4 (not 20 . . . *N–Q5? 21 R×P+!* and mate follows.) 21 P–Q4! (The opening of lines means that the black king will be exposed to the decisive crossfire of the white bishops.) 21 . . . P×P 22 N×P B×N 23 R×B! (Two bishops in combination here are well worth the sacrifice of the exchange.) 23

. . . N×R(*9*) (Now comes a finish among the most famous in chess history.)

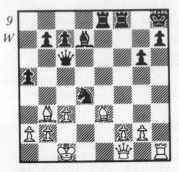

24 R×P+ K×R 25 Q–R1+ K–N2 26 B–R6+ K–B3 27 Q–R4+ K–K4 28 Q×N+ Black resigned. If 28 . . . K–B4 29 Q–KB4 is mate.

Comparison of this game and the next one points to three conclusions. First, the openings are played with greater exactitude today; the modern master would be unlikely to miss the chance to counter-attack in the centre which Chigorin did here at the 11th move. Secondly, the defensive technique of the modern master is much higher, but thirdly, a modern master could not surpass the imagination and dash of Steinitz's final attack.

A Ruy Lopez of Today
Ribli–Zuidema, Wijk aan Zee 1973

1 P–K4	P–K4
2 N–KB3	N–QB3
3 B–N5	P–QR3
4 B×N!?	

This is the Exchange Variation, which was once considered a drawing line by all but Emanuel Lasker. Regenerated in recent years by Fischer, it has become one of the most effective openings in master chess.

White's underlying idea is to break up Black's pawn structure on the wing where the latter will soon have a majority; in this way, White obtains the chance of winning endgames with his unsullied K-side majority, whereas Black (because of the doubled QBP) cannot force the creation of a passed pawn. This long-term threat has an almost hypnotic effect on many defenders of the Lopez who, rushing into piece exchanges, seal their doom at an early age. Logic requires that Black should complicate the game, in order to change the basis of the struggle; in particular, his bishop may be a factor, although in practice they rarely make themselves felt.

In this game, Black falls between two stools. He allows the queen exchange, and the swap of his KP for the white QP, that creates the local majorities. But then he castles Q-side and attempts to confuse matters (e.g. moves 9 and 14); the main upshot of this is that White is able to attack on the Q-side before Black can complete his development.

4 . . .	QP×B
5 0–0	

This move, by deferring exchanges for a move or two, imposes more tension on the game than did the old 'thematic' move, 5 P–Q4.

5 . . .	P–B3

Something has now to be done about the KP. Just about every move has been tried here, without it becoming clear which is best; 5 . . . B–KN5 has been the main alternative.

6 P–Q4	P×P

6 . . . B–KN5 is certainly more in accord with Black's aims, as outlined in the note to White's fourth move.

7 N×P	P–QB4

8 N–N3	Q×Q

Not forced, but clearly White is better prepared for a middle game, having made developing moves rather than . . . P–KB3 and . . . P–QB4.

9 R×Q	B–N5!?

A finesse, designed to weaken the . . . QR2 / . . . KN8 diagonal, and also, perhaps, to create a target for a later advance of the KNP. However, Black's plan is demonstrably inadequate, and he would have done better to develop his K-side with 9 . . . B–Q3, though White still stands well.

10 P–KB3	B–Q2
11 N–B3	0–0–0
12 B–B4	P–B5

Black is practically committed to this, since 12 . . . B–Q3 13 B×B loses a pawn.

13 N–R5	B–QB4+
14 K–R1	P–QN4

14 . . . B–QN5 fails to 15 B×P! K×B 16 N–Q5+.

15 N–Q5	P–B3

15 . . . B–N3 16 N×B+ P×N appears to win, but in reality White's mating threats outweigh the knight: 17 R–Q6! P×N 18 R–N6 B–K1 19 R–N8+ K–Q2 20 R–Q1+.

16 P–QN4!

Blow upon blow! Clearly 16 . . . P×N 17 P×B is unacceptable for Black, as White's passed pawns will join in the attack on the hapless king.

16 . . .	B–R2
17 N–B7	B–N1
18 N–K6(*10*)	
18 . . .	B×B

After this, Black's game collapses instantly. However, he also would have lost in the event of 18 . . . B×N 19 R×R+ K×R 20 N×P.B6+ K–B1 21 N×B K–N2 22 P–QR4 N–K2 23 P×P P×P 24 N–R6 followed by N–B5+ with

an extra pawn and the better ending.

19 N×P.B6!!

This is much more effective than 19 N×R or 19 N×B.

19 ...   B×N.K3

To take the other knight comes to the same thing. If 19 . . . R–K1 20 N–R7+ K–N1 21 N×B R–K2 22 N–Q5 R–B2 23 N–N6 and White should win.

20. N×R   ·B–Q2
21 N–B7   N–K2
22 N×R   B–K3

Two exchanges down, Black must attempt to encircle the knight. However, a few vigorous moves on the Q-side bring an early decision.

23 P–QR4   B–K4
24 P×P! ·   B×R
25 P×P   B–K4
26 R–Q8+!   Resigns

The QRP cannot be stopped anymore.

A Queen's Gambit of Seventy Years Ago
Pillsbury-Marco, Paris 1900

1 P–Q4   P–Q4
2 P–QB4   P–K3
3 N–QB3   N–KB3
4 B–N5   B–K2
5 P–K3   0–0
6 N–B3   ·P–QN3

Very popular at the end of the 19th Century, when it was thought that Black's attack on the queen's wing would develop faster than White's on

the king's. The system of play which Pillsbury first used against Tarrasch at Hastings in 1895 caused it to be abandoned. The idea still holds water today, but in combination with Black's general plan in most variations of the Queen's Gambit Declined, of exchanging off minor pieces and thus reaching a satisfactory endgame. 'Satisfactory' only; because this strategy gives Black, if few losing chances, even fewer ones of winning.

7 B–Q3   B–N2
8 P×P   P×P
9 N–K5(*11*)

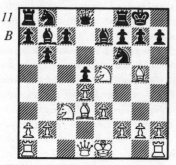

This is Pillsbury's attack. The premise, simply stated, is that White's attack is faster than Black's. At the turn of the century, masters did not realize the strength of the freeing system based on exchanging minor pieces. Here 9 . . . N–K5 (or 9 . . . P–KR3 first) is the best, although not as strong as 8 . . . N×P! would have been, since White can answer 9 . . . N–K5 by 10 B–KB4 N×N 11 P×N. The exchange of even one pair of minor pieces eases the defence, however, and furthermore Black has the possibility of slowing up the type of attack which White gets in the game, by a timely . . . P–KB4.

9 ...   QN–Q2
10 P–B4   P–B4
11 0–0   P–B5

12 B–B2	P–QR3
13 Q–B3	P–N4
14 Q–R3(*12*)	

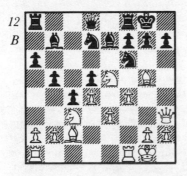

You will quite often have opportunities to reach this type of position with White in the games you play. Do so, for White's attack is very strong. Black cannot escape his difficulties by 14 . . . N–K5 because of 15 B×B Q×B 16 Q×N. To know what type of position to aim for in an opening is the hallmark which distinguishes the successful match and tournament player.

| 14 . . . | P–N3 |

White threatened 15 N×N.

| 15 P–B5 | |

Another characteristic of the Pillsbury Attack: White can force open the KB-file.

| 15 . . . | P–N5 |
| 16 P×P | RP×P |

17 Q–R4 P×N 18 N×N Q×N 19 R×N (Yet another common theme is revealed: weaknesses having been created, the attack is switched from KR7 to KN7.) 19 . . . P–R4 20 R1–KB1 R–R3 21 B×P P×B 22 R×R+ B×R 23 R×B+ K×R 24 Q–R8+ K–B2 25 Q–R7+ Black resigned.

A Queen's Gambit of Today
Mariotti-Radulov, Venice 1971

1 P–Q4	P–Q4
2 P–QB4	P–K3
3 N–QB3	N–KB3
4 P×P	

A popular variation nowadays; White stabilizes the central area.

4 . . .	P×P
5 B–N5	B–K2
6 P–K3	0–0
7 B–Q3	QN Q2

Black avoids . . . P–QB3 in order to bypass the 'minority attack' (see chapter 7), but gives White instead the opportunity of playing Pillsbury's Attack. The Italian master prefers a more original plan, which avoids any prepared idea of his opponent's.

| 8 KN–K2!? | |

A move which, in the Exchange Variation of the Queen's Gambit, invariably signals a K-side attack.

| 8 . . . | P–QN3 |
| 9 N–N3 | P–N3 |

White was threatening to establish his knight at KB5, but now he has a motive for attacking the king.

| 10 P–KR4 | P–KR4 |
| 11 Q–B2 | K–N2 |

Necessary, in view of 12 B×P! P×B 13 Q×P+ and N–B5.

| 12 N.B3–K2 | |

White spurns the 'automatic' move 12 0–0–0, since that would give Black counter-chances based on the advance of the QBP. Instead, White proceeds with his attack against the K-side weaknesses, reckoning that his king will be safe on the KB-file: a decision based not on general principles, but upon a concrete assessment of Black's position. White's king is protected by the bulk of his forces

12 . . .	B–N5+
13 K–B1	B–Q3
14 N–B4(*13*)	

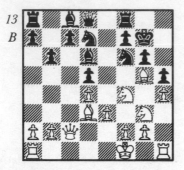

14 ...   B×N

If 14 ... B–N2 (to guard the QP), White has the promising sacrificial continuation 15 B×P! B×N (*15 ... P×B 16 N–K6+*) 16 N×P+ when: a) 16 ... K–N1 17 N×B P×B 18 P–R5!? Q–K2 19 P×P with dangerous threats; b) 16 ... N×N 17 B×Q P×B 18 P×B QR×N 19 Q×BP and for once three pieces are less than the queen, because White has the initiative and can quickly bring in his rooks via the K-file.

15 P×B!

Thus White gets a battering ram to hit the white squares like KN6 once more. The apparent danger on the K-file is comfortably neutralized, with exchanges that bring White's queen into a dominating position.

15 ...   P–B4
16 P–B5   P–B5

17 B–K2 Q–B2 (breaking the pin on his KN at last.) 18 Q–Q2 R–R1 19 R–K1 B–R3 20 B–B4 Q–B3 21 P–B3 QR–K1 22 K–B2 R–K2 (hoping to build up pressure, but White, having consolidated, can bring his KR into play quickly enough.) 23 B–Q1 R1–K1 24 R×R R×R 25 B–B2 B–B1 (Black still suffers from the greatly circumscribed field of action of his minor pieces.) 26 R–K1 R×R 27 Q×R

N–B1 (or *27 ... N–KN1 28 P×P P×P 29 Q–K8* and Black is immobilized.) 28 Q–K7 Q–K1 (not *28 ... Q–Q2 29 B–R6+ K×B 30 Q×N.B8+ K–R2 31 P×P+.*) 20 Q×RP Q–N4 30 Q–R3 B×P (*30 ... Q–K1 31 Q–Q6* is also hopeless.) 31 B–R6+ Black resigned.

How Openings Evolve

Having seen how, on a large time-scale, the conceptions involved in an opening like the Ruy Lopez or Queen's Gambit can alter, we shall now look at how this evolution comes about, as it were, on a day-to-day basis. The club player is perpetually amazed at the master's ability to discover innovations (or 'theoretical novelties', as the well-known *Chess Player* and *Informator* journals call them!), new moves in a well-trodden line of play which add an original twist and which frequently, taking the opponent by surprise, undermine his resistance.

Yet nearly all innovations are of two types. Firstly, in a complicated tactical situation, where the previously accepted best line involves very sharp play for both sides, it may happen that a resource for one side or the other will reverse the advantage. Secondly, innovations can come about in situations where White or Black has a clearly defined strategical object, but has not, in previous examples of the opening, been able to find a completely satisfactory method of carrying it out.

It follows that, if the club player can understand the basic strategy in a particular variation – and this should be well within his powers – he can also hope to discover new and strong moves for himself. This is a very worthwhile exercise, since the player who treats openings from his individual viewpoint, always providing that it is strategically sound, and does not take accepted authority as gospel, is far more likely to improve his playing strength than the man who simply follows the standard continuation without question. Here are some examples of innovations, with explanations of how they were discovered.

In the Two Knights' Defence, after the moves 1 P–K4 P–K4 2 N–KB3 N–QB3 3 B–B4 N–B3 4 N–N5 P–Q4 5 P×P N×P (*5 . . . N–QR4 is correct.*) 6 P–Q4, it has been known for many years that 6 . . . P×P 7 0–0 B–K2 8 N×BP! K×N 9 Q–B3+ K–K3 10 R–K1+ led to a decisive advantage for White. However, the American master, Pinkus, considered that Black could make the defence playable, after 6 P–Q4, by the finesse 6 . . . B–N5+ (taking away the square QB3 from the white knight) 7 P–B3 B–K2 since 8 N×BP K×N 9 Q–B3+ K–K3 is no longer clear for White. This recommendation was generally accepted for several years. One day, analysing with some friends at Oxford University, Leonard Barden demonstrated this line. When the position after 9 . . . K–K3 was reached, P. Keffler at once suggested 10 Q–K4!: a logical move, tying up all Black's pieces and threatening 0–0, P–B4 and BP×P with a winning attack, which nobody had previously thought of.

A few months later, Barden was able to play 10 Q–K4 at Hastings against the US master Weaver Adams, who had recommended 6 . . . B–N5+ in his book *Simple Chess*. The game had a conclusion which was drastic but also very easy to play for White, since the basic plan was already discovered in the earlier analysis at Oxford: 10 . . . B–B1

11 0–0 N3–K2 12 P–B4 P–B3 13 BP×P K–Q2 14 B–K2 K–K1 15 P–B4 N–B2 16 N–B3 B–K3 17 B–KN5 Q–Q2 18 QR–Q1 R–B1 19 B×N Q×B 20 P–Q5 Q–B4+ 21 K–R1 P×P 22 P×P B–Q2 23 P–K6 B–N4 24 Q–KB4 K–Q1 25 B×B N×B 26 N×N Q×N 27 P–Q6. A likely finish, forestalled by Black's resignation, would be 27 . . . R–B5 28 Q×B+ R×Q 29 R×R+ Q–K1 30 R×Q+ K×R 31 P–Q7+ K–Q1 32 P–K7+ K×P 33 P–Q8=Q+ etc.

Our second illustration is from the violent Four Pawns Attack against Alekhine's Defence: 1 P–K4 N–KB3 2 P–K5 N–Q4 3 P–QB4 N–N3 4 P–Q4 P–Q3 5 P–B4 P×P 6 BP×P N–QB3 7 B–K3 B–B4 8 N–QB3 P–K3 9 N–B3 B–K2 and now 10 P–Q5!? (*14*).

14
B

The first reaction to the discovery of this sacrifice was that Black is in trouble, in view of lines like 10 . . . P×P 11 P×P N–QN5 12 N–Q4 B–N3 13 B–QN5+ K–B1 14 0–0 (threatening *15 N–K6+*) 14 . . . K–N1 15 N–B5! However, Penrose realized that if Black could avoid the bishop check, the advanced white pawns might be very weak in view of White's retarded development, and he swiftly discovered the variation 10 . . . N–QN5! 11 N–Q4 B–N3 12 P–QR3 P–QB4! which seemed to put 10 P–Q5 out of business.

For over a decade the move was not played, until in 1970 the Yugoslav grandmasters Parma and Velimirović improved upon 10 ... N–QN5 11 N–Q4 with 11 R–B1! with complications perhaps favourable to White, e.g. 11 ... P×P 12 P–QR3 N–R3 13 P×P 0–0 14 P–QN4!? N–N1 15 B–K2 B–KN5 16 Q–Q4 B×N 17 B×B B–N4 18 0–0 B×B+ 19 Q×B P–QB3 20 QR–Q1 Q–K2 21 P–K6 P×P 22 P–Q6 Q–K1 23 B–R5! with a strong attack; Gorelov-Ignatiev, Moscow 1974. The latest twist for Black is to give up 9 ... B–K2 altogether, and to prefer play against White's centre by 9 ... N–N5 or 9 ... B–KN5 with chances of equalizing. If that is not good enough, Alekhine players will have to re-examine the line 9 ... B–K2 10 P–Q5 P×P!? 11 P×P N–QN5 12 N–Q4 B–Q2! (avoiding the check) as after the practically forced sequence 13 P–K6 P×P 14 P×P B–QB3 15 Q–N4 B–KR5+ 16 P–KN3 B×R 17 0–0–0 Q–B3! 18 P×B 0–0 19 B–K2 White, it appears from the games thus far played, has enough for his exchange but no safe way to play for a win.

In the late 1950s, Tal had a sensational rise to fame, culminating in winning the World Championship in 1960; one of his main weapons was the Modern Benoni Defence, 1 P–Q4 N–KB3 2 P–QB4 P–QB4 3 P–Q5 P–K3 4 N–QB3 P×P 5 P×P P–Q3 (*15*). Ever since, masters have been debating which is the best way to meet this defence. Black's basic idea is to use his 3:2 Q-side majority, in conjunction with his fianchettoed KB (and sometimes the half-open K-file) to get active counterplay, while White tries to maintain his space advantage and finally to break through either in the

centre (with P–K5) or on the K-side.

15 W

In early games with the Modern Benoni, White played routine developing moves and Black utilized this to advance on the Q-side with tempo. An example is Donner-Tal, Zürich 1959, which continued thus from diagram 15: 6 N–B3 P–KN3 7 P–K4 B–N2 8 B–Q3 0–0 9 0–0 P–QR3 10 P–QR4 B–N5 11 P–R3 B×N 12 Q×B QN–Q2 13 B–B4 Q–B2 14 Q–K2 KR–K1 15 B–R2 QR–B1 16 B–QB4 N–K4 17 P–B4 N×B 18 Q×N N–Q2 19 KR–K1 Q–N3 20 QR–N1 Q–N5 21 Q–B1 P–B5 22 R–K2 P–QN4 23 P×P P×P 24 K–R1 B×N 25 P×B Q×P 26 R×P Q–Q6 27 Q–K1 P–B6 28 R–N1 N–B4 White resigned.

At the Leipzig Olympiad the following year, Penrose (also against Tal) employed a superior plan involving a quick break in the centre: (from diagram 15) 6 P–K4 P–KN3 7 B–Q3 B–N2 8 KN–K2 0–0 9 0–0 P–QR3 10 P–QR4 Q–B2 11 P–R3 QN–Q2 12 P–B4 R–K1 13 N–N3 P–B5 14 B–B2 N–B4 15 Q–B3 KN–Q2 16 B–K3 P–QN4 17 P×P R–N1 18 Q–B2 P×P 19 P–K5! P×P 20 P–B5! B–N2 21 QR–Q1 B–QR1 22 N.B3–K4! N–R5 23 B×N P×B 24 P×P BP×P 25 Q–B7+ K–R1 26 N–QB5 Q–R2 27 Q×N Q×Q 28 N×Q R×P 29 N–N6 R–N6, 30

N×BP and White, with a sound extra piece, soon won..

Innovators realized that Black's 12 ... R–K1 was doubly useless – it did not stop P–K5 and it weakened the KB2 square. You can see the improvements in Black's plan in the next example, Garcia-Kavalek, Bucharest 1966: (first eight moves as in Penrose-Tal) 9 0–0 N–R3 10 N–N3 N–B2 11 P–KR3 R–N1! 12 P–QR4 P–QR3 13 P–B4 (*13 P–R5!*, to take the NP en passant, is critical.) 13 ... P–QN4 14 P×P P×P 15 Q–B3 P–N5 16 N–Q1 N–N4 17 B×N R×B 18 N–K3 N–Q2 19 N–B4 N–N3 20 N–R5 B–Q2 21 P–B5 Q–B3 22 B–B4 R–B1 23 N–B6 B×N 24 P×B N–B5 25 Q–K2 Q×NP 26 Q×N Q–Q5+ 27 Q×Q B×Q+ 28 K–R2 B×R 29 R×B P–N6 30 B×P P–N7 31 R–QN1 P–B5 32 B–R3 P–B6 33 N–K2 R×QBP 34 N×P R×N 35 R×P R×R 36 B×R R–B7 37 B–B6 P×P 38 P–K5 P–B5 39 P–R4? (In the long run, it's hopeless anyway.) 39 ... P–B6 40 K–N3 P–B7 White resigned.

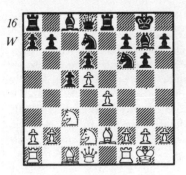

White innovators had to abandon the central rush, and played first to establish a knight on QB4. Early in the seventies, several games went 1 P–Q4 N–KB3 2 P–QB4 P–QB4 3 P–Q5 P–K3 4 N–QB3 P×P 5 P×P P–Q3 6 P–K4 P–KN3 7 N–B3 B–N2 8 B–K2 0–0 9 0–0

R–K1 10 N–Q2 QN–Q2 reaching diagram 16.

In the third Spassky-Fischer match game of 1972, Black played an interesting plan to get K-side pressure: 11 Q–B2 N–R4!? 12 B×N P×B 13 N–B4?! N–K4 14 N–K3 Q–R5. However, a few weeks later, the tables were turned at the Skopje Olympiad in the game Gligorić-Kavalek: (from diagram 16) 11 P–QR4 N–K4 12 Q–B2 N–R4 13 B×N P×B 14 N–Q1! Q–R5 15 N–K3 N–N5!? 16 N×N P×N 17 N–B4 Q–B3 18 B–Q2 (Black is short of counterplay now.) 18 ... Q–N3 19 B–B3 B×B 20 P×B P–N3 21 KR–K1 B–R3 22 N–Q2 R–K4 23 P–KB4! P×Pep 24 N×P R–R4 25 Q–B2 Q–B3 26 R–K3! R–K1 27 QR–K1 Q–B5 28 P–K5! P×P 29 R–K4 Q–B3 30 Q–N3+! K–R1 31 N×P R–KN1 32 R–KN4 R×R 33 N×R Q–N3 34 P–R4 R–B4 35 N–R6! R–B3 36 R–K8+ K–N2 37 R–KN8+ K×N 38 Q–R4+ Black resigned.

In the 1973 Leningrad Interzonal tournament, Taimanov (against Gligorić) tried to improve upon this by 14 ... P–N3 15 R–R3 P–B4 16 P×P B–QR3 17 N–K4! (not *17 R–K1 N–B5!*) 17 ... B×R 18 K×B N–B2 19 R–KN3 K–R1, but White has excellent attacking chances with either 20 P–B6 (as played) or with 20 R×B!? K×R 21 Q–B3+. This is not the last word, however, as many ideas for both players remain to be tried and the Benoni remains in a state of flux. A final example is Donner-Planinc, Amsterdam 1973: (first eight moves as in Gligorić-Kavalek) 9 0–0 B–N5! 10 B–B4 R–K1 11 Q–B2 P–QR3 12 P–QR4 Q–K2 13 KR–K1 QN–Q2 14 P–R3 B×N 15 B×B P–B5 16 P–R5 N–B4 17 R–K2 N3–Q2 18 R–R3 N–N6

19 Q–Q1 N–K4 20 B×N B×B 21 N–R4
N–Q5 22 R–K1 N–N4 23 R–R1
QR–B1 24 R–QB1 B–Q5 25 R–K2
Q–Q1 26 R2–B2 Q×P 27 R×P R×R 28
R×R B–N2 29 P–QN4 Q–Q1 30 P–N3
N–R6 31 R–B1 P–QN4 32 N–B3 Q–N3
33 B–K2 B–Q5 34 Q–N3 B×P+ 35
K–N2 Q–K6 White resigned.

A Study Plan

We have accepted in this book a broad
distinction between two kinds of chess
players, 'positional' and 'combinative'.
It is most important that a player
should adopt an opening which leads to
the type of game suited to his own
individual style. Some players have a
flair for combination and are happiest
when conducting an attack against the
enemy king. For them we recommend,
as White, study of one of the open
games from chapter 3, 2 P–QB3 against
the Sicilian (p. 64), the Four Pawns
Attack against the King's Indian (p.
143) and so on. With Black, the Sicilian
Defence and the Yugoslav Variation of
the King's Indian are recommended.

The other type of player, who prefers
a more steady kind of game, with
accumulation of slight advantages and
pressure against definite weak points in
his opponent's game, needs a different
opening repertoire. He should adopt, as
White, the Ruy Lopez or the Queen's
Gambit, the Averbakh Variation
against the King's Indian (p. 144), the
Tarrasch Variation against the French
(p. 77) etc. With Black he can try the
French or Pirc Defences, according to
whether he prefers blocked or open
positions, while against 1 P–Q4 he
should employ the Nimzo-Indian and
Bogoljubow lines.

When you have decided on your
repertoire, or at least on a particular

opening or defence that you wish to try,
how should you set about learning it?
The best time to study an opening is
immediately before and/or immediately after a game, because then
the stimulus to learn is at a peak. A good
idea is to play semi-blitz games (15–20
minutes per player) against an
opponent of equal strength, with the
openings agreed on beforehand. If you
can try the opening in a few postal
games, so much the better, since you are
allowed to consult openings books (but
not friends) which will prevent you
from going badly wrong. Of course it is
true that correspondence games can
take several months to play, but you
can use the leisurely pace to make a
thorough study of the opening, with the
desire to win the game providing a
strong motivation. When you come to
play the same opening 'over-the-
board', you should then be clearer
about the strategic ideas and main
variations than if you had relied solely
on learning sequences of moves by
heart.

Players keen to improve should have
periodicals like *The Chess Player* or
Informator to hand as reference material.
These will include recent grandmaster
games with your openings, and you
should play through these (and the
players' notes) with care. Another
helpful practice is to analyse critical
lines with a reasonably strong partner,
if possible taking opposite points of
view. But keep the analysis under
control; don't let 'investigation'
degenerate into a skittles game.

Some players make their opening
moves confidently, but collapse when
the game gets 'out of the book'. So our
final piece of advice is not to make a
hasty reply when your opponent makes

an unexpected move in the opening (or indeed at any time), even if it appears very weak or very strong; remember that 'obvious' checks and recaptures are not always the best moves. The first step is always to work out what your opponent is threatening, and to see whether you have any threats that he cannot meet. Three or four 'candidate moves' will probably suggest themselves to you, and you must next analyse and evaluate these. Even if your opponent's new move is 'the latest Russian improvement', this methodical approach will always provide you with a mental buffer and give you a good chance of finding the best plan in reply. Even at quite fast time-limits, it is worth spending ten minutes at this critical stage when the opening becomes the middle game. And it is only by thought taken in the true testing-ground, serious play, that you will obtain real understanding.

1	P–K4	P–K4
2	N–KB3	N–QB3
3	B–N5	

This, the Ruy Lopez, has reigned supreme among the K-pawn openings this century. The main reason for its popularity is its sound strategic basis, which makes it particularly hard for Black to equalize. Although the Lopez has a reputation for leading to slow manoeuvring games, exchanges or sacrifices are liable at any moment to transform the game into a tense combinational struggle. An additional factor that contributes to the richness of the opening is the opportunity it allows to Black to create complications, for example by the 3 . . . P–B4!? (Schliemann) defence whereby, at some positional risk, Black seeks the initiative.

White's problem in the Lopez, therefore, is that he has to be prepared, chessically and psychologically too, for a variety of replies. In the main lines, he needs the patience gradually to build up a K-side attack against the hedgehog defence, or if need be to see the right moment for switching his threats to the other side of the board. On the other hand, he must be ready for sharp piece play in open situations, which some of the irregular defences call for. Black's problem is easier, since he can usually pick his line of defence beforehand to suit his style of play, and in most cases it is impossible for White to avoid any particular defence. But, for all these difficulties, the Ruy Lopez offers more prospects of lasting pressure than any other opening, even supposing a good defence by Black.

The Worrall Attack

We recommend White to adopt this variation as the main string to his bow for two main reasons. Firstly, it leads to positions strategically similar to the main (R–K1) lines, without being so well-known, thus minimizing the danger that Black will be able to play a pet line or one prepared out of the latest foreign magazines. Secondly, by avoiding several of the sharp counter-attacking lines (the Open, the Marshall, the Archangel), White spares both his nerves and his memory. Nor has it been proved that the Worrall Attack is inferior to the more-analysed lines. Alekhine, Keres and Hübner often played the Worrall and it still appears in top tournaments from time to time.

1	P–K4	P–K4
2	N–KB3	N–QB3
3	B–N5	P–QR3
4	B–R4	N–B3
5	Q–K2	

The most common move here is 5 0–0. In conjunction with 5 . . . B–K2 6 R–K1, many leading grandmasters consider it White's major continuation after 1 P–K4 P–K4. This very popularity, however, is a disadvantage for club and junior players who should prefer lines where they feel at home and where their opponents cannot so readily draw upon book learning.

Examples of the massive published analyses following 5 0–0 can be seen in the Batsford books *The Closed Ruy Lopez*, *The Marshall Attack* and *Ruy Lopez: Breyer System*. Leonard Barden's book *The Ruy Lopez* is a good general treatment of the opening.

By playing 5 Q–K2 (instead of 5 0–0 B–K2 6 Q–K2) White avoids the complications arising from 5 0–0:
a) 5 . . . N×P 6 P–Q4 P–QN4 7 B–N3 P–Q4 8 P×P B–K3 – the Open Lopez;
b) 5 . . . P–QN4 6 B–N3 B–N2 (or 6 . . . B–B4!?) 7 R–K1 B–B4 8 P–B3 0–0 9 P–Q4 B–N3 – the Archangel Variation.

These lines may or may not be objectively good for White. The point is that Black usually knows them well (else he would not go in for them), and is liable to come up with troublesome innovations in practical play.

     5 . . .   P–QN4

Black occasionally tries:
a) 5 . . . B–B4? 6 B×N QP×B 7 N×P Q–Q5 (or 7 . . . 0–0 8 P–Q3) 8 N–Q3 B–R2 9 P–KB3 0–0 10 N–B3 R–K1 11 P–QN3! P–B4 12 B–N2 P–B5 13 N–B4 P–QN4 14 0–0–0 is good for White, Bisguier-H. Steiner, New York 1949.
b) 5 . . . B–K2 6 P–B3 P–Q3 7 0–0 0–0 8 P–Q4 B–Q2 9 B–B2 (*9 B–N3* is also good.) 9 . . . P×P 10 P×P N–QN5 11 N–B3 N×B 12 Q×N B–N5 13 N–K1! P–B3 14 P–KR3 B–Q2 15 B–K3 and White has a spatial advantage, Brinckmann-Bogoljubow, Aachen 1933.

     6 B–N3   B–K2

Rarely seen are:

a) 6 . . . B–B4 (not a bad move) 7 P–B3 (*7 P–QR4 B–N2!=*) 7 . . . 0–0 8 P–Q3 P–Q3 9 0–0 B–K3 10 B–N5 Q–K2 11 QN–Q2 P–R3 12 B–K3 B–R2 (Gereben-Eliskases, Vienna 1935) when White, instead of continuing quietly, might have tried 13 P–Q4!? e.g. 13 . . . P×P 14 P×P P–Q4 15 P–K5.
b) 6 . . . N–QR4 7 N×P N×B 8 RP×N Q–K2 9 P–Q4 P–Q3 10 N–B6 Q×P 11 Q×Q N×Q 12 0–0 B–B4 13 P–QB4 with some Q-side pressure.

     7 0–0(*22*)

With this, we arrive at the normal position of the Worrall Attack. Before proceeding with the detailed analysis, let us look at some typical positions of this variation.

Favourable Positions for White
Alekhine-Sämisch, Bad Nauheim 1937

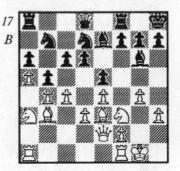

Black's knights have been driven into passivity, and now White opens up the Q-side with great advantage in piece activity.

Spassky-Donner, Santa Monica 1966 (*18*).

Black advanced his QP recklessly to Q5, but could not maintain it there. White now has full control of the centre, and targets (K6, QN5).

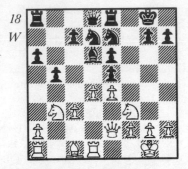

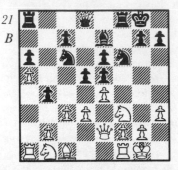

A keen struggle is in prospect all over the board.

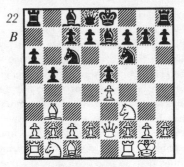

Favourable Positions for Black
Hübner-Geller, Palma 1970

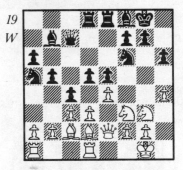

Black has maintained the central tension and built up his forces appropriately. White is cramped and has weakened his K-side.

Vorotnikov-Havsky, Leningrad 1964

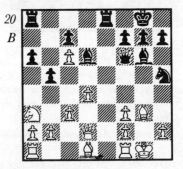

White has defended badly against Black's counter-gambit; now he is pole-axed by 1 ... B–B5!

Black now plays one of:

7 ... *P–Q3* – solid
7 ... *0–0* – sharp

The Solid Line

7 ...   P–Q3
8 P–QR4

One of the main ideas in the Worrall: White opens a second front on the Q-side. None of the possible defences of the QNP are wholly satisfactory, so Black offers it as a sacrifice.

8 ...   B–N5!?

Others:

a) 8 ... R–QN1 9 P×P P×P 10 P–B3 B–K3 11 B×B P×B 12 P–Q4 P×P 13 P×P Q–Q2 14 B–N5 and White has central pressure and the QR-file.

b) 8 ... P–N5? 9 Q–B4 or 9 B×P+ K×B 10 Q–B4+.

c) 8 ... B–N2 9 P–B3 0–0 10 P–Q4 N–QR4 11 B–B2 with a small advantage to White.

d) 8...B–K3 9 B×B P×B 10 P×P P P×P 11 R×R Q×R and the capture of the QNP is inadvisable; but 10 P–B3 (intending P–Q4) may be strong.

9 P B3

White's extra pawn is worthless after 9 P×P P P×P 10 R×R Q×R 11 Q×P 0–0 (threatening *12 ... N–R2*) 12 Q–K2 N–QR4 13 P–Q3 N×B etc.

9 ...   0–0

Black can rarely do without this move in the Ruy Lopez. If 9 ... P–N5 10 P–R5 isolates the black QRP.

10 P–R3

The beginning of Alekhine's plan, which aims at limiting the scope of Black's QB. 10 P–Q3 and 10 R–Q1 (intending P–Q4) are reasonable, but less ambitious continuations.

10 ...   B–R4

Others:

a) 10 ... B×N 11 Q×B N–QR4 12 B–B2 P–B4 13 R–K1 Q–N3 14 P–Q3 QR–K1 15 P×P P×P 16 N–Q2 Rabar-Bely, Marianske Lazne 1960, White had a slight advantage

b) 10 ... B–Q2 11 P–Q4 P–N5 12 B–QB4 P×P 13 P×P and again we prefer White's chances

c) 10 ... N–QR4?! is critical. Play can go on 11 B×P+! R×B 12 P×B N×NP *(or 12 ... N–N6 13 R–R3 N×B 14 R×N N×P 15 P×P* etc. 13 P×P P×P 14 Q×P B–R5, which was analysed in 1966 in the magazine *Shakhmaty v SSSR* ('Chess in the USSR'). When this line was followed in a 1967 Soviet game Kulmaya-Tomson, White won after 15 Q–Q5! P–B3 16 Q–K6 B×P+ 17 R×B N×R 18 K×N Q–N3+ 19 K–N3! (The

article had only considered *19 P–Q4 R1–KB1* 'with the initiative for Black'.) 19 ... R1–KB1 20 P–N4 etc. This is a grim warning not to believe uncritically everything you read in chess literature!

11 P–N4   B–N3

11 ... N×NP? fails to 12 P×N B×P 13 Q–K3, unpinning.

12 P–Q3   N–QR4

Not 12 ... P–KR4 13 N–R4

13 B–B2   P–B4

13 ... N–Q2? (to prevent N–R4) leaves White with a free hand, e.g. 14 P–N4 N–N2 15 N–R3 P–QB3 16 B–N3 N–N3 17 P–R5 N–Q2 18 B–K3 K R1 (*18... P–Q4!? 19 P×P P–QB4 20 P–Q6!* – Alekhine) 19 P–B4! reaching diagram 17.

The text move, suggested by Alekhine himself, envisages ... Q–B2 and centralization of the other pieces; a heavyweight encounter lies ahead. If White is patient, he should find this a congenial position. As a rule, Black avoids this line by playing instead:

The Sharp Line

7 ...   0–0

White should now experiment with both:

Variation 1: *8 P–B3* and

Variation 2: *8 P–QR4*

8 P–Q4 is premature, Black obtaining a comfortable game by 8 ... N×QP! 9 N×N P×N 10 P–K5 N–K1 11 P–B3 P–QB4.

Variation 1

8 P–B3   P–Q4

If 8 ... P–Q3 then 9 P–QR4 can lead to A. With the text move, Black offers a pawn in return for development and threats against the white king.

9 P–Q3! *(23)*

9 P×P is risky. Black can follow up with one of:

a) 9 ... N×P 10 N×P N×N! (*10 ...
N–B5?! 11 Q–K4 N×N 12 P–Q4!*) 11
Q×N B–N2 12 P–Q4 P–QR4 =
Kashdan-Bisguier, New York 1949.

b) 9 ... B–KN5 10 P×N P–K5 11 P–Q4
P×N 12 P×P B–R4! with good
attacking chances; if White slips up,
diagram 20 can result.

With the text move, White aims to
keep a solid position. The KR can go to
Q1, and Black must be careful how he
continues.

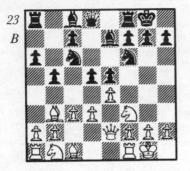

23
B

9 ...   R–K1

Black has also tried:

a) 9 ... P–Q5? 10 R–Q1 (*10 P×P!?* is
also quite promising) 10 ... B–K3 (*10
... B–KN5* might minimise his
disadvantage.) 11 QN–Q2 R–K1 12
B×B P×B 13 N–N3 P×P 14 P×P B–Q3
15 P–Q4 N–Q2 16 B–N5 (continuing
from diagram 18) 16 ... Q–B1 17 P–B4!
with advantage to White.

b) 9 ... B–N2!? 10 R–Q1!? (However,
White can try instead *10 QN–Q2, 10
B–N5!?* or *10 R–K1*, when *10 ... R–K1*
transposes to the main line) 10 ...
R–K1 11 QN–Q2 B–KB1 12 N–B1
N–QR4 13 B–B2 P–B4 Black has some
advantage in space, but the
complications lie ahead. Some
inaccuracies by White led to diagram
19.

10 R–K1
Keres suggested 10 R–Q1.
10 ...   B–N2
11 QN–Q2   Q–Q2?
Keres suggested 11 ... B–KB1 12
N–B1 N–QR4 13 B–B2 P–B4. The
game Flatau-Stern, 9th German Corres
Ch 1965–7, continued 14 N–N3 P–Q5
15 N–B5 (*15 P–N4!? N–B3!? 16 NP×P
P×P* probably favours Black.) 15 ...
P×P 16 P×P P–B5! 17 B–N5 Q–N3 18
P–QR4, and Black took the initiative
by 18 ... P×P 19 B×P N–N6 although
the game was drawn in the end. Better
would be 18 QR–N1, with an unclear
position; there is scope in this line for
the reader to discover ideas of his own.
12 N–B1   QR–Q1
13 B–N5
In retrospect, Keres thought 13
N–N3 might be better.
13 ...   N–QR4
14 B–B2   P×P
15 P×P   N–B5
16 N–K3
Not 16 P–QN3 N–R6 17 N×P
Q–K3.
16 ...   N×NP?
16 ... N×N 17 Q×N N–N5 with
balanced chances is better. Now we
shall follow the game Keres-Geller,
Budapest 1952.
17 N×P   Q–K3
18 N×P!
This combination forces liquidation
into a won ending.
18 ...   Q×N
19 B–N3   N–B5
20 N×N   P×N
21 B×P   N–Q4
22 B×B   Q×B
23 P×N   Q×Q
24 R×Q   R×R
25 B×R   B×P
26 P–QR4!

Preparing to activate the rook: not 26 R–Q1? R–K1. 26 B×P R–R1 27 P–QB4 also makes the win problematic, in view of 27 . . . R×B 28 P×B R–R4 29 P–Q4 K–B1 or 27 . . . B×NP!? 28 K×B R×B.

26 . . .   R–Q3

Or 26 . . . P–QR4 27 R–Q1 R–K1 28 R×B R×B 29 P–N3 R–B7 30 R–QB5 – Keres.

27 R–Q1   K–B2

The bishop ending after 27 . . . B–N2 28 R×R P×R 29 P–R5 would be hopeless.

28 P–R5!

Keres saw that he could bring about a pawn ending by 28 R×B R×R 29 B–B4 K–K3 30 K–B1 K–Q3 31 B×R K×B 32 K–K2, but also that after 32 . . . K–B5 33 K–Q2 K–N6 his QRP would fall. After the text move, White wins without much difficulty.

28 . . .   R–K3
29 B–B1   B–N6
30 R–Q7+   K–B1

31 R×BP R–K4 32 R–B6 R×P 33 R–QN6! B–B7 34 R×P R–QB4 35 R–R3 (the point of move 33) 35 . . . R–Q4 36 P–B3 R–Q8 37 K–B2 R–QB8 38 P–R4 B–N3 39 B–B4 K–K2 40 P–N4 P–R3 41 B–Q5 Black resigned.

Variation 2

8 P–QR4 (*24*)

By comparison with the solid line, Black has a more developed position, but the text is still a worthwhile alternative to 8 P–B3.

8 . . .   P–N5!?

Although not disastrous, this move is still suspect, because it concedes the c4 square to White. Reasonable alternatives are:

a) 8 . . . R–N1 9 P×P P×P e.g. 10 N–B3 P–Q3! 11 P–R3 B–Q2 12 P–Q3 Q–K1 as in Treybal-Alekhine, Pistyan 1922.

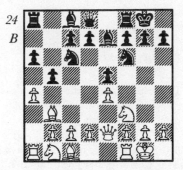

White might consider 10 P–B3 P–Q3 11 P–Q3, with a careful build up for P–Q4.

b) 8 . . . P–Q4!? can be met by 9 B×P!? (*9 P–Q3 B–KN5*=) as suggested by Matanović.

9 P–R5!

9 P–Q4 P–Q4! and 9 P–Q3 P–Q3 are interesting, but less dangerous.

9 . . .   P–Q3

Here 9 . . . P–Q4!? is dubious; after 10 P×P:

a) 10 . . . N×QP?? 11 Q–B4 forks two knights.

b) 10 . . . P–K5?! 11 N–N5!

c) 10 . . . B–KN5 11 P×N P–K5 12 P Q3 is unclear, while 12 P–Q4!? P×N 13 Q–Q3 P×P 14 R–K1 is worth trying.

10 P–R3

Not 10 P–B3 R–N1 11 B–QB4 P–Q4 when White can no longer keep a pawn at K4.

10 . . .   B–K3
11 B×B   P×B
12 P–B3   P–Q4
13 P–Q3= (diagram 21)

The Exchange Variation

In this section, we briefly indicate an alternative way for White to handle the Ruy Lopez. Then we shall discuss, in the remainder of the chapter, some methods by which Black may try to avoid the Worrall Attack.

1 P–K4	P–K4
2 N–KB3	N–QB3
3 B–N5	P–QR3
4 B×N	QP×B
5 0–0	

This is particularly effective against players who like an early simplification. See our comments on pp. 8–9.

5 . . .	P–B3

5 . . . B–KN5 is the main alternative, and can lead to an amusing draw after 6 P–KR3 P–KR4 7 P–B3 Q–Q6 8 P×B P×P 9 N×P B–Q3! 10 N×Q! B–R7+ 11 K–R1 B–N6+ etc. White can try to improve on this with 7 P–Q3!, e.g. 7 . . . Q–B3 8 QN–Q2 (or *8 B–K3!?*) 8 . . . N–K2 9 N–B4 B×N 10 Q×B Q×Q 11 P×Q as in Kagan-Ree, Havana 1966.

6 P–Q4	B–KN5

For 6 . . . P×P see the game Ribli-Zuidema in chapter 1 (pp. 8–9).

7 P×P!	Q×Q
8 R×Q	B×N

8 . . . P×P only transposes after 9 R–Q3 B×N 10 P×B! One of White's ideas is to create a passed pawn by eventually playing P–KB4. The rook goes to Q3 to avoid being obstructed by the knight, and to stand by to attack on the Q-side.

Adorjan-Tringov, Varna 1972, now continued 9 P×B P×P 10 R–Q3 N–B3 11 N–Q2 P–QN4 12 P–QR4 B–Q3 13 N–N3 0–0 14 N–R5 P–B4 15 P–QB4. White was well on top, thanks to the weak black pawns.

Other Lopez Defences for Black

So far we have only considered lines in which Black meets the Ruy Lopez by 3 . . . P–QR3 and 4 . . . N–B3. No other defences have retained the same popularity as that (the so-called Morphy Defence), but others are tried from time to time by players whose particular style is suited to them. These are of two types: a) the strong-point defences; b) the combinative counter-attacks.

The strong-point defences are those in which Black bases his play on the defence of a particular key central square (usually, his K4). He is willing to suffer a long White initiative in the hope of later reaching a good ending or going over to a counter-attack. The most important of these is the Steinitz Defence Deferred, 3 . . . P–QR3 4 B–R4 P–Q3.

Most of the combinative defences, as we have already observed, can be avoided by White, if he goes into the Worrall Attack by 5 Q–K2. The most important of the unavoidable counter-attacks is the Schliemann, 3 . . . P–B4, which is still seen from time to time, even in master tournaments. As it requires sharp and accurate play from White right from the start, it is the main threat to the equilibrium of the Exchange Lopez die-hards. Like most of the defences considered under this rubric however, the Schliemann is probably unsound from an analytical point of view.

1 P–K4	P–K4
2 N–KB3	N–QB3
3 B–N5	

We consider:

3 . . . B–B4 – Classical
3 . . . N–B3 – Berlin
3 . . . KN–K2 – Cozio
3 . . . P–Q3 – Steinitz
3 . . . P–QR3 – to Steinitz Deferred
3 . . . P–B4 – Schliemann

Classical Defence

3 . . .	B–B4

An apparently active square for the bishop: attacking White's KB2 and delaying White's P–Q4. But it has drawbacks.

4 P–B3 N–B3

Occasionally seen are:

a) 4 ... P–B4?! 5 P–Q4 BP×P 6 B×N QP×B 7 KN–Q2 B–Q3 (7 ... *Q–N4 8 P×B Q×P 9 Q–R5+*) 8 P×P P–K6 9 P×P (*9 N–K4!?*) 9 ... B–QB4 10 Q–R5+ P–KN3 11 Q–B3 with some advantage to White.

b) 4 ... KN–K2 5 0–0 B–N3 6 P–Q4 P×P 7 P×P P–Q4 8 P×P N×P 9 R–K1+ B–K3 10 P–QR4 (or *10 B–N5*) 10 ... P–QR3 11 B×N+ P×B 12 B–N5 Q–Q3 13 QN–Q2 0–0 14 N–B4 Nei-Anitsenko, Minsk 1963. White has a strong initiative.

5 P–Q4 P×P

Or 5 ... B–N3 6 Q–K2 P×P 7 P–K5 0–0 8 P×P (not 8 P×N? R–K1) 8 ... R–K1 9 B–K3 N–Q4 10 N–B3 N×B 11 P×N P–Q4 12 0–0 B–N5 13 Q–B2 B–KR4 14 B–R4 Tal-van Geet, Wijk aan Zee 1968. White has a firm and centre and good prospects of a K-side attack.

6 P–K5 N–K5
7 0–0 P–Q4
8 KP×Pep 0–0
9 QP×P Q–B3!
10 B×N P×B
11 P×P

a) 11 ... B–Q3? 12 R–K1 B–KB4 13 N–B3 KR–K1 14 N×N B×N 15 B–N5! and White won, Stein-Spassky, 28th USSR Ch 1961.

b) 11 ... B–N3 12 R–K1 B–KB4 13 N–B3 KR–K1 14 N×N B×N 15 B–N5! Q–Q3! 16 B–Q8 B×BP still gives Black drawing chances, despite the pawn minus – Euwe.

Berlin Defence

3 ... N–B3
4 0–0

Black now has the choice between:

a) 4 ... P–Q3 (strong-point style) 5 P–Q4 B–Q2 6 N–B3 P×P 7 N×P B–K2 8 B–B4! (avoiding wholesale exchanges) 8 ... N×N 9 Q×N 0–0 10 QR–Q1 B×B 11 N×B P–QR3 12 N–B3 Holmov-Sandor, Bucharest 1954; White dominates the centre.

b) 4 ... N×P (simplifying. This is the true Berlin Defence.) 5 R–K1 N–Q3 6 N×P B–K2 7 B–Q3 0–0= but the sharper 5 P–Q4 gives some prospects of an initiative.

c) 4 ... B–B4 (complicating) 5 P–B3 0–0 6 P–Q4 B–N3 7 B–N5 P–KR3 8 B–KR4 P–Q3 9 P–R4 P–QR4 10 R–K1 B–N5 11 B5×N P×B 12 P×P P×P 13 QN–Q2. The liability of Black's weak Pawns outweighs his possession of the two bishops.

Cozio Defence

3 ... KN–K2

This is the ancient Cozio Defence, revived of late by Larsen and Wade. The main idea is to transpose to the Steinitz Defence Deferred, while avoiding the Exchange Variation:

a) 4 P–B3 P–QR3 5 B–R4 P–Q3 6 P–Q4 B–Q2 is level.

b) 4 0–0 is met by 4 ... N–N3 – Larsen. This needs more tests.

c) 4 P–Q4 N×P 5 N×N P×N 6 Q×P N–B3 7 B×N QP×B 8 Q×Q+ K×Q (Mestel-Larsen, London 1973) is an improved Exchange variation for Black, in view of the extra pair of knights exchanged.

Steinitz Defence

3 ... P–Q3

This move is often played by novices, who think that they have to defend their KP immediately. However, after 4 P–Q4 B–Q2 5 N–B3 N–B3 6 B×N

B×B 7 Q–Q3!, the attack on the KP does become real, and Black has to give up the centre, allowing White attacking chances after 7 . . . P×P 8 N×P B–Q2 9 B–N5 B–K2 10 0–0–0 0–0 11 P–B4 N–K1 12 B×B Q×B 13 N–Q5 Q–Q1 14 P–KN4! Spielmann-Maroczy, Göteborg 1920.

Steinitz Defence Deferred

3 ...	P–QR3
4 B–R4	P–Q3(*25*)

Black, if need be, is now able to play . . . P–QN4 in order to maintain the strongpoint at K4. There is no space here to go into all the ramifications of the defence, which is one of Black's soundest positional methods of meeting the Lopez. However, a few examples should give a basic idea of the chances of the two players.

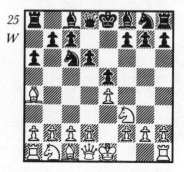

25
W

From the wide choice available to White at this stage, we choose the move that does most to cut across Black's plans:

5 B×N+

Old-fashioned but probably the best. We shall follow the game Richter-Naegeli, Munich 1936.

5 ...	P×B
6 P–Q4	P–B3
7 Q–Q3!	P–KN3

Critical is 7 . . . N–K2 8 N–B3 (*8 P–KR4 B–N5!?*) 8 . . . N–N3 9 P–KR4 P–KR4 10 B–K3 B–Q2 11 0–0–0 with good attacking chances for White; Stulik-Podgorny, Karlovy Vary 1948.

8 P–KR4!	P–KR3
9 N–B3	B–K3
10 B–K3	N–K2

11 0–0–0 B–N2 12 N–R2! (White is now ready to launch a storming attack of his K-side pawns.) 12 . . . Q–N1 13 P–B4 Q–N5 (rather than 'castle into it', Black prefers to keep his king in the centre and counter-attack along the QN-file – but White is too solidly entrenched.) 14 P–QR3 Q–B5 15 Q–Q2 (threatening *16 P–QN3*, winning the queen!) 15 . . . P–QR4 16 P–QN3 Q–R3 17 BP×P BP×P 18 P×P B×KP 19 N–B3 B–N5 20 N×B! (a fine exchange sacrifice which opens up the way for White's pieces into the heart of the enemy position.) 20 . . . B×R 21 R×B P×N 22 Q–Q7+ K–B2 23 Q×P.B7 R–KR2 24 Q×KP R–K1 25 P–R5! Q–B1 26 R–Q6! P–N4 27 R–B6+ K–N1 28 B–Q4 Q–Q2 29 R×RP! N–B4 30 Q–R8+!! Black resigned.

A beautiful finish. If 30 . . . R×Q 31 R×R+ K–B2 32 R–R7+ K–K3 33 P×N+ K–Q3 34 R×Q+ K×R 35 P–R6 R–K2 36 B–N7 and wins.

Schliemann Counter-Attack

3 . . .   P–B4

The Schliemann, a double-edged sword indeed!

4 N–B3

This sound developing move is now generally thought to be White's best preparation for the inevitable complications. 4 P×P is too wild after 4 . . . P–K5, but the sharp 4 P–Q4 and the cautious 4 P–Q3 may also give White somewhat the better of things.

4 ...   PxP

Sometimes Black tries:

a) 4 ... N–Q5 5 B–R4 N–B3 6 0–0 B–B4 7 NxP 0–0 (*7 ... PxP?! 8 P–Q3!*) 8 PxP P–Q4 9 N–K2 Q–K2 10 NxN QxN 11 N–B3 QxBP 12 P–Q4 B–Q3 13 P–QB3 Zurakhov-A. Zaitsev, USSR 1963. Black's K-side pressure seems insufficient compensation for the lost pawn.

b) 4 ... N–B3 5 PxP B–B4 6 0–0 0–0 7 NxP! NxN 8 P–Q4 BxP 9 QxB P–Q3 10 B–KB4 (or *10 B–Q3*) 10 ... BxP 11 BxN PxB 12 QxKP BxP 13 B–B4+ K–R1 15 N–N5 Stein-Nadezhdin, USSR 1963. White has the more active pieces.

5 QNxP   P–Q4

6 NxP!?

White gets slightly better chances also with the conservative 6 N–N3, meeting 6 ... B–KN5 by 7 P–KR3 BxN 8 QxB N–B3 9 P–Q3 B–Q3 10 N–R5.

6 ...   PxN

7 NxN   Q–Q4

White has a clear plus after either:

a) 7 ... PxN? 8 BxP+ B–Q2 9 Q–R5+ K–K2 10 Q–K5+ B–K3 11 P–KB4! PxP ep (*11 ... N–R3 12 P–B5!*) 12 0–0 R–QN1 13 P–Q4 N–B3 (*13 ... N–B7!?*) 14 P–Q5 Gipslis-Tringov, Varna 1962, or

b) 7 ... Q–N4 8 Q–K2 N–KB3 9 P–KB4! Q–R5+ 10 P–N3 Q–R6 11 N–K5+! P–B3 12 B–B4 Hazai-Szell, Hungary 1973.

8 P QB4   Q–Q3

9 NxP+

Black is the only one with winning chances after 9 Q–R5+ P–N3 10 Q–K5+ QxQ 11 NxQ+ P–B3 12 B–R4 B–N2!

9 ...   B–Q2

10 BxB+   QxB

11 Q–R5+!   P–KN3

11 ... K–Q1 allows some advantage after 12 Q–R5 (or even *12 N–N5*) 12 ... K–K1 13 0–0 N–B3 14 P–Q3 PxP 15 B–K3.

12 Q–K5+   K–B2

13 N–N5   P–B3

14 Q–Q4! Ciocaltea-Malich, Romania–E. Germany 1964. Black cannot justify his deficit of two pawns – if 14 ... Q–N5 simply 15 0–0 is best.

3 OTHER KING-SIDE OPEN GAMES

Games that begin 1 P–K4 P–K4 share certain common characteristics. The central files are liable to be quickly opened, so that the kings are often subject to direct attack. Skill at hand-to-hand fighting with the pieces is at a premium. These openings were more popular than any others in the 19th Century, and many of their secrets were discovered by the great masters of that era: Morphy, Anderssen, Steinitz and Chigorin. Nowadays these openings are relatively infrequent in master play, but in correspondence chess, where it is more usual for Black to reply 1 ... P–K4, knowledge of them is important. But a season or two of playing open games is an essential stage in the development of anybody who aspires to all-round and to international ability; one should study these openings before going on to the more fashionable defences and closed games.

The Vienna Game

1 P–K4   P–K4
2 N–QB3

The Bishop's Opening, 2 B–B4, is closely related to the Vienna. The usual continuation is 2 ... N–KB3 when:
a) 3 N–QB3 transposes to the Bishop's Variation following.
b) 3 P–Q3 is best met by 3 ... P–B3 and now:
b1) 4 Q–K2 B–K2 5 N–KB3 (*5 P–B4 P–Q4*) 5 ... P–Q3 or

b2) 4 N–KB3 B–K2 5 0–0 (5 N×P?? Q–R4+) 5 ... P–Q3 6 QN–Q2 0–0 7 R–K1 QN–Q2 8 P–B3 P–QN4 9 B–N3 P–QR4 and Black has good counter-chances; Hartston-Clarke, London 1973.

The chief characteristic of the Vienna is White's desire to attack the centre by P–KB4, either immediately, or after B–B4 and some further preparation. It is not easy for Black to equalize against either form of the Vienna, for he has to worry about not only the pressure on the KB-file (especially his KB2, a typical weakness in all open games), but also the pin on his KN by B–KN5 and the pressure which the white queen can exert by coming to KN3 via K1. Black must respond aggressively from the very first, if he is not to incur a positional disadvantage.

2 ...   N–KB3 (*26*)

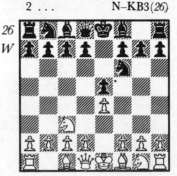

26
W

2 ... N–QB3 allows White to play 3 B–B4 without risking the critical

3 . . . N×P!? 2 . . . B–B4 3 N–B3 P–Q3 4 P–Q4 gives White a slight but definite initiative in the centre.

White must now choose between:

3 B–B4 – Bishop's Variation

3 P–B4 – Vienna 'Gambit'

3 P–KN3 is occasionally seen. A sample line is 3 . . . B–B4 4 B–N2 N–B3 5 N–B3 P–Q3 6 P–Q3 0–0 (*6 . . . B–KN5 7 N–QR4 N–Q2* is also good.) 7 P–KR3 P–QR3 8 0–0 B–K3 9 K–R2 P–R3 10 B–K3 B×B 11 P×B P–Q4, Kolobov-Bykhovsky, Moscow 1964, when Black has equal chances.

Bishop's Variation

3 B–B4

Diagrams 27, 28 and 29 show typical positions from this variation.

Good Position for White
Larsen-Lengyel, Amsterdam 1964

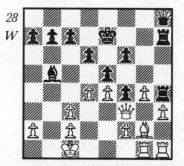

28
W

In return for the pawn sacrificed, Black has obtained a strong grip on the K-side. The white king has fled across the board, but even on QR1 he will be vulnerable to the attack based on · . . . B–B5, and . . . Q–K1–R5. Relatively best now would be 1 P–B4, returning the pawn in order to gain scope for the white queen.

An Even Position
Larsen-Letelier, Havana 1967

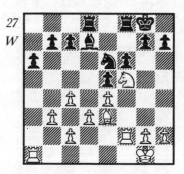

27
W

White is in control of the half-open QR-and KB-files, and his minor pieces have more scope than Black's. The ideal pawn structure gives White a solid centre, with the possibilities of P–Q4 or P–QN5 at the right time; he duly won in the endgame.

Good Position for Black
Adams-A. R. B. Thomas, Hastings 1950–1

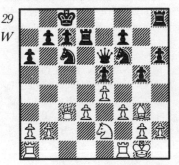

29
W

This is a complicated middle game, with kings castled on opposite sides. Black has pressure on the Q-file, but White has compensation for this, as by advancing his QNP he can create threats against the black king.

After 3 B–B4, Black has three main plans:

3 . . . N–B3 – Variation 1

3 . . . B–B4 – Variation 2

3 . . . N×P!? – Variation 3

Variation 1

3 ...   N–B3

4 P–Q3

4 P–B4!? is a trappy alternative. Black's best is probably 4 ... N×P 5 N–B3 N–Q3! 6 B–N3 (*6 B–Q5!? P×P!*) 6 ... P–K5 7 Q–K2 (*7 N–KN5 P–KR3 8 N5×KP N×N 9 Q–K2 Q–K2*) 7 ... Q–K2 8 N–KN5 N–Q5 9 Q–K3 N×B! for now the seemingly devastating 10 N–Q5 is immediately defeated by 10 ... N×R!. After 10 RP×N N–B4 11 Q–R3 P–Q4! 12 N×QP Q–Q1 Black has much the better development; Prins-Stoltz, Stockholm 1952.

4 ...   B–N5

Instead 4 ... N–QR4 5 KN–K2 N×B 6 P×N B–B4 7 0–0 P–Q3 8 Q–Q3 gives White a firm control of the centre.

5 N–B3

Also playable are:

a) 5 N–K2 P–Q4 6 P×P N×P 7 0–0 B–K3 8 B×N B×B 9 P–B4 0–0 10 P–B5 P–B3 11 Q–K1 with chances of a K-side attack, although Black has a solid position with the two bishops.

b) 5 B–KN5 P–KR3 6 B×N B×N+ 7 P×B Q×B 8 N–K2 N–K2 9 Q–Q2 (*9 0–0 P–KN4 10 N–N3 P–KR4!* led to diagram 28) 9 ... P–KN4 10 Q–K3 P–Q3 11 P–B3 N–N3 12 P–N3 B–K3 13 B–N3 Wade-Jones, British Ch 1952; White plays a waiting game. At the right moment, P–KB4 may prove effective.

5 ...   P–Q3

Black dare not win material: 5 ... P–Q4 6 P×P N×P 7 0–0! N×N? 8 P×N B×P? 9 N–N5! White also stands better after 8 ... B–K2 9 Q–K1 Q–Q3 10 P–QR4! 0–0 11 B–R3 or 8 ... B–QB4 9 P–Q4!

6 ́0–0   B×N

7 P×B   N–QR4

It is safer to play 7 ... 0–0, as 8

B–KN5 is not an effective reply. White should first play 8 Q–K2 and 9 N–Q2, followed by Q–N3 and P–KB4 if Black fails to prevent this.

8 B–N3   N×B

9 RP×N   0–0

10 P–B4

Larsen has shown that this position is favourable for White; a possible sequel is 10 ... Q–K2 11 N–Q2 N–Q2 12 Q–R5 N–B4 13 P–B4 P×P 14 R×P Q–K4 15 Q×Q P×Q 16 R–B2 N–K3 17 N–B3 P–KB3 18 B–K3 P–QR3 19 N–R4 B–Q2 20 N–B5 QR–Q1, reaching diagram 27.

Variation 2

3 ...   B–B4

4 P–Q3

Not 4 P–B4? B×N! 5 R×B N×P! 6 N×N P–Q4 and Black stands very well.

4 ...   P–Q3(*30*)

4 ... N–B3 can be met by 5 P–B4, 5 B–KN5 or 5 B–K3; but now 5 B–K3 can be met by 5 ... QN–Q2!

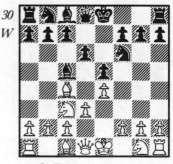

5 Q–B3!?

An interesting alternative to:

a) 5 N–R4 B–N5+! 6 P–B3 P–Q4! 7 P×P B–Q3 with promising play for the pawn – Keres.

b) 5 P–B4 P–Q3 6 N–B3 P–QR3! = See p. 34.

c) 5 B–KN5 P–KR3 6 B–R4 P–KN4 7 B–N3 N–B3 = – Nimzowitsch.

5 ...	N–B3
6 KN–K2	P–KR3
7 B–K3	B×B

Or 7 ... B–KN5 8 Q–N3 B×B 9 P×B N–QR4 10 B–N3 N×B 11 RP×N 0–0 12 0–0 B×N 13 N×B N–R2 14 N–B3 Q–Q2 15 P–N4 P–R3 16 N–Q5 with good chances for White, Harding-Karafiath, corres 1973–5.

8 P×B	N–QR4
9 B–N3	N×B

10 RP×N P–B3 11 0–0 0–0 12 N–N3 P–Q4 13 P×P P×P 14 P–Q4 and Black's position is devoid of active counter-chances; Larsen-Petersen, Danish Ch 1964.

Variation 3

3 ...	N×P!?
4 Q–R5	

Not 4 N×N P–Q4 because Black gets the upper hand in the centre, while 4 B×P+ K×B 5 N×N P–Q4 6 Q B3+ K–N1 is also dubious (7 P–Q4 B–K2 8 Q–N3 N–B3).

4 ...	N–Q3
5 B–N3	N–B3

5 ... B–K2 does not equalize, because of 6 N–B3 (*6 Q×KP* is also possible.) 6 ... N–B3 (*6 ... 0–0? 7 P–KR4! N–B3 8 N–KN5 P–KR3 9 Q–N6!*) 7 N×P N×N (or *7 ... 0–0 8 N–Q5 N–Q5 9 0–0 N×B 10 RP×N N–K1 11 Q–K2 B–B3 12 N–QB4* or *11 ... N–B3 12 N–B6!*) 8 Q×N 0–0 9 N–Q5! R–K1 10 0–0 B–B1 11 Q–B4 Alekhine-Euwe, match 1935. White had the initiative and went on to win.

6 N–N5	P–KN3
7 Q–B3	P–B4
8 Q–Q5	Q–K2
9 N×P+	K–Q1
10 N×R	P–N3(*31*)

By a virtually forced sequence, this complex and unclear position has been reached. Black has, in effect, sacrificed the exchange, in return for which he has chances against the white king and queen.

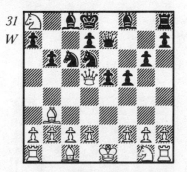

31
W

As an illustration, we give the continuation of the game Hansen-Nunn, Students' Olympiad, Teesside 1974:

11 P–Q3

White has also tried here 11 Q–B3, 11 P–Q4, 11 N×P and others.

11 ...	B–QN2
12 P–KR4	P–B5
13 Q–B3	B–KR3!
14 Q–N4?	

Better may be 14 N–K2 N–Q5 15 Q–R3 e.g. 15 ... N×N (*15 ... P–K5 16 N×N P×P+ 17 N–K6+!*) 16 K×N P–B6+ 17 P×P B×B and 18 ... R–B1 with complications.

14 ...   P–K5!

15 B×P P×P+ 16 K–B1 B×B 17 Q×B R–B1 18 Q–N3 (Not *18 Q–N5? R×P+! 19 K×R N–K5+*) 18 ... N–K5 19 Q–B7+ K–K1 20 N–R3 (if *20 N–B3–or 20 P–KB3 Q–B4!– 20 ... N–Q7+ 21 K–N1* Black mates by *21 ... R×N! 22 P×R N×P+ 23 K–N2 Q–K5* threatening 24 ... N–K8+ etc.) 20 ... N×P! 21 N×N Q–K7+ 22 K–N1 Q×N+ 23 K–R2 Q×RP+ 24 K–N1 Q–Q5+ 25 K–R2 N–K4 26 KR–KB1 N–N5+ 27 K–N3 (*27 K–N1 B×P+ 28*

K×B N–K6+ soon leads to mate.) 27 ... Q–K6+ 28 K×N P–KR4+ 29 K–R4 P–KN4+ 30 K×RP R–R1+ 31 K–N6 B–K5+ 32 R–B5 B×R+ 33 K×B R–B1+ 34 K–N6 Q–K5+ 35 K–N7 Q–K2+ 36 K–N6 Q–B3+ 37 K–R5 Q–R1+ 38 K–N4 Q–R5 mate.

Vienna 'Gambit'

3 P–B4(*32*)

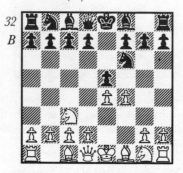

3 ...   P–Q4

Inexperienced players sometimes choose:

a) 3 ... P–Q3? 4 N–B3 N–B3 5 B–B4 and Black's KB is passively placed within the pawn chain, or

b) 3 ... P×P? 4 P–K5 Q–K2 5 Q–K2 forcing the ignominious retreat 5 ... N–N1.

4 BP×P   N×P

The fundamental ideas of this position are simple. White wishes to drive away the black knight, and form a strong pawn centre by P–Q4. Black wants, if possible, to maintain his knight at K5. If not, he has a choice of two plans or a combination of them: to try to set up a centre of his own by ... P–QB4 (and possibly ... P–Q5), or to attack the spearhead of the white forces by ... P–KB3.

5 P–Q3 .

5 N–B3 is usually played, but Black then gets good chances to equalize by 5 ... B–KN5 6 Q–K2 N×N. The text has the advantage of containing tactical possibilities, in which the player with the more detailed knowledge of the opening comes off best.

5 ...   N×N

Other moves lead to wild complications, tending in White's favour:

a) 5 ... Q–R5+? 6 P–N3 N×P 7 N–KB3 Q–R4 8 N×P! and now two game continuations:

1) 8 ... N×R 9 N×P+ K–Q1 10 N×R B–K2 11 B–N2 B–R5+ 12 K–B1 N–B3 13 P–Q4! and White remains at least a pawn ahead; Baretic-Nikolic, Hastings Challengers 1964.

2) 8 ... B–KN5 9 B–N2 N×R 10 N×P+ K–Q2 11 N×R N–B3 12 B–K3 P–B3 13 P–Q4 P×P 14 P–Q5! with Black's king is in the greater danger, Milner-Barry – Sergeant, Margate 1938.

b) 5 ... B–QN5!? 6 P×N Q–R5+ 7 K–K2 B–N5+ 8 N–B3 B×N 9 P×B P×P 10 Q–Q4! B–R4! (*10 ... P×N+? 11 P×P* and the bishop is lost.) 11 K–K3! B×N 12 B–N5+ (*12 P×B Q–K8+ 13 K–B4 Q–R5+* is perpetual check!) 12 ... P–B3 13 P×B when:

b1) 13 ... Q–R3+! is best played in Chigorin-Caro, Vienna 1898; objectively correct then is 14 K–K2 Q–R6 15 R–Q1 P×P+ 16 K–B2 Q×P+ 17 K–K3 Q–R3+ with perpetual check – Vuković.

b2) 13 ... P×B? 14 Q×KP (*14 B–R3!?* is wild.) 14 ... Q×Q+ 15 K×Q N–Q2 with reasonable drawing chances for Black, although White's centralized king gives him the better ending – Marco.

6 P×N   P–Q5

This is best, but also interesting are:

a) 6 ... B–K2 7 P–Q4! 0–0 8 B–Q3!
P–KB3 9 Q–R5 P–KN3 10 B×B P×B
11 Q×P+ K–R1 12 N–B3!? – Eales and
Henderson in *Chess*.

b) 6 ... P–QB4 7 N–B3 N–B3 8 B–K2
B–K2 9 0–0 B–K3 10 P–Q4 P–B5
(Gardner-Persitz, Oxford 1955) 11
R–N1 with some chances for White –
Persitz.

7 N–B3	P–QB4!?

Consistent, but it is better to simplify
by 7 ... N–QB3 8 P×P B–N5+! (*8 ...
N×QP? 9 P–B3*) 9 B–Q2 B×B+ 10
Q×B N×QP 11 P–B3 N×N+ 12 P×N
Q–Q4! and White's position is loose, M.
Prizant-A. Phillips, Surrey v. Kent
1973; formerly, 12 ... Q–R5+ was
played, with an edge to White.

8 B–K2	B–K2
9 0–0	0–0
10 Q–K1	P–B3

Not 10 ... N–B3 11 Q–N3 K–R1 12
N–N5! with a strong attack. Sax-
Ciocaltea, Vrnjacka Banja 1974.

11 Q–N3

Also dangerous is 11 KP×P B×P 12
Q–N3 offering a pawn for the sake of
swift development, but Black can reply
12 ... N–B3 13 B–N5 N–K2! to bring
the knight into the white position.

11 ...	BP×P?

11 ... N–B3 or 11 ... K–R1! should
be tested.

12 B–R6	B–B3
13 N–N5!	Q–K2
14 B–B3!	

White has a ferocious attack:
a) 14 ... K–R1 15 N×P! P×B (*15 ...
K×N 16 B–K4!* and *17 Q–N6*) 16 N×R
Q×N 17 B–Q5 N–Q2 18 Q–N6 Q–N2
19 Q–K8+ N–B1 20 R×B Black
resigned. Beckers-Denckens, Belgian
Corres Ch 1959–60.

b) 14 ... P×B 15 N–K6+ K–R1 16
N×R Q×N 17 B–Q5 N–Q2 18 R–B3
Q–N2 19 QR–KB1 etc.

The King's Gambit

1 P–K4	P–K4
2 P–KB4	(*33*)

This ancient opening has experienced a definite resurgence of
popularity, thanks to Fischer, Spassky,
and Bronstein. It has the power to
inspire a fanatical loyalty in certain
players, who are temperamentally
suited to its complications.

The idea of sacrifice of material in
return for an attack has rarely taken a
simpler form. White offers his KBP to
divert Black's KP from the centre.
Then he occupies the centre and hopes
to regain the pawn, or to break through
on the KB-file later on. In the 19th
century, Black almost always tried to
hold on to his gains by 2 ... P×P 3
N–KB3 P–KN4. All kinds of
complications result from this, in which
White has many opportunities for
combinative attack. We shall only look
at a few lines for Black: those which give
him good chances of counter-attack.

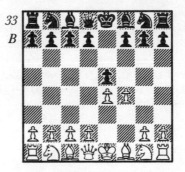

Black can try:
2 ... *P–Q4!?* – Falkbeer
2 ... *B–B4* – Declined
2 ... *P×P* – Accepted

Falkbeer Counter-Gambit

    2 ...   P–Q4!?
    3 QP×P   P–K5

The Falkbeer Counter-Gambit, which has fallen upon evil days. Black will have a hard job to improve on this line, given by Keres: 4 P–Q3! N–KB3 5 P×P! N×KP 6 N–KB3! B–QB4 7 Q–K2 B–B4 8 N–B3 Q–K2 9 B–K3 B×B (or *9 ... N×N 10 B×B N×Q 11 B×Q N×P 12 B–R3!*) 10 Q×B N×N 11 Q×Q+ K×Q 12 P×N B–K5 13 N–N5! B×QP 14 0–0–0 and White's minor pieces are very active.

If Black wishes to play the Falkbeer, we think he should consider Nimzowitsch's idea 3 ... P–QB3, e.g. 4 N–QB3 BP×P 5 P×P P–Q5 6 N–K4 Q–Q4 7 Q–K2 N–QB3.

King's Gambit Declined

    2 ...   B–B4

The most reliable move.

    3 N–KB3   P–Q3

3 ... N–QB3 is bad, because of 4 N–B3! P–Q3 5 N–QR4 B–KN5 6 N×B P×N 7 B–N5! – Korchnoi and Zak.

    4 P–B3

4 N–B3 N–KB3 5 B–B4 N–B3 6 P–Q3 can arise from the Vienna, too. 6 ... P–QR3! preserves the valuable KB from exchange and thus ensures Black good chances. A sample line is 7 P–B5 P–R3 8 Q–K2 B–Q2 9 B–K3 N–Q5 10 B×N P×B 11 N–Q1 0–0 12 0–0 P–Q4; Tolush-Furman, Leningrad 1946.

    4 ...   N–KB3
    5 P×P

Not 5 P–Q4 P×QP 6 P×P B–QN5+!

    5 ...   P×P
    6 N×P

6 P–Q4 P×P 7 P×P is well met by Euwe's line 7 ... B–QN5+ 8 B–Q2 Q–K2! 9 P–K5 N–Q4.

    6 ...   Q–K2

    7 P–Q4   B–Q3

The chances are equal:

a) 8 N–B3 N×P 9 B–K2 0–0 10 0–0 P–QB4 11 QN–Q2 N×N 12 B×N Charousek-Janowski, Berlin 1897.

b) 8 N–B4 N×P 9 N×B+ P×N! – Korchnoi and Zak.

King's Gambit Accepted

    2 ...   P×P
    3 N–KB3   P–Q4

Fischer showed that White can try to keep the pawn by 3 ... P–Q3!?, the main idea being to keep the white knight out of e5. Black's chances in the complications are certainly not worse, e.g.:

a) 4 P–Q4 P–KN4 5 P–KR4 P–N5 6 N–N5?! P–KB3! 7 N–R3 P×N 8 Q–R5+ K–Q2 9 B×P Q–K1! 10 Q–B3 K–Q1 is dubious, and so is

b) 4 B–B4 P–KR3 5 P–Q4 P–KN4 6 P–KN3!? N–QB3 7 P×P P–N5 8 N–N1 Q–R5+ 9 K–B1 N–B3 10 N–QB3 P–N6 Spassky-Portisch, Leningrad – Budapest 1967.

The text move is popular but should turn out good for White.

    4 P×P   N–KB3
    5 B–N5+   P–B3
    6 P×P   N×P!?

Or 6 ... P×P 7 B–B4 N–Q4 8 N–B3! preventing ... B–Q3

    7 P–Q4   B–Q3
    8 0–0!

Not:

a) 8 P–Q5? N×P 9 Q×N?? B–QN5+ wins the white queen.

b) 8 Q–K2+ B–K3 9 N–K5 (*9 N–N5 0–0*) 9 ... 0–0 10 B×N P×B 11 B×P N–Q4 12 B–N3 P–B3 with a clear advantage for Black; Hartston-Spassky, Hastings 1965–66.

    8 ...   0–0

9 QN–Q2!   B–KN5
10 N–B4   B–B2
11 P–B3 N–Q4 12 Q–Q3. White threatens 13 B×N P×B 14 N3–K5, so it is doubtful whether Black can equalize.

The Italian Game and Two Knights' Defence

1 P–K4   P–K4
2 N–KB3   N–QB3
3 B–B4(*34*)

This opening contains two basic ideas: to attack directly the weak point at KB7 (always vulnerable at the beginning of the game, since it is defended only by the king), and to advance the QP, supported by the QBP, in order to obtain two pawns abreast in the centre. Black's counter lies almost always in . . . P–Q4, and in the following variations the student should notice how often this occurs. Against careless play, White quickly obtains an overwhelming initiative, e.g. 3 . . . B–B4 4 P–B3 N–B3 5 P–Q4 P×P 6 P×P B–N3? 7 P–Q5 N–QN1 8 P–K5 N–N1 9 0–0 N–K2 10 P–Q6 N–N5 11 N–N5 0–0 12 Q–R5 and Black will soon have to sacrifice his queen to avoid mate.

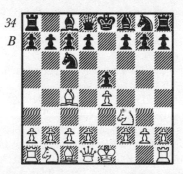

34
B

In the Italian Game, White has a wide choice of attacks, and we recommend the match player who is concerned about finding a standard defence to 3 B–B4 to concentrate on the Two Knights' Defence instead. Objectively, this defence offers equal chances; in many lines, Black is able to seize a dangerous initiative at the cost of a pawn or two.

We consider in turn:
3 . . . B–B4 – Italian
3 . . . N–B3! – Two Knights'

The Italian Game

3 . . .   B–B4

Internationally, White's and Black's first three moves are known as the Italian Game, though English-speaking countries refer to it as the Giuoco Piano.

White's main attacking lines now are:
4 P–QN4 – Evans Gambit
4 P–B3 – Main Line

Evans Gambit

4 P–QN4   B×NP
5 P–B3   B–R4

This is the best way to meet the famous Evans Gambit. Another defence that may equalize is 5 . . . B–K2, meeting 6 P–Q4 by 6 . . . N–R4 7 N×P N×B, returning the pawn but obtaining the two bishops.

6 P–Q4   P×P

6 . . . P–Q3 7 Q–N3 gives White chances for an initiative. White can still play 7 Q–N3 after the text move, offering another pawn or two for a speculative attack. More usual, however, is:

7 0–0   KN–K2!(*35*)

Now Black has very little to fear. For example:
a) 8 N–N5 P–Q4 9 KP×P N–K4 10 Q×P P–B3.

b) 8 P×P P–Q4 9 P×P N2×P 10 Q–N3
(10 B–R3 B–K3 11 B–QN5 B–QN5=)
10 ... B–K3! 11 Q×P N4–N5 12
B–QN5 B–Q4! 13 B–R3 0–0!
threatening ... R–QN1.

35
W

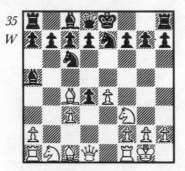

Main Line

4 P–B3	N–B3
5 P–Q4	P×P
6 P×P	B–N5+
7 B–Q2	

7 N–B3!? is complicated, but not
really sound. Black gets the better of it
after 7 ... N×KP 8 0–0 B×N 9 P–Q5
B–B3 10 R–K1 N–K2 11 R×N P–Q3 12
B–KN5 B×B 13 N×B P–KR3! (*13 ...
0–0 14 N×RP!* should lead to a draw.)
14 B–N5+ B–Q2! 15 Q–K2 B×B 16
Q×B+ Q–Q2; Barczay-Portisch,
Budapest 1969.

7 ...	B×B+
8 QN×B	P–Q4

9 P×P KN×P 10 Q–N3 N3–K2 11 0–0
0–0 12 R–K1. White has good practical
chances in the middle game, but Black
can equalize with care: 12 ... P–QB3
13 P–QR4 Q–N3! 14 P–R5 Q×Q 15
N×Q R–Q1 16 N–B5 R–N1 17 N–K5
K–B1; Rossolimo-Unzicker, Heidel-
berg 1949.

Two Knights' Defence

3 ...	N–B3!(*36*)

36
W

The Two Knights' Defence, which,
in practice, is met by one of:
4 N–N5 – Attacking
4 P–Q4 – Centre Play

Attacking Line

4 N–N5	P–Q4

A very tricky counter-attack is the
Wilkes-Barre Variation, 4 ... B–B4!?
which Leonard Barden recommended
in *The Guardian Chess Book*. Black will
meet 5 N×BP with 5 ... B×P+!
obtaining good chances in the wild
goings-on that ensue. Although this
variation remains a good practical
chance for club players, it has been
analysed very deeply in the last few
years. After 5 B×P+! K–K2 (KB1 is
needed for the KR) 6 B–Q5!, White
probably has the better game, as he can
open the centre (by P–B3 and P–Q4) to
expose the black king.

5 P×P	N–QR4

Others:

a) 5 ... N×P? is an instructive error.
See Barden-Adams on page 13.
b) 5 ... P–QN4!? 6 B–B1! N–Q5! 7
P–QB3 N×P 8 N–K4! also leads to a
very sharp game where, although
theoretically White's chances are to be
preferred, Black does quite well in
practice with 8 ... N–K3 or 8 ...
Q–R5!? 9 N–N3 B–KN5!? 10 P–B3
P–K5!

6 B–N5+

Almost always played, although Morphy's move 6 P–Q3 also leads to an interesting game. The critical line runs 6 ... P–KR3 7 N–KB3 P–K5 8 Q–K2 N×B 9 P×N B–QN4 10 P–KR3 0–0 11 N–R2 P–B3! (*11 ... P–K6* and *11 ... N–R2* are also playable.) 12 P×P P–K6! 13 B×P B×B 14 P×B N–K5 15 N–B1! with a very unclear position.

6 ...	P–B3 ↔
7 P×P	P×P
8 B–K2	

8 Q–B3 was at one time recommended by many experts, but it has been practically refuted by the second pawn offer 8 ... R–QN1! 9 B×P+?! (*9 B–Q3 P–KR3!* also favours Black) 9 ... N×B 10 Q×N+ N–Q2 11 P–Q3 B–K2. Black has an advantage in development, two bishops, and chances of attacking either by bringing his QR to the K-side via b6, or with an eventual ... P–KB4–5.

8 ...	P–KR3
9 N–KB3	P–K5
10 N–K5(*37*)	

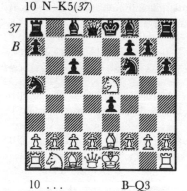

37
B

10 ...	B–Q3

This is the most flexible attacking move. Another example of these complications is 10 ... B–QB4!? 11 P–QB3 Q–B2 12 P–KB4 N–N2 13 P–QN4! when White may have some advantage – Estrin.

11 P–KB4   P×Pep
12 N×P.B3   0–0!

Estrin-Strand, corres 1966; Black has sufficient counterplay for his pawn. Both rooks will soon seize open files, while White remains backward in his development.

Centre Play

4 P–Q4	P×P
5 0–0(*38*)	

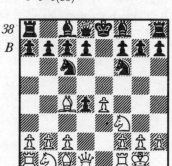

38
B

White can also try:

a) 5 P–K5 P–Q4! (The invariable counter-attack in the centre) 6 B–QN5 N–K5 7 N×P B–Q2 8 B×N P×B 9 0–0 B–QB4=.

b) 5 N–N5 P–Q4 6 P×P Q–K2+! 7 K–B1 N–K4 8 Q×P N×B 9 Q×N.B4 P–KR3! 10 N–KB3 Q–B4 11 Q×Q B×Q 12 P–B4 B–Q2! and Black's active position is well worth the sacrificed pawn – Estrin.

5 ...   N×P

The Max Lange Attack, 5 ... B–B4!?, is extremely complicated, although tending in White's favour, e.g. 6 P–K5 P–Q4 (*6 ... N–KN5?!* 7 *B–B4!* favours White) 7 P×N P×B 8 R–K1+ B–K3 9 N–N5 Q–Q4 (not *9 ... Q–Q2?? 10 N×B P×N 11 Q–R5+*) 10 N–QB3 Q–B4 11 N3–K4 0–0–0 12 P–KN4! Q–K4 13 N5×B P×N 14 B–N5!? P–KR3? (*14 ... P–KN3!* 15

P–B7 B–K2) 15 N×B! Q×N (*15 . . .
Q×B 16 P×P!*) 16 P×P P×B 17
P×R=Q R×Q 18 R×P and White
won, Cafferty-Sombor, Bognor Regis
1965.

6 R–K1	P–Q4
7. B×P	Q×B
8 N–B3	Q–QR4
9 N×N	B–K3
10 B–Q2	

Also 10 N4–N5 0–0–0 11 N×B P×N
12 R×P has been tried. Now 12 . . .
Q–KB4 ensures dead equality, while
after 12 . . . B–Q3 13 B–N5 QR–K1 14
Q–K2 K–Q2 15 R–K1 Q×R+! and 16
. . . R×R the rooks and the queen are
worth about the same.

10 . . .	Q–Q4!
11 B–N5	B–Q3!
12 B–B6	0–0!=

Marić-Djurašević, Yugoslav Ch
1956.

The Scotch Game and Gambits

1 P–K4	P–K4
2 N–KB3	N–QB3
3 P–Q4	P×P (*39*)
4 N×P!	

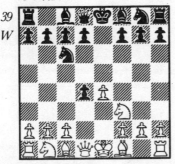

39
W

Black's best reply to 4 B–QB4 is 4 . . .
N–B3, transposing into the Two
Knights' Defence, above.

The Göring Gambit, 4 P–B3!?, has
had quite a vogue in recent years, the
influence of Penrose doubtless having

an effect. To avoid duplication of lines
given in *The Guardian Chess Book*, we just
give here a recommendation for Black:
4 . . . P×P when:

a) 5 B–QB4 P×P 6 B×NP P–Q3! (*6 . . .
B–N5+* is unclear.) 7 0–0 (*7 Q–N3
B–K3! 8 Q×P KN–K2!* embarrasses the
queen.) 7 . . . B–K3 8 B×B P×B 9
Q–N3 Q–Q2 10 N–N5 N–Q1 11 P–B4
N–KB3 is a double-edged variation
that needs more tests.

b) 5 N×P B–N5 6 B–QB4 P–Q3 7 0–0 (*7
Q–N3 B×N+! 8 P×B Q–Q2!*) 7 . . .
B×N 8 P×B N–B3 9 P–K5! (*9 B–R3?
B–N5!* and White's attack is
insufficient; Penrose-Smyslov, Munich
1958) 9 . . . N×P 10 N×N P×N 11
Q–N3 Q–K2 12 B–R3 P–B4 13 B–N5+
(*13 Q–N5+?! N–Q2* Penrose-Unzicker,
Leipzig 1960) 13 . . . K–B1 14 P–B4
P–K5 15 P–B5 P–KR4 with a difficult
game, Smederevac-Minić, Yugoslav
Ch 1959.

The text move, introducing the
Scotch Game, is often underestimated.
White, with the correct follow-up, gets
a definite initiative, based on his spatial
advantage in the centre.

4 . . .   B–B4

White can meet 4 . . . N–B3 (*4 . . .
Q–B3?! 5 N–N5!*) by 5 N×N! NP×N 6
P–K5 Q–K2 7 Q–K2 N–Q4 8 N–Q2!
as played by – Mieses – although the
result will largely depend upon the
relative middle game skills of the two
players. White will play P–QB4,
fianchetto the QB and usually castle on
the Q-side. 6 B–Q3 is another plan.

5 N–N3	B–N3
6 P–QR4	P–QR3
7 N–B3	KN–K2

Probably a mistake. Other possibilities are:
a) 7 . . . Q–B3 8 Q–K2 KN–K2 9 N–Q5
N×N 10 P×N+ N–K2 11 P–R5 B–R2

12 P–R4 P–R3 13 R–R4! and Black is in trouble.

b) 7 . . . P–Q3 (*8 B–Q3 N–B3!*) seems relatively best.

8 B–KN5   0–0?

Here or next move, 8 . . . P–B3 is essential, although White should retain the advantage.

9 N–Q5   B–R2
10 N–B6+!!(*40*)

A surprising and utterly decisive coup.

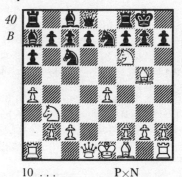

10 . . .   P×N

11 B×P Q–K1 12 Q–R5 N–Q1 13 Q–R6 N–K3 14 0–0–0 B×P 15 R–Q3 N–N3 16 R–R3 B–R5 17 R×B N×R 18 Q×N Black resigned. There is no answer to the threat of P–K5, B–Q3 and Q×P mate; Botterill-Thomas, British Ch 1974.

The Four Knights' Game

1 P–K4   P–K4
2 N–KB3   N–QB3
3 N–B3   N–B3(*41*)

This old-fashioned opening is a real rarity, nowadays. Like most of its kind, it conceals traps for the unwary.

White may now play:

4 P–Q4 – Scotch Four Knights
4 B–N5 – Lopez Four Knights

Beginners sometimes try 4 B–B4, a move too late! Black can equalize by 4 . . . N×P (*5 N×N P–Q4*), or preserve

the symmetry a little longer: 4 . . . B–B4 5 P–Q3 P–Q3 6 B–KN5 N–QR4! 7 N–Q5 N×B 8 P×N P–B3! 9 N×N+ P×N 10 B–K3 (*10 B–R4 Q–Q2!*) 10 . . . Q–N3 Korchnoi-Bronstein, 20th USSR Ch 1952.

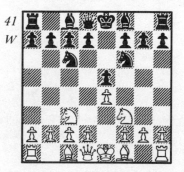

Scotch Four Knights

4 P–Q4   P×P

An alternative way, which takes much of the sting out of the Scotch Four Knights, is 4 . . . B–N5, e.g.:

a) 5 P–Q5 N–K2 6 N×P P–Q3 7 B–QN5+ K–B1! 8 N–Q3 B×N+ 9 P×B N×P 10 Q–B3 N–KB3 Hort-Trifunović, Sarajevo 1964.

b) 5 N×P N×KP! 6 Q–N4 N5×N 7 Q×NP R–B1 8 P–QR3 N×P!? 9 P×B N×P+ 10 K–Q2 N×R 11 K×N P–QR4! 12 P×P? P–QB4 13 N–B4 Q–K2 14 N–K3 Q–K5! 15 B–B4 P–Q4! with a good game, Strauss-Littlewood, Islington 1971.

5 N–Q5!?

The Belgrade Gambit. 5 N×P is an inferior line of the Scotch: 5 . . . B–N5 6 N×N NP×N / B–Q3 P–Q4 8 P×P P×P 9 0–0 0–0 10 B–KN5 P–B3 11 Q–B3 B–Q3!:

a) 12 B×N Q×B 13 Q×Q P×Q gives Black the better ending, for the weakness in his pawn formation is more than outweighed by his two bishops, and the prospects which his rooks have on the QN- and K-files.

b) 12 QR–K1 R–N1! 13 N–Q1 R–N5!, threatening 14 ... B–KN5 with fine counterplay for Black.

c) 12 B–B5 B×B 13 Q×B= Alexander-Unzicker, Amsterdam 1954.

     5 ...   B–K2!

This is the best reply, which takes away all White's attacking possibilities.

     6 B–KB4

Also possible is 6 B–QN5 P–QR3 (*6 ... P–Q3* is playable.) 7 B×N QP×B 8 N×N+ B×N 9 P–K5 B–K2 10 Q×P Q×Q and Black's two bishops may be a potent force in the ending.

     6 ...   P–Q3

     7 N3×P

Or 7 B–QN5 0–0 8 Q–K2 P–QR3 9 B–R4 B–Q2 10 0–0–0 R–K1 11 KR–K1 P–R3 12 B–N3 N×N 13 B×N B–B3= Miles-Clarke, Birmingham 1972.

     7 ...   KN×N
     8 P×N   N×N
     9 Q×N   0–0
     10 0–0–0   B–B3

11 Q–Q2 P–QB4! 12 P×Pep Q–N3 13 P–QB3 P×P 14 B×P R–Q1 15 B–QB4 (Firmenich-Glattacker, corres 1953) 15 ... B–B4! and Black has fine attacking chances.

Lopez Four Knights
     4 B–N5   N–Q5(*42*)

Rubinstein's move. 4 ... B–N5 is also playable, but it gives White a more prolonged initiative than the text move.

     5 N×P

The boldest course. Others are:

a) 5 N×N P×N 6 P–K5 P×N 7 P×N Q×P 8 QP×P Q–K4+ 9 Q–K2 Q×Q+ 10 B×Q is a variation often used by masters, when they are feeling lazy and want to draw quickly.

b) 5 B–R4 B–B4 6 N×P 0–0 7 N–Q3

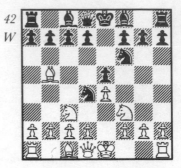

42
W

B–N3 8 P–K5 N–K1 9 0–0 P–Q3 10 P×P N–KB3!? 11 P–Q7 (*11 P×P Q–Q3!* with a tremendous attack) 11 ... B×P 12 B×B Q×B 13 N–K1 QR–K1 gives Black lasting pressure in return for the sacrificed pawn.

c) 5 B–B4 B–B4 6 N×P Q–K2 7 N–B3 P–Q4! 8 N×P Q×P+ 9 N–K3 B–KN5 10 B–K2 N×B 11 Q×N 0–0–0 12 P–Q3 Q–K3 again gives Black full value in terms of initiative for the pawn.

     5 ...   Q–K2
     6 P–B4   N×B

7 N×N P–Q3 8 N–KB3 Q×P+ 9 K–B2 N–N5+ 10 K–N1 (*10 K–N3 Q–N3!* is too risky.) 10 ... Q–B3 11 Q–K2+ B–K2 12 P–KR3 Q–N3+ 13 P–Q4 N–B3 14 K–R2 B–Q2 15 R–K1 0–0. Black has completed his development and acquired the two bishops – a fully satisfactory state of affairs for him.

Petroff's Defence
     1 P–K4   P–K4
     2 N–KB3   N–KB3

Unlike the other openings in this chapter, the Petroff Defence will be considered from White's point of view, since it is a defence which the regular Ruy Lopez player will have to contend with from time to time. The Petroff is a tricky defence to deal with in actual play, for it has the psychological advantage that it has many variations leading to a draw. This means that very often White will go into some artificial line of play, in order to avoid one of the drawing variations, and against artificial lines the Petroff gives excellent opportunities for rapid and overwhelming counter-attack.

   3 N×P

3 P–Q4 is also good.

3 ...	P–Q3
4 N–KB3	N×P
5 N–B3	

The alternatives 5 Q–K2 and 5 P–Q4 are more frequently played than the text-move, but 5 N–B3 has the advantage of being no weaker and not so well-known.

5 ...	N×N

5 ... P–Q4 loses a pawn to 6 Q–K2, and the retreat 5 ... N–KB3 allows White to remain ahead in development: 6 P–Q4 B–K2 7 B–N5 B–N5 8 Q–Q2 0–0 9 0–0–0.

6 QP×N!	B–K2
7 B–K3	

Another good line is 7 B–KB4 N–B3 8 Q–Q2 B–N5 9 B–K2 Q–Q2 10 P–KR3 B–R4 11 0–0–0 e.g. 11 ... 0–0–0 12 KR–K1 P–QR3 13 Q–Q5 B–N3 14 N–Q4 N×N 15 Q×N K–N1 16 B–N4, Foltys-Szapiel, Sczawno-Zdroj 1950. If Black castled K-side instead, he would find his Q-side pawn storm held up by White's extra QBP.

With the text move, we follow the game Atkins-Sherrard, Southport 1905.

7 ...	N–B3
8 P–KR3	P–QR3

9 Q–Q2 B–K3 10 0–0–0 P–QN4 11 K–N1 R–QN1 12 P–KN4 P–QR4. Black is going ahead with his development as fast as possible, which makes Atkins' method of dealing with it most interesting. First of all, he weakens

Black in the centre, and forces the advantage of the two bishops, before proceeding with his own attack. 13 N–N5 Q–Q2 14 N×B P×N 15 P–KB4 0–0 16 B–N2 P–N5 17 P–B4 P–R5 18 P–KB5! N–Q1. White's attack steadily gains momentum, while Black has no means of forcing open lines leading to the white king. If *18 ... P×P 19 Q–Q5+.* 19 B–K4 P×P Henceforth, Black is completely on the defensive. But if instead *19 ... P–N6 20 QBP×P RP×P 21 P–R3* and White's king is quite snug. 20 B×P Q–K1 21 QR–K1 P–N3 22 B–K4 P–B3 23 P–R4 N–K3 24 P–R5 P–N4 25 B–KB5 N–B5 26 B×N P×B 27 Q–Q3. Contrast the two attacks now! Black made three attacking moves before White even got started; now White has broken the black king's defences, and is preparing to invade along the K-file as well. 27 ... P–R3 28 R–K6 R–B3 29 KR–K1 R×R 30 R×R Q–KB1 31 R–N6+ Black resigned.

Other Open Games

The remaining openings of this group can be dismissed briefly, as they are rarely played, except for a few loyal devotees.

Latvian Counter-Gambit

1 P–K4	P–K4
2 N–KB3	P–KB4!?

A lot of detailed – but often suspect – analysis has been done on this opening. White's safest course is 3 N×P Q–B3 4 P–Q4 P–Q3 5 N–B4 P×P 6 B–K2!; Bronstein-Mikenas, Rostov 1941.

Queen's Pawn's Counter-Gambit

1 P–K4	P–K4
2 N–KB3	P–Q4!?

An extreme measure! White can

practically refute it by 3 P×P! P–K5 4 Q–K2 N–KB3 5 P–Q3 B–K2 6 P×P 0–0 7 B–KN5! Prüss-Wills, corres 1966.

Philidor Defence

1 P–K4	P–K4
2 N–KB3	P–Q3

This is a solid if passive defence. As it is usually only played by those who know it well, we recommend 3 B–B4, getting off the beaten track. Then if 3 ... B–K3 (Best is *3 ... B–K2.*) 4 B×B P×B 5 P–Q4 P×P 6 N×P gives White an edge, Grob-Tartakower, Ostend 1937.

Ponziani Opening

1 P–K4	P–K4
2 N–KB3	N–QB3
3 P–B3	

An ancient opening, with much latent sting. Black's best practical method lies in a reversed Vienna: 3 ... P–B4!? 4 P–Q4 (*4 P×P Q–B3!*) 4 ...

BP×P 5 N×P N–B3 and 6 ... Q–K2.

Centre Game

1 P–K4	P–K4
2 P–Q4	P×P
3 Q×P	

An offshoot is the Danish Gambit, 3 P–B3, which is well met by 3 ... P×P 4 B–QB4 P×P 5 B×NP P–Q4 6 B×QP N–KB3 7 B×BP+ K×B 8 Q×Q B–QN5+ etc.

3 ...	N–QB3
4 Q–K3	

4 Q–Q1 and 4 Q–QR4 also allow comfortable equality.

4 ... N–B3 =

Black need only know that 5 P–K5!? N–KN5 6 Q–K4 is answered by 6 ... P–Q4! 7 P×Pep+ B–K3 8 B–QR6?! (*8 P×P Q×P* is most satisfactory.) 8 ... Q×P! 9 B×P Q–N5+ 10 Q×Q N×Q (Levin-Beilin, Lubov 1949) e.g. 11 B×R N×P+ 12 K–B1 N×R or 11 N–R3 R–QN1 12 B–K4 N×QRP, favouring Black.

4 THE SICILIAN DEFENCE: A FIGHTING DEFENCE TO 1 P–K4

The outstanding characteristic of the Sicilian Defence is that, with his first move, Black begins a counter-attack on the Q-wing. From very early in the game, Black has the better chances on that flank, and in consequence White must either attack fiercely on the K-side, or else obtain so tight a grip on the centre that Black's counterplay is smothered. In exceptional cases, White may be able to exploit his majority of pawns on the Q-side.

Various principles occur time and again in different variations of the opening. When White attacks, he does so by the advance of his KBP (and sometimes the KNP and KRP), aiming eventually to choke Black's KB by the thrust P–KB6. When he tries to control the centre, he does so by either preventing Black's ... P–Q4 or rendering it harmless; then he can build up an attack himself on the centre files, by putting his major pieces on Q2, Q1 or K1 and then proceeding by N–Q5, or, if Black has any loose pieces on the Q-file, by P–K5.

Black, meanwhile institutes counter-attacks on the QB-file, perhaps supported by a fianchettoed KB, and making especial use of ... QB5, which he will try to occupy with the QN. At every move he must look out for a chance to play ... P–Q4 or even ... P–K4. In the long run, Black's play on the Q-side will become very powerful if

White defends passively, since he can, given time, place his rooks on the QN- and QB-files (or double them on the QB-file) and press home an advance of his Q-side pawns in order to open a file into the heart of the white position. That is why the Sicilian is particularly good against those players (and there are many) who sit tight and undertake nothing constructive after the opening moves. The player of 1 P–K4 must expect to meet the Sicilian more often than not, so should study this chapter with especial care.

The Dragon Variation

The Dragon is characterized by the fianchetto of Black's KB. This piece has great potential on the long diagonal, especially in the double-edged modern lines where castles Q-side. White's main ideas are a K-side pawn storm, and the manoeuvre B–K3, Q–Q2 and B–KR6 which is designed to exchange the Dragon bishop. The next five diagrams, 43 to 47, show some typical positions from this variation.

    1 P–K4   P–QB4

    2 N–KB3

We now consider.

2 ... P–Q3 – to Dragon
2 ... N–QB3 – Accelerated
2 ... P–K3 (Scheveningen Variation) is discussed on page 60.

Favourable Positions for White
Gusev-Averbakh, Moscow 1951

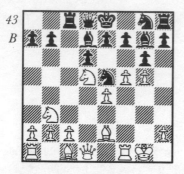

43
B

The K-side pawn advance has driven back Black's pieces in disorder.

Mecking-Joksić, Vrsac 1871

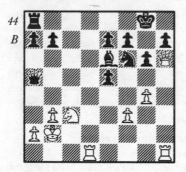

44
B

Black has a nominal material advantage, but White's mating threats (based on N–K4 and P–N5) are much more concrete than Black's vague chances on the Q-side.

Favourable Positions for Black
From Analysis by Hollis

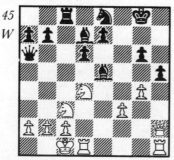

45
W

Black's two bishops are very potent. If now 1 P–B4 B×NP or if 1 Q–Q2 R×N, in either case with complications where White will have to fight hard for a draw.

Sherwin-Brasket, Milwaukee 1953

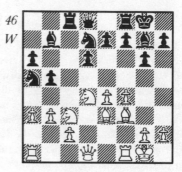

46
W

White has vacillated, and allowed his opponent time to organize Q-side counterplay.

An Even Position
Schmid-Bogoljubow, Southsea 1950

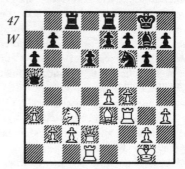

47
W

Each side has attacking chances.

Leading to Dragon

2 ...	P–Q3
3 P–Q4	P×P
4 N×P	N–KB3
5 N–QB3	P–KN3(*48*)

White has several methods of proceeding from here. We shall limit ourselves to three of these:

6 B–K2 – Classical
6 B–K3 – Rauzer
6 P–B4 – Levenfish

Classical

6 B–K2

This is the classical treatment of the Dragon. White will develop his pieces, castle K-side and then advance his pawns on that wing: the 'Stockholm Attack'.

6 ...	B–N2
7 B–K3	N–B3
8 0–0	0–0
9 N–N3	

If White plays 9 P–B4 at once, then 9 ...Q–N3! (threatening 10 ...N×P) is awkward to meet.

9 ...	B–K3
10 P–B4	N–QR4

Tartakower's 10 ... Q–B1 is also interesting:

a) 11 Q–K1 P–QR4! 12 P–QR4 N–QN5 13 N–Q4 B–N5 14 P–B5 N–Q2 and Black's minor pieces obtain good play; Pachman-Gadalinsky, Spindleruv Mlyn 1948.

b) 11 P–KR3 R–Q1 12 B–B3 B–B5 13 R–B2 P–K4 gaining the important square K4 for a black knight. After 14 R–Q2 P×P 15 B×BP N–K4 16 K–R2

B–QR3 17 B×N P×B 18 R×R Q×R 19 N–B5 the game is fully equalized; Matanović-Geller, Belgrade 1956.

11 P–B5

Experience has shown that this gives White a strong attack.

11 ...	B–B5
12 N×N	

Or 12 P–KN4!? R–B1! 13 B×P! (*13 P–K5 QP×P!*) 13 ... B×B 14 Q×B N–B5 =.

12 ...	B×B
13 Q×B	Q×N(*49*)

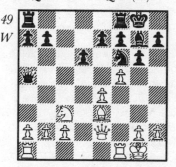

14 B–Q4!

The older move 14 P–KN4?! enables Black to get counterplay by 14 ... QR–B1! 15 P–N5 R×N! 16 P×N (*16 P×R N×P* leaves White's game in ruins.) 16 ... R×B 17 Q×R B×P 18 P–B3 R–B1 as analysed by Simagin. Black's exchange sacrifice has broken the white attack and his Q-side possibilities make up for the slight material deficit.

The text move keeps control of the position. A good example is the game Knox-Lemon, British Ch 1970:

14 ...	QR–B1
15 QR–Q1	N–Q2
16 B×B	K×B
17 K–R1	Q–QB4
18 P–KN4	

White's attack gets under way at last.

The game continued 18 . . . P–KR3 19 R–Q2 N–N3 20 N–Q5 N×N 21 P×N Q–R4 22 P×P K×P 23 Q–K4+ K–N2 24 R–N2 Q–N4 25 R1–KN1 (The pressure on the KN-file is decisive.) 25 . . . R–B5 26 Q–Q3 Q–B4 27 P–N5 P–KR4 28 P–N6 P–B3 29 Q–K2 P–K4 30 P×Pep Q–Q4 31 P–K7 R–K1 32 R–Q1 R–Q5 33 R×R Q×R 34 Q×RP Black resigned.

Rauzer-Yugoslav Attack

6 B–K3	B–N2
7 P–B3	N–B3
8 Q–Q2	0–0
9 B–QB4	

White plans an all-out attack, based on castling Q-side and then the advance P–KR4–5, opening the KR-file, will be a very strong threat. This line of play is probably more often played than any other against the Dragon nowadays.

9 0–0–0 pays insufficient attention to the centre. After 9 . . . P–Q4 10 P×P (*10 N×N P×N 11 B–KR6 Q–R4!*) 11 N4×N P×N:

a) 12 N×N P×N 13 Q×P Q–B2! when: a1) 14 Q×R B–B4 15 Q×R+ K×Q 16 R–Q2 P–KR4 and Black should retain some initiative.

a2) 14 Q–QB5 Q–N1 (*14 . . . Q–N2* is also good.) 15 P–QN3! P–QR4! 16 Q–N6 Q–K4 17 B–Q4 Q–B5+ 18 B–K3 Q–K4 with a draw by repetition.

b) 12 B–Q4 P–K4 13 B–B5 B–K3 14 N–K4 (*14 B–B4 N×N* also gives balanced chances.) 14 . . . R–K1 15 P–KR4 P–B4! 16 N–N5 B–R3 with interesting possibilities; Keres-Hartston, simul 1962.

9 . . .   B–Q2(*50*)

The consequences of this position have been very deeply analysed in the last 10 years or so, and hundreds of

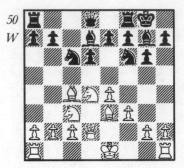

master games have been played. The possibilities are far from exhausted, but the evidence suggests that Black's chances are no worse.

10 P–KR4!

One advantage of this move is that it is little-known. The usual moves 10 B–N3 and 10 0–0–0 are probably no stronger; with best play, the same position often results later on, anyway.

10 . . .   Q–R4!

Attempts to take advantage of White's king in the centre are unconvincing:

a) 10 . . . Q–N1 11 N–Q5! or 11 P–R5.

b) 10 . . . R–B1 11 B–N3 and now two ideas:

1) 11 . . . P–KR4 12 0–0–0 N–K4 13 B–R6! (*13 P–N4 P×P!*) 13 . . . B×B 14 Q×B R×N 15 P×R Q–R4. This exchange sacrifice usually works against an early B–R6 by White, but here Black's voluntary weakening of his K-side means that, after 16 K–N2 R–B1 17 Q–K3 Q–N2 18 Q–K2! White has some advantage – Sokolov.

2) 11 . . . N–K4 12 P–R5 (*12 0–0–0* is more usual) 12 . . . N×RP 13 P–N4 (*13 N–Q5!? P–K3!*) when 13 . . . N–KB3 14 N–Q5! N×N 15 P×N gives White a dangerous attack, and Keene's 13 . . . R–B5!? 14 P×N R×N.5!? has been generally recommended; however,

after 15 Q–K2! it is White who has winning chances.

   11 0–0–0   KR–B1
   12 B–N3   N–K4

12 ... P–KR4 is, once more, too slow: 13 K–N1 N–K4 14 Q–K2 P–R3 (*14 ... P–QN4 15 N–Q5! N×N 16 B×N!*) 15 QR–N1 P–QN4 16 P–N4 N–B5 (*16 ... P×P 17 P–R5!*) 17 P×P N×NP 18 P×P Q×N 19 P×P+ K–B1 (Ristoija-Asplund, Denmark 1968) 20 B–R6! with a winning attack for White - Lilienthal.

   13 P–R5

This pawn offer is again the key to White's attack. Others:

a) 13 B–R6?! N–B5 and Black's attack is at least as quick.

b) 13 P–N4 N–B5 14 B×N R×B 15 P–R5 R1–QB1 16 N–N3 Q–R3! 17 P×P BP×P 18 P–K5 N–K1 19 Q–R2 P–R4 20 B–Q4 R×B! 21 N×R B×KP! reaching diagram 45.

c) 13 K–N1 N–B5 14 B×N R×B 15 N–N3 Q–Q1 16 B–R6 B×B! 17 Q×B Q–KB1 18 Q–K3 P–QR4= – Keene & Levy.

   13 ...   N×RP(*51*)

A very complicated position where White can try:

14 B–R6 Variation 1
14 P–N4 – Variation 2
14 K–N1 – Variation 3

Variation 1

   14 B–R6   B×B!

Exalted claims have been made for the dramatic coup 14 ... N–Q6+!? White meets this best by 15 K–N1! N×P! (*15 ... B×N? 16 N–Q5!* is worse.) 16 K×N B×B 17 Q×B R×N (better than *17 ... Q×N+ 18 K–N1 P–R4 19 R–Q3*) 18 P–N4 N–B3 19 P–K5! P×P 20 N–K2 R×B+ 21 RP×R B–K3 22 N–B3! reaching diagram 44; the Mecking-Joksić game ended 22 ... P–K5? (Relatively best is *22 ... R–QB1* or *22 ... R–Q1.*) 23 N×P R–QB1 24 K–N1 R–B3? 25 P–N5! Black resigned.

   15 Q×B   R×N
   16 P×R

White can draw immediately by 16 R×N P×R 17 Q–N5+ K–R1 18 Q×KP R–K1 19 Q–B6+ etc.

   16 ...   R–QB1!

17 N–K2! N–KB3 18 R–Q5 Q–R6+ 19 K–Q2 P–R4! 20 N–B4 Q–N7 21 R×N Q×P.B6+ 22 K–K2 Q×R 23 N×P B–N4+! 24 K–Q1! Q–R8+ Drawn. Schutt-Alexander, corres. 1968–9.

Variation 2

   14 P–N4   N–KB3
   15 B–R6

The game Ezmakov-Keene, USSR – GB corres 1969-70, went instead 15 K–N1 R×N 16 Q×R Q×Q 17 P×Q R–QB1 18 K–N2 P–QR4 with a typical Dragon exchange sacrifice endgame. As White has already committed himself to P–KN4, weakening the K-side, his task is rather the harder, and he lost in forty-four moves.

   15 ...   R×N!
   16 P×R   B×B

17 R×B! R–QB1 18 K–N2 Q–N3 (*18 ... N–B5+*, proposed by Tal, leads to unfathomable complications.) 19 K–B1 Q–R4 20 K–N2 P–R4! Analysis by

Larsen; Black has winning chances (21
R1–R1 P–K3!).

Variation 3

14 K–N1	R×N
15 Q×R	Q×Q

16 P×Q R–QB1 17 K–N2 P–R4 18
P–R3 N–KB3 19 B–KB4 N–K1 20
B–N5 P–R5 21 B–R2 N–QB3! Spassky-
Stein, RSFSR – Ukraine 1967. The
continuation is a good example of how
Black should play these endings: 22
R–Q2 N–B3 23 N×N B×N 24 R–Q4
P–R4 25 K–B1 K–B1 26 K–Q2 R–R1
27 R N4 R R4 28 B–K3 P–K3 29
P–QB4 N–Q2 30 P–B3 B–B3 31 B–KN1
B–KN4+ 32 B–K3 B×B+ 33 K×B
K–K2 34 K–B2 N–B4 35 R4–N1 N–Q2
36 R–N4 N–B4 37 R4–N1 N–Q2
Drawn.

Levenfish Attack

6 P–B4 *(52)*

This is an aggressive system
calculated to disrupt Black's normal
Dragon development, by making an
early thrust in the centre.

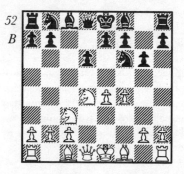

52
B

6 ...	N–B3

Although the last word has not been
said, it seems unlikely that this is Black's
soundest procedure. These rare

alternatives should also be studied
attentively:

a) 6 . . . Q–N3?! 7 B–K2 N–B3 8 B–K3!
P–K4? 9 P×P P×P 10 N×N! with the
win of the black queen, or 10 . . . Q×B
11 Q–Q8 mate.

b) 6 . . . QN–Q2 7 B–K2 B–N2 8 B–K3
0–0 9 B–B3 N–N3 (*9 . . . P–QR3* with a
form of Najdorf Variation, is also
interesting.) 10 Q–K2 P–K4 11 N–N3
may be alright for Black. Keene and
Levy suggest such plans as 11 . . . B–K3,
11 . . . N–N5 or even 11 . . . P×P 12
B×P N–R4.

c) 6 . . . B–N2 7 P–K5! was Levenfish's
main idea. Now:

c1) A trap that regularly claims victims
is 7 . ∴ . P×P 8 P×P N–N5 9 B–N5+
K–B1? (But *9 . . . N–B3* is also very good
for White.) 10 N–K6+ etc. winning.

c2) 7 . . . N–R4!? 8 B–N5+ B–Q2 9
P–K6 P×P 10 N×P B×N+ 11 P×B and
now Mestel has suggested 11 . . . Q–B1!!
with complications, as another line
where Black may be able to overturn
'theory'.

7 B–QN5

Or 7 N×N P×N 8 P–K5 with some
advantage to White.

7 ...	B–Q2
8 B×N	P×B

If 8 . . . B×B 9 Q–K2, again
threatening P–K5.

9 P–K5	P×P
10 P×P	N–N5

This is a more active defence than 10
. . . N–Q4 11 N×N P×N 12 Q–B3!
P–K3 13 0–0 B–N2 14 B–Q2 Q–N1 15
B–B3 0–0 16 QR–K1 Nezhmetdinov-
Ilivitsky, USSR 1951, White stands
well.

11 Q–K2	B–N2
12 B–KB4	Q–N1
13 0–0–0	

Not 13 N–B3? Q×NP: this was why

the black queen went to . . . N1 and not
. . . B2!

| 13 . . . | B×P |
| 14 B–N5 | |

White has good attacking chances for the sacrificed pawn; Schmid-Gilg, Dusseldorf 1951.

Accelerated Dragon

2 . . .	N–QB3
3 P–Q4	P×P
4 N×P	P–KN3

This is a way to head for Dragon-type positions, while avoiding the Levenfish. However, White can now adopt the Maroczy Bind formation, with pawns at K4 and QB4 controlling the centre and restricting Black to cramped manoeuvres. Black tries to exploit the black-square holes in the white position, but in 1974–6 the balance of master results was definitely in White's favour.

5 P–QB4

If 5 N–QB3 B–N2 6 B–K3 N–B3 7 B–QB4 Black can, if he wishes, avoid the Yugoslav Attack by 7 . . . 0–0.

| 5 . . . | N–B3 |
| 6 N–B3 | |

This position often occurs via the English Opening: 1 N–KB3 N–KB3 2 P–B4 P–B4 3 N–B3 N–B3 4 P–Q4 P×P 5 N×P P–KN3 6 P–K4.

6 . . .   B–N2

A good idea against the popular system 6 . . . N×N 7 Q×N P–Q3 is 8 B–N5 B–N2 9 Q–Q2 0–0 10 B–Q3 P–QR4 11 0–0 P–R5 12 QR–B1 B–K3 13 Q–B2 N–Q2 14 P–B4 and White built up a winning K-side attack; Portisch-Reshevsky, Petropolis 1973.

7 B–K3	N–KN5
8 Q×N	N×N
9 Q–Q1	N–K3

9 . . . P–K4 is under a cloud after this

brilliancy by the Women's World Champion: 10 N–N5 0–0 11 B–K2 Q–R5? 12 N×N P×N 13 B×P Q×KP 14 B×B Q×NP? 15 Q–Q4! Q×R+ 16 K–Q2 Q×R 17 Q–B6 Black resigned; Gaprindashvili-Servaty, Dortmund 1974.

10 R–B1   P–Q3(*53*)

If Black tries to anticipate White's next with 10 . . . P–QR4, then 11 P–B5! is a good reply, while if 10 . . . Q–R4 11 B–Q3! offers the QRP for good attacking chances.

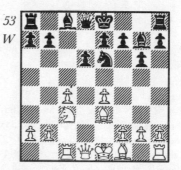

Portisch-Pfleger, Manila 1974, now went 11 P–QN4! 0–0 12 B–K2 P–QR4 13 P–QR3 P×P 14 P×P B–Q2 15 0–0 B–QB3 16 Q–Q2 R–R6 (If *16 . . . B×N 17 Q×B B×P 18 B–R6 R–K1 19 KR–K1* threatening B–Q3 and R×N.) 17 N–Q5 K–R1 18 B–N6 Q–Q2 19 P–B4 P–B4 20 P×P P×P 21 B–B3 R1–R1 (This file is Black's only hope for active play.) 22 QR–K1 R–R8 23 P–N5 (Wins a pawn, and obtains the two bishops on an open board.) 23 . . . B×N 24 Q×B N–Q1 25 R×R R×R 26 R×R B×R 27 P–B5! P–K3 28 P–B6 (avoiding the last trap: *28 Q×QP? B–Q5+* followed by . . . Q×Q and . . . B×B) 28 . . . P×P 29 P×P P×Q 30 P×Q B–B3 31 B×P K–N2 32 B–B4 B–K2 33 K–B2 K–B3 and Black resigned. White's simplest win is to march his king up to QB8.

Orthodox Development by Black

At master level, the soundest Sicilian variation is probably that in which Black develops naturally, keeping pawn moves to a minimum and obliging White to show his hand first. This system is generally known according to what plan White adopts at move 6 after:

1	P–K4 ·	P–QB4
2	N–KB3	N–QB3
3	P–Q4 .	P×P
4	N×P	N–B3

4 ... P–K4!? 5 N–N5 P–QR3 6 N–Q6+ B×N 7 Q×B Q–B3 8 Q–Q1 Q–N3 9 N–B3 KN–K2 10 B–K3 and White has the two bishops, although Black has tactical chances.

    5 N–QB3   P–Q3 *(54)*

5 ... P–K4!? 6 N4–N5 P–Q3 7 B–N5 P–QR3 8 N–R3! is sharp and difficult for both players, but White should have the advantage through control of Q5. One crucial line runs 8 ... P–QN4 9 B×N P×B 10 N–Q5 P–B4.

54
W

 .The three main possibilities are:

6 B–KN5 – Richter-Rauzer Attack
6 B–QB4 – Sozin Attack
6 B–K2 P–K4 – Boleslavsky Variation

Before proceeding with the analysis, let us consider some typical positions in the orthodox system.

Favourable Positions for White
Tal-Ilivitsky, USSR Teams Ch 1953

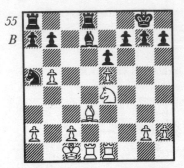

55
B

White has a strongly centralized position, with chances on both sides of the board. From the Rauzer Attack.
Harding-Pickett, London 1974

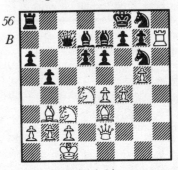

56
B

Black has helped his opponent to open the KR-file. White's pieces are strongly placed to besiege the black king. From the Sozin.

Favourable Positions for Black
Unzicker-Taimanov,   Saltsjobaden 1952

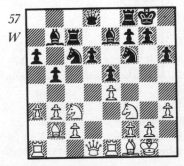

57
W

White has played too passively, and Black can prepare at leisure (by ... Q–R1 and ... R–Q1) for ... P–Q4. From the Boleslavsky.

Enklaar-Ribli, Amsterdam 1973

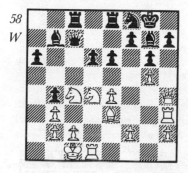

58
W

The Sozin bishop has been exchanged, and White's pressure on the KR-file amounted to nothing. Now Black's counter-attack in the centre and on the QB-file is much too strong for White's misplaced pieces.

Two Balanced Positions
Boleslavsky-Taimanov, USSR 1970

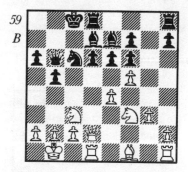

59
B

Both kings are comparatively safe. Black has two bishops and chances on the black squares, while White has rather better pawns and white square

pressure. The black central pawn mass is a common sight in Rauzer positions.

Boleslavsky-Euwe, Zürich 1953

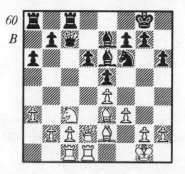

60
B

From Boleslavsky's Variation; both players have a very solid game.

Richter-Rauzer Attack

6 B–KN5   P–K3

A continuation that has gained in popularity of late is 6 ... B–Q2, since 7 B×N (giving Black two bishops and the KN-file) is no longer considered effective. A likely continuation instead is 7 Q–Q2 R–B1 8 0–0–0 N×N 9 Q×N Q–R4 10 P–B4 (*10 B Q2 P–QR3* is also critical.) 10 ... R×N!? (*10 ... P–K3* is perhaps even better.) 11 P×R P–K4 12 Q–N4 Q×Q 13 P×Q N×P 14 B–R4 P–KN4! 15 P×P B–K2!= Unzicker-Gheorghiu, Ljubljana 1969.

7 Q–Q2(*61*)

Richter used to play 7 N×N P×N 8 P–K5, with the idea of the dangerous pawn-offer 8 ... P×P 9 Q–B3! However, the variation is now considered to be refuted by 8 ... Q–R4! 9 B–N5 P×B 10 P×N P–N5! 11 N–K4 Q–K4 12 P–KB3 P–Q4 13 Q–Q2 P–KR3 (not *13 ... P×N?? 14 0–0–0* winning) 14 B–R4 P–KN4 15 B–N3 Q×NP and White has the worst of it, both materially and positionally.

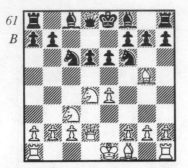

61
B

Black must now decide between rapid development and Q-side activity.

7 ... *B–K2* – Variation 1
7 ... *P–QR3!* – Variation 2

Variation 1

 7 ...   B–K2
 8 0–0–0 0–0
 9 P–B4   P–KR3

This zwischenzug usually improves Black's chances to some extent. However White's game is preferable:

 10 B–R4

To win a pawn by 10 B×N B×B 11 N×N P×N 12 Q×P Q–N3! is too risky here, as in most similar situations.

 10 ...   N×P
 Others:

a) 10 ... N×N 11 Q×N Q–R4 12 Q–Q3 R–Q1 13 K–N1! B–Q2 14 P–KN4 B–B3 15 B–N2! and White stands well; Zagorovsky-Hybl, 5th World Corres Ch 1965–8.

b) 10 ... P–K4 11 N–B5 B×N 12 P×B Q–R4 13 K–N1 QR–Q1 14 B×N! B×B 15 N–Q5 Q×Q 16 R×Q P×P 17 N×B+ P×N 18 B–K2 KR–K1 19 R–KB1 R–K5 20 B–B3 R–K2 21 P–QR3 N–K4 22 B–Q5 N–N5 23 R×P N–K6 24 B–B3! and White won the ending, Rittner-Stern, 6th World Corres Ch 1969–71.

 11 B×B   N×Q
 12 B×Q   N7×B

13 N×N P×N 14 B–K7 R–K1 15 KR×N R×B 16 R×P B–N2. Opinions vary, on whether Black should hold this ending or not. White at least has the better pawns and possession of the only open file.

Variation 2

 7 ...   P–QR3!

Prepares ... P–QN4, and safeguards the QP against N4–N5.

 8 0–0–0 B–Q2
 9 P–B4   B–K2

Another important line is 9 ... P–N4, e.g. 10 B×N P×B 11 N×N P×N 12 P–B5!? and 12 ... P–N5 13 N–K2 B×P is dubious in view of 14 P×P P×P 15 N–Q4 – Gligorić and Sokolov.

 10 N–B3

10 N–N3 also has been tried by some American masters.

 10 ...   P–QN4
 11 B×N   P×B

It is also possible to sacrifice by 11 ... B×B!? 12 Q×P B–K2 13 Q–Q2 P–N5, but there have been insufficient tests of this as yet.

 12 P–B5   Q–N3
 13 K–N1   0–0–0
 14 P–KN3

We have reached diagram 59.

Sozin Attack

 6 B–QB4 P–K3!(*62*)

The most logical move against the Sozin, restricting the scope of the white KB. 6 ... B–Q2 instead can lead into the Dragon, while if 6 ... Q–N3 7 N–N3 P–K3 8 B–K3 Q–B2 9 P–B4 P–QR3 10 B–Q3 P–QN4 11 Q–B3 B–N2 12 0–0 B–K2 13 P–QR4 White may retain some initiative, but the position is admittedly very complex.

The main lines now are:

7 *B–N3* – Original Sozin

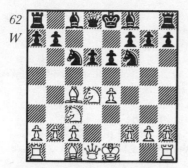

62
W

7 B–K3 – Velimirović Attack

7 0–0 has no independent significance, but 7 P–QR3 (to retreat the bishop to QR2) deserves to be taken seriously.

Original Sozin

| 7 B–N3 | B–K2 |
| 8 0–0 | |

Fischer experimented with 8 P–B4!? 0–0 9 B–K3 N×N! 10 B×N, but after the sacrifice 10 ... P–K4! (recommended by Euwe) White should have no vestige of an advantage, and could even stand worse.

8 ...	0–0
9 9 B–K3	P–QR3!
10 P–B4	N×N!
11 B×N	P–QN4
12 P–K5	

Or 12 P–QR3 B–N2 13 Q–Q3?! P–QR4! 14 P–K5 (*14 P–B5 P–N5!*) 14 ... P×P 15 P×P N–Q2 16 N×P N–B4! 17 B×N! B×B+ 18 K–R1 Q–N4 Fischer-Spassky, 4th match game 1972; White had to fight hard for a draw.

| 12 ... | P×P |
| 13 P×P | N–Q2 |

This is a typical position from the original line of the Sozin. White controls a little more space, but his KP is weak and his king not entirely secure in view of the open KR1 QR8 diagonal; chances are balanced. In recent years,

White has tended to prefer a still more double-edged plan, involving Q-side castling.

Velimirović Attack

7 B–K3

Black has chiefly tried:
7 ... P–QR3 – Variation 1
7 ... B–K2 – Variation 2

Variation 1

7 ...	P–QR3
8 Q–K2	Q–B2
9 0–0–0	B K2
10 B–N3	N–QR4
11 P–N4	P–QN4
12 P–N5	N×B+
13 RP×N	N–Q2

Black leaves his king in the centre, believing it to be safer there than on the K-side. First he has eliminated the Sozin bishop and got his own pawn storm under way. The position is unclear; typical continuations are:

a) 14 Q–R5 N–B4 15 P–N4 N–R5 16 R–Q3 Q–N2! Vogt-Tringov, Bulgaria 1973.

b) 14 N B5!? P×N 15 N–Q5 Q–Q1 16 P×P B–N2 (*16 ... 0–0? 17 P–B6!*) 17 KR–N1 B×N 18 R×B 0–0 19 P–B6 N×P! 20 P×N B×P!=.

c) 14 P–R4 P–N5 15 N–R4 N–B4 16 P–R5!? N×KP 17 P–N6! is critical.

Variation 2

7 ...	B–K2
8 Q–K2	0–0
9 0–0–0!(*63*)	
9 ...	P–QR3

Black gets a somewhat passive game if he tries to do without this any longer. To illustrate this, here is the game Jovcić-Radoicić, Yugoslavia 1969: 9 ...Q–R4 10 B–N3 N×N 11 B×N B–Q2 12 K–N1 B–B3 13 P–B4 QR–Q1 14

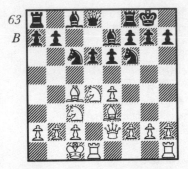

63

B

KR–B1 P–QN4 15 P–K5! (In Fischer-Geller, Skopje 1967, White played *15 P–B5*, which also is strong, if followed up correctly.) 15 ... P×P 16 P×P N–Q2 17 Q–N4! (Threatening *18 B×KP*, and *18 R–Q3* followed by *R–KN3*.) 17 ... P–N5 18 R×P!! K×R (White reaches a winning ending after *18 ... R×R 19 Q×KP R1–KB1 20 R–KB1 N–B3 21 P×N B×BP 22 B×B* etc.) 19 Q×KP+ K–K1 20 Q×B.6 P×N 21 P–K6 Q–R4 22 P×N+ R×P 23 P–N4! Q–N3 (or *23 ... Q×NP 24 Q–B8+ B–Q1 25 R–K1+ R–K2 26 R×R+ K×R 27 B–B5+ K–K1 28 B–R4+ Q×B 29 Q–K6+ B–K2 30 Q×B mate* – analysis by the winner) 24 B–B6! R×B 25 Q×R.7+ K–B1 26 Q–B8+ Q–K1 27 Q–B4 Q–B2 28 Q×Q+ R×Q 29 B×R K×B 30 R–Q7 Black resigned.

10 B–N3   Q–B2

This removes the queen from the perilous Q-file, protects the QN and prepares to launch a counter attack.

11 P–N4

The popular alternative 11 KR–N1 is too slow, in view of 11 ... N–QR4! 12 P–N4 P–QN4 13 P–N5 N×B+ (It is important to enforce capture with the RP, else after K–N1 White might occupy the QB-file with his rooks.) 14 RP×N N–Q2 15 Q–R5 P–N3 16 Q–R6 (*16 Q–R4 P–N5!*) 16 ... R–K1 and

White has insufficient attacking resources.

11 ...   N×N
12 R×N   P–QN4!

12 ... P–K4 13 R–B4 or 13 N–Q5 is rather risky.

13 P–N5   N–Q2
14 P–B4

14 Q–R5 R–Q1! 15 R–N1 P–N3 halts White's attack.

14 ...   N–B4
15 Q–B2   R–Q1

Probably better is 15 ... P–B4 16 KP×P R×P 17 Q–Q2 (Planinc-Langeweg, Wijk aan Zee 1974) 17 ... B–Q2 with balanced chances.

With the text move, we follow Planinc-Enklaar, from the same event.

16 P–B5   R–N1
17 R–B1 B–B1 18 P–N6!? (This gives White a typically dangerous attack.) 18 ... N×B+ 19 RP×N P–N5?! (Proves to be a waste of time, but Black's position is anyway hard to defend.) 20 Q–R4! RP×P (or *20 ... BP×P 21 P×NP P–R3 22 B–N5* with a threatening position.) 21 P×NP P×P 22 B–N5 R–K1 23 R–Q3 (threatening *24 R–R3* and so forcing Black's next, which negates his 19th move.) 23 ... P–K4 24 N–Q5 Q–N2 25 R3–KB3 B–K3 (White was threatening 26 R×B+ mating, but White has another shot left.) 26 R1–B2! (guarding the rook, and so threatening *27 R×B+! R×R 28 N–K7+* etc.) 26 B×N 27 R–R3 Black resigned.

Boleslavsky Variation

6 B–K2   P–K4 (*64*)

This is a move which would have shocked the theorists of 1900, or even of 1930. Black accepts a backward QP for some time to come, relying for compensation on chances of attack on the Q-side. The QRP may be advanced, even as far as QR6, and there are good possibilities of the second advance . . : P–Q4 which, if carried out without ensuing difficulties, results in the superior position for Black in the centre. A further motif is the exchange of the black-squared bishops on each side, which gives Black possibilities of exploiting the slight weakness of White's Q4, K3 and KB4. Black frequently obtains a minimal advantage in the middle game which needs care and patience to be evaluated in the endgame. Consequently, the Boleslavsky Variation is to be recommended particularly to steady positional players.

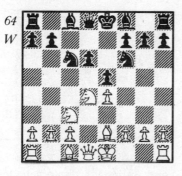

White has three main possibilities in diagram 64:

7 N–B3 – Variation 1
7 N×N – Variation 2
7 N–N3 – Variation 3

Variation 1

    7 N–B3   P–KR3

This is best, else B–KN5 is hard to meet.

    8 0–0   B–K2
    9 R–K1

Simple development is no better: 9 B–K3 0–0 10 Q–Q2 B–K3 11 QR–Q1 Q–Q2 12 Q–K1 (trying to prevent . . . P–Q4) 12 . . . KR–Q1 13 B B1 B–B1 14

P–QN3 Q–B1 with good prospects.

    9 . . .   0–0
    10 P–QN3

Diagram 57 was reached by 10 P–KR3 P–R3 11 B–B1 P–QN4 12 P–R3 B–N2 13 P–QN3 QR–B1 14 B–N2 R–B2.

    10 . . .   P–R3
11 P–QR4 B–K3 12 B–N2 R–QB1 13 P–R3 Q–R4 14 B–KB1 KR–Q1= Castaldi-Unzicker, Munich 1954.

Variation 2

    7 N×N   ·   P×N
    8 0–0

8 P–B4 at once is premature: 8 . . . N–Q2 9 P–B5? Q–N3! and the white king is awkwardly exposed in the centre of the board.

    8 . . .   N–Q2!

8 . . . B–K2 is usually played, but it is less accurate because of 9 P–B4! N–Q2 10 P–B5! 0–0 11 Q–Q3 N–N3 12 Q–N3 B–R5 13 Q–N4 K–R1 14 R–B3 with a strong attack, Donner-Trott, Beverwijk 1953.

    9 Q–Q3   B–K2
10 Q–N3 0–0 11 P–B4 P×P 12 B×P N–B4 (*12 . . . N–K4* is also good.) 13 B–B4 N–K3 14 B–K3 B–B3 15 QR–Q1 B–K4 16 Q–B2 Q–R4 17 B×N B×B 18 B–Q4= Walther-Euwe, Zürich 1954; White's knight has almost the same value as Black's bishop here.

Variation 3

    7 N–N3   B–K2
    8 0–0   0–0(*65*)

The immediate 8 . . . P–QR4 has been tried here, but after 9 B–K3 P–R5 10 N–Q2 P–R6 11 P×P! B–K3 12 N–B4 B×N 13 B×B 0–0 14 R–N1! R×P 15 R–N3 R×R 16 BP×R and White's formidable grip on the Q-file, and especially Q5, gives him the better game; Wade-Barden, Nottingham 1954.

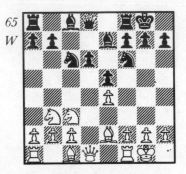

65
W

9 B–K3

Others:

a) 9 B–B3 P–QR4 or 9 ... B–K3 requires further tests.

b) 9 P–B4 P–QR4! 10 P–QR4 (*10 B–K3 P–R5*) 10 ... N–QN5! 11 K–R1 (not *11 B–K3 B–K3* threatening the surprise combination *12 ... N×BP!* and *13 ... Q–N3+*) 11 ... B–K3 12 P–B5 B–Q2 13 B–KN5 R–B1 14 B–B3 B–B3 15 Q–K2 P–R3 16 B–R4 Q–B2 followed by ... KR–Q1 and Black, fully prepared for the liberating ... P–Q4, has an excellent game; Lokvenc-Gligorić, Agram 1949.

9 ...   B–K3

9 ... P–QR4 is also playable.

10 B–B3   P–QR4

11 N–Q5

Not 11 P–QR4, because Black's QN occupies the excellent square QN5.

11 ...   B×N

12 P×B   N–N1!

The beginning of a subtle idea: Black intends to lure on White's pawns to white squares. Then he will exchange off the black-squared bishops and occupy the weakened black squares with his knights.

13 P–QR4

Weaker is 13 P–QB4, e.g. 13 ...

N–R3 14 B–Q2 Q–N3 15 B–B3 N–B4 16 N×N NP×N 17 Q–K1 N–Q2 18 B–Q1 P–R5 favouring Black; Pilnik-Geller, Göteborg 1955.

13 ...   N1–Q2

14 B–K2   N–N3

15 P–QB4 N.N3–Q2 16 N–Q2 N–K1 17 K–R1 B–N4. Pilnik-Petrosian, Buenos Aires 1954; Black is well on the way to achieving his strategical objectives.

The Najdorf Variation

1 P–K4	P–QB4
2 N–KB3	P–Q3
3 P–Q4	P×P
4 N×P	N–KB3
5 N–QB3	P–QR3(*66*)

66
W

This variation has achieved considerable notoriety[*] in the last 15 years. Following the example of Fischer, a whole generation of young players have been attracted to the double-edged play that ensues after Black's provocative fifth move. The original idea of the Najdorf was to play ... P–K4 (much as in the Boleslavsky), but against modern procedures for White (variations 4 and 5) other plans have had to be developed. Black will expand rapidly on the Q-side and put pressure on White's KP if he can; White will play to expose the black king, which often remains in the centre throughout the game.

Favourable Positions for White
Karpov-Polugayevsky, match 1974

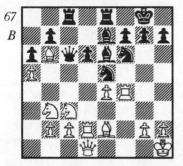

Black cannot begin his Q-side counterplay.

Tringov-Reshevsky, Amsterdam 1964

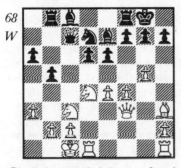

Black has castled into a ferocious attack: 1 P–N6! RP×P 2 N×KP! etc.

Favourable Positions for Black
Bellin-Portisch, Teesside 1972

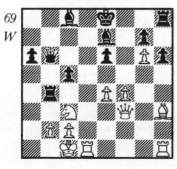

The K-side situation has been stabilised and White's king is now in the greater danger: 1 N–Q5 P×N 2 B×B 0–0!

Byrne-Fischer, Sousse 1967

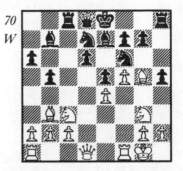

Black has a solid centre and pressure on both flanks.

An Even Position
Flores-Najdorf, Mar del Plata 1955

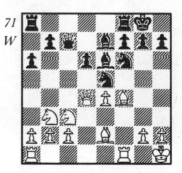

Black's strong knight on e5 adequately compensates for his isolated QP.

White has a very wide choice of replies to the Najdorf. We shall look at:

6 B–K2 – Variation 1
6 P–KN3 – Variation 2
6 P–B4 – Variation 3
6 B–QB4 – Variation 4
6 B–KN5 – Variation 5

Variation 1

6 B–K2	P–K4
7 N–N3	B–K2

An older line is 7 . . . B–K3 8 0–0 QN–Q2 (*8 . . . B–K2* see below.) 9 P–B4 Q–B2 10 P–B5!? B–B5 11 P–QR4 R–B1 12 B–K3 B–K2 13 P–R5 (once thought favourable to White) 13 . . . P–QN4! 14 P×P ep N×NP with adequate play for Black; Geller-Fischer, Curaçao 1962.

8 0–0   B–K3

If 8 . . . 0–0 9 P–QR4 B–K3 10 P–B4 Q–B2 11 K–R1 with an edge to White.

9 P–B4	Q–B2
10 P–QR4	QN–Q2

11 K–R1 0–0 12 B–K3 P×P 13 R×P N–K4 14 P–R5 KR–K1! (Polugayevsky earlier tried *14 . . . KN–Q2?!*) 15 B–N6 Q–Q2 16 R–R4!? QR–B1! 17 R–Q4 Q–B3? (Polugayevsky later suggested *17 . . . R×N!? 18 P×R Q–B3!* with fair chances) 18 R–Q2! and we have reached diagram 67, which favours White.

Variation 2

6 P–KN3	P–K4
7 N4–K2	P–QN4

This is probably better than 7 . . . B–K3 or 7 . . . B–K2.

8 B–N2	B–K2
9 0–0	0–0

10 P–KR3 B–N2 11 N–Q5 N×N 12 P×N N–Q2 13 P–QR4 N–N3= Black has adequate Q-side prospects; Konstantinopolsky-Geller, 20th USSR Ch 1952.

Variation 3

6 P–B4

This allows Black a variety of replies, although some care is necessary.

6 . . .   QN–Q2

Of the alternatives, 6 . . . P–K4 7 N–B3 QN–Q2 8 P–QR4 is most often seen. After 8 . . . P–QN3 9 B–B4 B–K2 10 0–0 0–0 11 P×P P×P 12 B–KN5 B–K2 13 Q–K2 White has the more active pieces, but Black has no serious difficulties.

7 B–Q3

Or 7 P–QR4 (*7 N–B3 P–K3* or *7 B–B4 P–QN4*) 7 . . . P–KN3 8 B–Q3 B–N2 9 N–B3 0–0 10 0–0 N–B4!? 11 Q–K1 R–N1 12 Q–R4 P–QN4 13 P×P P×P= Ghizdavu-Karpov, European Team Ch, Bath 1973.

7 . . .	P–QN4
8 0–0	B–N2
9 P–QR3	P–N3
10 Q–K1	B–N2
11 K–R1	N–B4

Black has a comfortable game without weaknesses. White must find a good plan or he will drift into an inferior position. For example, here is the game Penrose-Ljubojevic, European Team Ch 1973: 12 N–B3 0–0 13 B–Q2 R–B1 14 R–Q1 Q–B2 15 P–QN4 N×B 16 P×N P–K4! 17 R–B1 Q–K2 18 Q–R4 R–B2 19 P×P P×P 20 B–K3 R1–B1 21 B–B5 Q–K1 22 N–K2 P–R3 23 B–K3? (Overlooking the strength of the reply, but Black was threatening . . . Q–K3–QN6 etc.) 23 . . . R–B7! 24 R×R R×R 25 N–N3? (*25 Q–K1* was less desperate.) 25 . . . P–N4 26 N×NP P×N 27 B×P N–R2! 28 N–B5 P–B3 29 B–R6 B×B 30 N×B+ K–R1 31 P–R3 B–B1 White resigned.

Variation 4

6 B–QB4	P–K3
7 B–N3	

This sharp line was introduced by Fischer early in his career. Current theory gives the nod to Black, however.

7 . . .	P–QN4
8 0–0	

Or 8 P–B4 when:

a) 8 ... B–N2 9 P–B5 P–K4 10 N4–K2 QN–Q2 11 B–N5 B–K2 12 N–N3 R–QB1! 13 0–0 P–KR4! reaching diagram 70.

b) 8 ... P–N5!? 9 N–R4 N×P 10 0–0 N–KB3! with complications not unfavourable to Black.

8 ...	B–K2
9 P–B4	0–0
10 P–K5	P×P
11 P×P	N3–Q2
12 Q–R5(*72*)	

This move, discovered by Mestel, is White's last hope in the 6 B–QB4 variation.

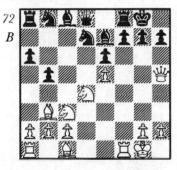

72
B

| 12 ... | N–B4! |

White's main idea is seen in the line 12 ... P–N3 13 Q–K2 B–B4 14 B–K3 B–N2 15 R×P! with a winning attack:

a) 15 ... R×R 16 N×KP B×B+ 17 Q×B Q–N3 18 Q×Q N×Q 19 N–Q8 N–B5 20 P–QR4!

b) 15 ... B×N 16 B×P B×B+ 17 Q×B R×R 18 R–KB1 Q–N3 19 Q×Q N×Q 20 R × R Walther-Gereben, Switzerland 1971.

However, 12 ... N–B3 13 N×N Q–N3+ may also be strong.

| 13 B–K3 | N×B |

Eliminating any danger of the rook sacrifice.

| 14 RP×N | B–N2 |

This was Mestel-Browne, Hastings 1972–3; Black's position after 15 R–B2 (*15 R–B4?! B–N4*) 15 ... B–N2 16 R1–KB1 Q–K1 is temporarily cramped, but very solid.

Variation 5

| 6 B–KN5 | P–K3 |
| 7 P–B4(*73*) | |

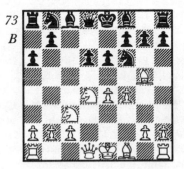

73
B

This position frequently arises, and it certainly offers great scope to the combinative player with either colour. Objectively, White probably has rather the better of it, but the major drawback for him is that Black has at this point a wide choice of lines, all of which require careful study – whereas Black need only specialize in one of them.

| 7 ... | QN–Q2 |

Others include:

a) 7 ... P–QN4 (Polugayevsky) 8 P–K5 P×P 9 P×P Q–B2 10 P×N Q–K4+ 11 B–K2 Q×B 12 0–0 with good attacking chances for White.

b) 7 ... Q–N3 8 Q–Q2 Q×P (Fischer's favourite 'poisoned pawn' line) can be defended by Black, but it is not easy against 9 R–QN1 Q–R6 10 P–B5! N–B3 11 P×P P×P 12 N×N P×N 13 P–K5!

c) 7 ... P–R3 8 B–R4 is similar to the main line; if 8 ... Q–N3 9 Q–Q3!

d) 7 ... B–K2 8 Q–B3 P–R3 9 B–R4 P–KN4 10 P×P KN–Q2 11 Q–R5

N–K4 12 B–N3 B×P 13 B×N P×B 14 N–B3 with a sharp game, somewhat better for White.

| 8 Q–B3 | Q–B2 |
| 9 0–0–0 | B–K2 |

Or 9 . . . P–R3 (9 . . . *P–N4!?* is also interesting.) 10 B–R4 B–K2 11 B–K2! R–QN1 (*11 . . . P–QN4 12 P–K5!*) 12 Q–N3 R–N1 (*12 . . . P–QN4!?*) 13 KR–B1 P–QN4 14 N×KP!! P×N 15 Q–N6+ K–Q1 16 P–K5 P×P 17 P–B5! P×P 18 B×N B×B 19 N–Q5 Q–B3 20 R×P R–B1 21 B–N4! R–N3 22 R×B! P×R 23 Q–N7 R–N2 24 Q–K7 mate; Lombardy-Quinteros, Manila 1973.

10 P–KN4

The main alternative is 10 B–Q3 P–QN4 11 KR–K1 with obscure complications. The text move is probably just as good, and has the merit that White is unlikely to be downed by a surprise innovation.

10 . . .	P–N4
11 B×N	N×B
12 P–N5	N–Q2
13 P–QR3	

This is sounder than the pawn offer 13 P–B5!?

13 . . .   R–QN1

If 13 . . . 0–0–0 14 B–R3 preparing to sacrifice on K6.

14 B–R3!

The fashionable 14 P–KR4?! leads to diagram 69 after 14 . . . P–N5 15 P×P R×P 16 B–R3 Q–B4 17 N–N3 Q–N3 18 P–R5 N–B4 19 N×N P×N! 20 P–N6 BP×P 21 P×P P–R3!

14 . . .   N–B4

Neither 14 . . . 0–0? (diagram 68), nor 14 . . . P–N5?! 15 P×P R×P 16 B×P! (Harding-van Dop, Amsterdam 1973) are tenable for Black.

15 KR–N1	P–N5
16 P×P	R×P
17 P–B5	Q–N3

The alternative 17 . . . Q–N2 18 P–B6 P×P 19 P×P B–B1 20 P–N3 P–QR4 (O'Kelly) probably loses after 21 N–Q5!! P×N 22 B×B! etc.

| 18 P×P | P×P |
| 19 N×P! | |

White follows up with N–Q5, N×R and P–K5 reaching positions with some winning chances; Balashov-Danov, ½-final 33rd USSR Ch 1965.

Scheveningen and Other 2 . . . P–K3 Variations

1 P–K4	P–QB4
2 N–KB3	P–K3
3 P–Q4	P×P
4 N×P(*74*)	

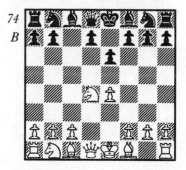

74
B

In recent years, some of · Black's possibilities from this diagrammed position have enjoyed a revival. Although Black gets rather passive-looking positions, it is not easy for White to prevent equality, and the swashbuckling attacks one often sees against the Dragon or Najdorf Variations rarely succeed here. The players build up their positions more slowly, and the game takes on a positional character.

Black's plan involves . . . P–QR3 (to allow . . . Q–B2 and . . . P–QN4), or sometimes . . . B–B4; or he can leave the QRP untouched and play . . . N–KB3,

... N–QB3, ... B–Q2, ... QN×N and
... B–B3, on the look-out to hit back in
the centre with ... P–K4 or (more
rarely ... P–Q4), after a knight may be
securely posted on K4. White usually
makes moves like B–K3, B–K2, 0–0,
P–B4, Q–K1, R–Q1 (to hold back
Black in the centre) and Q–N3, ready
always to obtain a decisive break by
P–K5 or P–B5. Also White is sometimes
able to play P–QB4, obtaining some
extra space, or the sharp P–KN4, to cut
across Black's harmonious development.

The three main lines you need to
know are:

4 ... N–KB3 – Scheveningen
4 ... N–QB3 – Taimanov
4 ... P–QR3 – Kan

Scheveningen Variation

4 ...	N–KB3
5 N–QB3	P–Q3

This, with 6 B–K2, is so-called
because of its introduction by Euwe in a
tournament at Scheveningen, Holland
in 1923.

Two other moves are occasionally
seen here:

a) 5 ... B–N5?! 6 P–K5! N–Q4 7 Q–N4
P–KN3 8 N–N5! N–QB3 9 B–Q2 B×N
10 P×B! and Black has serious
weaknesses on the black squares. 10 ...
N×P fails to 11 Q–Q4 P–Q3 12 P–QB4
P–QR3 13 P×N P×N 14 B×P+ B–Q2
15 B×B+ Q×B 16 P–KB4.

b) 5 ... N–B3 (Sicilian Four Knights'
Game) 6 N4–N5 B–N5 7 P–QR3
B×N+ 8 N×B P–Q4 is a line offering
Black good chances of drawing, but
none of winning. He has to play to
neutralize White's two bishops, but the
IQP that arises after 9 P×P P×P! is not
a serious handicap. As it is hard for
White to do much with his slight

advantage, this makes the line a good
one for a player who wants half a point
to become club champion and has
Black in the last round!

6 B–K2

Keres' move 6 P–KN4 will appeal to
attacking players. One fair line for
Black is 6 ... N–B3 (Petrosian favours *6
... P–KR3!?*) 7 P–N5 N–Q2 8 B–K3
B–K2 9 P–KR4 0–0! (a courageous
move, enabling Black to get Q-side
counterplay) 10 Q–Q2! (*10 B–QB4
N–N3!* or *10 P–B4 P–QR3=*) 10 ...
P–QR3 11 0–0–0 N×N 12 B×N P–N4
13 P–R3 B–N2 14 P–B4 R–B1! meeting
15 P–B5 by 15 ... N–K4 or 15 B–R3 by
15 ... N–B4 and 16 ... Q–B2=.

6 ...	N–B3
7 B–K3	B–K2
8 0–0	P–QR3

Also often played is 8 ... B–Q2 9
P–B4 0–0 10 Q–K1 (*10 N–N3 may be
more testing.*) 10 ... N×N 11 B×N
B–B3 12 Q–N3 P–KN3! 13 B–Q3
N–R4! 14 Q–B2 N×P 15 Q×N P–K4=
(*16 B×P? B–KN4!*). The text move is
not so drawish.

9 P–B4	Q–B2
10 Q–K1 (*75*)	

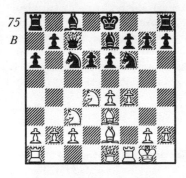

75
B

10 ...	B–Q2

Up to here, the order of moves has
not been important (except that ...
P–QR3 must be played before ...

Q–B2, in order to prevent N–N5), but here this seems definitely the most accurate:

a) 10 ... N×N 11 B×N P–QN4 12 P–K5! P×P 13 P×P N–Q2 14 N–K4 B–N2 (Aronin-Kotov, 19th USSR Ch 1959) 15 N–Q6+ B×N 16 P×B Q×P 17 R–Q1 Q–B2 18 Q–B2 and wins – Tolush.

b) 10 ... 0–0 11 Q–N3 B–Q2 12 N–B3! P–QN4 13 P–K5! P×P 14 P×P with a dangerous initiative – Nikitin.

11 R–Q1

Now 11 Q–N3 could be met by 11 ... P–KR4!? (*12 Q×P R–KN1 13 Q–R6 R–N3* drawing), or 11 P–KN4 by 11 ... P–KR3! when Black's king is safe in the centre, and he can counter-attack by an eventual ... P–K4.

11 ...   0–0
12 Q–N3   P–QN4

12 ... P–KR4!? might still be worth trying.

13 P–QR3   QR–Q1
14 N–B3

If instead 14 K–R1, Black obtains sufficient counter-chances against the white KP by 14 ... N×N 15 B×N B–B3 16 B–B3 Q–N2 17 R–Q2 P–QR4; Simonović-Pirc, Yugoslav Ch 1946.

After the text move, White retains a slight advantage, because of his greater command of space and the constant threat to open up the position by P–K5, e.g. 14 ... P–N5 15 P×P N×NP 16 P–K5!

Taimanov Variation

4 ...   N–QB3

The variation devised by the Soviet grandmaster Taimanov, which has the merit of not committing the KN and KB to specific squares. The

disadvantage is that White, being under no obligation to defend his KP, can take a firm grip on the centre.

5 N–N5   P–Q3

Forced, in view of 5 ... P–Q4? 6 P×P P×P 7 Q×Q 8 N–B7+.

6 P–QB4

6 B–B4 P–K4 7 B–K3 N–B3 8 B–N5 was favoured by Fischer, but in his first match game against Petrosian (1971) there followed 8 ... B–K3 9 N1–B3?! P–QR3 10 B×N P×B 11 N–R3 P–Q4! 12 P×P B×N 13 P×B Q–R4! 14 Q–Q2 0–0–0! with the initiative in Black's hands.

6 ...   N–B3

This is usually played, but tends to lead to positions where, after the opening moves, Black can find no active plan. The Soviet theoretician Nikitin recommends 6 ... P–QR3 7 N5–B3 B–K2 8 B–K2 N–B3 9 0–0 0–0 10 B–K3 R–N1! with balanced chances.

7 N1–B3   P–QR3
8 N–R3   B–K2
9 B–K2   0–0
10 0–0   P–QN3

Black had better try 10 ... B–Q2 e.g. 11 B–K3 R–N1 or 11 B–B4 N–K4!, with more chances of satisfactory counterplay, although White retains his advantage in space.

11 B–K3   B–N2
12 R–B1   N–K4

A well-known position – but White's next move is little-played.

13 P–B4   N4–Q2

If 13 ... N–N3, White can play 14 B–Q3 R–B1? 15 Q–N3 N–Q2 16 N–R4.

14 B–B3   R–N1

15 Q–K2 R–K1 16 KR–Q1 Q–B2 17 P–KN4 R.K1–Q1 18 P–N5 N–K1 19 N–Q5! P×N 20 BP×P N–B4 21 P–N4 and Black's wall has been breached; Spassky-Langeweg, Amsterdam 1973.

Kan Variation

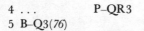

4 ...	P–QR3
5 B–Q3(*76*)	

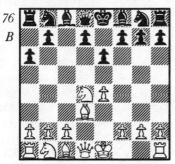

White's knight would only be a target on QB3. Now Black has two distinct ideas:

5 ... *B–B4* – Variation 1
5 ... *N–QB3* – Variation 2

5 ... N–KB3 6 0–0 leads to positions similar to the Scheveningen.

Variation 1

5 ...	B–B4
6 N–N3	B–R2

7 Q–K2 N–QB3 8 0–0 P–Q3 9 B–K3 B×B 10 Q×B N–B3 11 P–QB4 0–0 12 R–Q1 (preventing ... P–Q4) 12 ... Q–B2 13 N–B3 N–K4 14 QR–B1 P–QN3 15 B–K2 B–N2 16 P–B4 N–N3 17 P–N3 KR–Q1 18 P–QR3 QR–B1 19 N–Q4 B–R1 (19 ... Q–B4 20 P–QN4) 20 P–QN3 N–K2 21 B–B3 Karpov-Hübner, Student Olympiad, Graz 1972; White has a clear advantage.

Variation 2

5 ...	N–QB3
6 N×N	NP×N

6 ... QP×N (intending 7 ... *P–K4* with a drawish position) can be met by 7 B–KB4 N–K2 8 B–N3 N–N3 9 N–Q2 B–Q3 10 N–B4 B×B 11 RP×B P–N4 12 N–K3 P–QB4 13 Q–R5 P–B5 14 B–K2

B–N2 15 B–B3 Q–Q5 16 P–QB3 Q–K4 17 P–QR4 with the initiative; Murei-Ignatiev, Zenit club Ch 1971.

7 0–0	P–Q4
8 P–QB4!	

Black is behind in development, so White seeks to open up the position. We are following the 7th Fischer-Petrosian match game, 1971.

8 ...	N–B3

Botvinnik suggested 8 ... P×BP 9 B×P Q×Q 10 R×Q N–B3 11 N–B3 B–B4 12 B–KN5 P–K4 with the defending Black's Q4 square.

9 BP×P	BP×P
10 P×P	P×P

Others:

a) 10 ... N×P 11 B–K4 B–K2 12 N–B3 B–N2 13 Q–N3 – Lilienthal

b) 10 ... Q×P 11 N–B3 Q–Q2 (Botvinnik) is somewhat better. However, White still got a plus in the game Vasyukov-Vooremaa, Uzhgorod ½-final 40th USSR Ch 1972: 12 B–B2 Q×Q 13 R×Q B–K2 14 B–B4 with Q-side chances in the endgame.

11 N–B3!	B–K2
12 Q–R4+!	Q–Q2

Or 12 ... B–Q2 13 Q–Q4! with an advantageous transfer of the white queen to a central square.

13 R–K1!	

To take the exchange by 13 B–QN5 P×B 14 Q×R 0–0 would give Black undeserved counterplay.

13 ...	Q×Q
14 N×Q	B–K3
15 B–K3	

This ending is unpleasant for Black, although it is the error at move 20 that makes the loss certain. White has a Q-side pawn majority, and has firmly blockaded the black QP. Fischer now increases his advantage by exchanging the black-squared bishops.

15 ...   0–0
16 B–B5! KR–K1 17 B×B R×B 18
P–QN4! K–B1 19 N–B5 B–B1 20 P–B3
R2–R2? (Necessary was *20 ... R×R+
21 R×R N–K1.*) 21 R–K5! B–Q2 22
N×B+ R×N 23 R–QB1 R–Q3 24
R–B7 N–Q2 25 R–K2 P–N3 26 K–B2
P–KR4 27 P–B4 P–R5 28 K–B3 P–B4
29 K–K3 P–Q5+ 30 K–Q2 N–N3 31
R2–K7 N–Q4 32 R–B7+ K–K1 33
R–QN7 N×NP 34 B–B4 Black
resigned.

The Alapin Variation
1 P–K4   P–QB4
2 P–QB3(*77*)

We recommend this line to anybody
who, as White, wishes to avoid the well-
analysed paths of the open Sicilian.

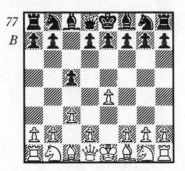

77
B

Black can reply:
2 ... *P–Q4* – Variation 1
2 ... *N–KB3* – Variation 2

It is surprising how many opponents
look flustered, and then concede the
centre by 2 ... P–Q3? 3 P–Q4 etc.
Possible, however, is 2 ... P–K3 3
P–Q4 (or *3 N–B3*) P–Q4 4 P–K5
transposing to the French Defence.

Variation 1
2 ...   P–Q4

The natural move, but it causes
Black some trouble.

3 P×P   Q×P
4 P–Q4   N–QB3
Or 4 ... P–K4 5 P×KP Q×KP+ 6
B–K3 N–KB3 7 N–B3 Q–B2 8 N–R3!
5 N–B3   P×P
Or 5 ... P–K3 (5 ... B–N5 6 B–K2)
6 B–Q3 N–B3 7 0–0 B–K2 8 P–B4
Q–Q1 9 P×P 0–0 10 N–B3 B×P 11
B–KN5 B–K2 12 Q–K2 Q–R4 13
N–K4 N×N 14 B×B N×B 15 B×N
P–B3 16 KR–Q1 Zak-Krasnov, USSR
1973; White stands slightly better.

6 P×P   B–N5
Or 6 ... P–K4 7 N–B3 B–QN5 8
B–Q2 B×N 9 B×B P–K5 10 N–K5
N×N 11 P×N N–K2 12 P–K6!? White
now has a slight edge with 7 B–K2, or a
promising pawn offer in:
7 N–B3!?   B×N
If the queen moves, then 8 P–Q5!
8 P×B   Q×QP
9 Q×Q   N×Q
10 N–N5!
a) 10 ... N–K3 11 P–B4 P–QR3 12
P–B5 (*12 0–0–0!?*) 12 ... P×N 13
B×P+ K–Q1 14 P×N P×P 15 B–K3
and White should win.
b) 10 ... N–B7+ 11 K–Q1 N×R 12
N–B7+ K–Q1 13 N×R P–K4 14 B–K3
P–QN3 15 B–QR6! is also winning for
White.
c) 10 ... 0–0–0 11 N×N R×N 12 B–K3
R–N5 may be Black's best chance.
d) 10 ... P–K4!? 11 N–B7+ K–Q2 12
N×R B–N5+ and Black tries to take
the initiative at the cost of the
exchange; this line needs further tests,
but 13 K–Q1! should be a sufficient
defence.

Variation 2
2 ...   N–KB3
This is the reply you should expect to
meet.
3 P–K5   N–Q4

4 P–Q4	P×P
5 P×P	

After 5 Q×P P–K3 6 N–KB3 (*6 B–QB4 N–QB3 7 Q–K4 P–Q3!*) 6 ... N–QB3 7 Q–K4 Black can try Taimanov's 7 ... P–B4!?

5 ...	P–Q3
6 N–KB3	N–QB3
7 N–B3	

Markland prefers 7 Q–N3, e.g.:

a) 7 ... P×P 8 N×P N×N 9 P×N P–K3 10 N–B3 B–N5 11 B–QN5+ B–Q2 12 0–0 with an unclear position.

b) 7 ... P–K3 8 B–QN5 B–Q2 (*8 ... B–K2!?*) 9 N–B3 N×N 10 P×N P×P 11 B×N B×B 12 N×P when, in practice, White has a slight edge.

7 ...	N×N?!

With this and the next move, Black falls into a book trap. One critical line is 7 ... P×P 8 P×P (*8 B–QN5!?* should be tried.) N×N? 9 Q×Q+ when the ending gives White tactical chances. The Hungarian master Csom, in particular, has played the white pieces with success here. However, 8 ... N4–N5! is a big improvement for Black.

8 P×N	P×P?

8 ... P–K3 was the last chance of equalizing.

9 P–Q5!	P–K5
10 N–N5!	N–K4
11 N×KP	

Black is disorganized and lacks a toehold in the centre. Relatively best is 11 ... P–K3 but we shall follow the game Chiburdanidze-Andreyeva, from the 1973 Tbilisi women's international tournament; the winner was only 12 years old at the time!

11 ...	Q–B2
12 Q–Q4	B–Q2
13 B–R3	P–B3
14 P–Q6!	Q–B3

15 P×P B×P 16 B×B K×B 17 Q–N4+

K–B2 18 P–KB4 KR–K1 19 P×N (not *19 N–Q6+? Q×N! 20 Q×Q N–B5+*) 19 ... R×P 20 0–0–0! R×N 21 R×B+ K–K1 22 R–K7+! Black resigned, for 22 ... R×R 23 B–N5+ wins the queen.

Other Sicilian Variations

A few other lines of the Sicilian are worth a brief mention, although there is no space to discuss them thoroughly.

The Close Sicilian

1 P K4	P–QB4
2 N–QB3	

This has often been played by ex-World Champion Smyslov. The two players build up almost independently of one another, and the weight of the struggle is deferred until the middle game. Black has a choice of formations.

2 ...	N–QB3
3 P–KN3	P–KN3
4 B–N2	B–N2
5 P–Q3	P–Q3
6 P–B4	P–B4!?
7 N–B3	N–R3

Black has prevented White's main attacking idea (P–KB5) and, after K-side castling, will have good prospects on the Q-side. This set-up for Black is sound enough, and has the merit of being relatively unknown.

The Morra Gambit

1 P–K4	P–QB4
2 P–Q4	P×P
3 P–QB3	

White hopes for a strong initiative if the gambit is accepted: 3 ... P×P 4 N×P N–QB3 5 N–B3 P–Q3 6 B–QB4 followed by 0–0, Q–K2 and B–KB4 or B–KN5. Although Black can defend this attack, it is much safer to decline by 3 ... N–KB3 4 P–K5 N–Q4 5 P×P

P–Q3, transposing to Variation 2 of the Alapin, above.

The B–QN5 Variation

1 P–K4	P–QB4
2 N–KB3	N–QB3

Or 2 . . . P–Q3 3 B–N5+ N–QB3 (*3 . . . B–Q2* is also playable.) transposing.

3 B–N5   P–Q3

Also playable are 3 . . . P–KN3, 3 . . . P–K3 and other moves, but they are more common and White will be prepared to meet them. Here Black plans to turn the opening into a kind of Ruy Lopez: 4 0–0 B–Q2 5 R–K1 (or *5 P–B3 N–B3 6 R–K1 P–QR3 7 B–B1 P–KN3*) 5 . . . P–K4 6 P–B3 P–QR3 7 B–R4 P–QN4 8 B–B2 B–K2 9 P–Q4 (Lokvenc-Milić, Vienna 1951–2) 9 . . . N–B3=

The 4 Q×P Variation

1 P–K4	P–QB4
2 N–KB3	P–Q3
3 P–Q4	P×P
4 Q×P	

This is another evasive system which is beginning to attract some attention.

Black's most reliable line is 4 . . . N–QB3 5 B–QN5 B–Q2 6 B×N B×B when:
a) 7 N–B3 N–B3 8 B–N5 P–K3 9 0–0–0 B–K2 10 KR–K1 0–0 (*10 . . . Q–R4 11 N–Q5!?*) 11 P–K5! P×P 12 Q–KR4 Q–B2 13 N×P KR–Q1= Vasyukov-Tal, 40th USSR Ch 1972.
b) 7 P–B4 N–B3 8 N–B3 P–KN3! 9 0–0 B–N2 10 Q–Q3 0–0 11 N–Q4 Q–N3 Andersson-Benko, Las Palmas 1972; once again, Black maintains equality by vigorous methods.

The Nimzowitsch Variation

1 P–K4	P–QB4
2 N–KB3	N–KB3!?

This interesting counter-attack has resisted decades of effort at refutation by 3 P–K5 N–Q4 etc.

3 N–B3

The safest reply. There can follow:
a) 3 . . . P–Q4 4 P×P N×P 5 B–N5+ with an edge to White.
b) 3 . . . N–B3 4 P–Q4 P×P (*4 . . . P–Q4!?* may equalize.) 5 N×P transposing to regular lines.

5 THE FRENCH DEFENCE: A RESILIENT DEFENCE TO 1 P–K4

You should not adopt the French Defence if you are afraid of being attacked. It is an opening which recommends itself to those who like a patient, long-drawn-out struggle, and who do not mind being on the defensive. Time after time in the games of great masters like Yanofsky and Uhlmann with the French Defence, we see them being violently attacked, but later in the game going over to a victorious counter-attack. Even very fine attacking players find great difficulty in dealing with it.

The Basic Pattern

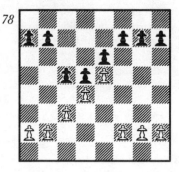

The pawn formation in the diagram is one which occurs again and again as a result of this opening. The plans which you have in mind during French Defence games should be in harmony with the possibilities inherent in this formation.

Plans for White

1) As a general principle, K-side attack is indicated, with the development of the KB at Q3. White aims in addition at Q–KN4.

2) Attack the base of Black's pawn formation by P–KB5, possibly prepared by P–KN4. If this advance can be carried through without Black obtaining equivalent compensation elsewhere, White will have the chance of driving the wedge further into Black's position, by P–KB6 etc. This plan is strongly to be recommended in every case where Black plays the French Defence passively, for instance without . . . P–QB4 or . . . P–KB3. For this attack, it is important to secure the base of White's pawn chain at Q4; the reason is that if Black answers P–KB5 by . . . KP×P, then White's KP is weak unless it is supported by the QP. So the set-up of pieces at which to aim is: bishop at Q3, knights at K2 and KB3, pawns at QB3, Q4, K5, KB5 and KN4.

3) A more positional way of treating this pawn formation is to relieve the pressure on Q4 by playing QP×QBP. This has the advantage that Q4 is now free for the white knights, and that White can aim at an ending in which he will have a strong knight on Q4 against Black's QB, hemmed in by its own pawns.

Plans for Black

1) Our remarks on the effectiveness of the white K-side attack against passive play lead to the conclusion that Black must counter-attack vigorously. Normally, this is done by pressure on the white QP, with the black QN on QB3, the pawn at QB4, queen at QN3 and sometimes the KN at KB4. Note that Black must not play . . . P–QB5, which many club players do almost automatically; this releases all the pressure on white's centre, allowing him to pursue his K-side assault without interruption.

2) Black can attack the apex of White's pawn formation by . . . P–KB3. This will generally have the effect of taking the sting from White's P–KB5. If White allows . . . KBP×KP, he must either retake with the QP (when the black rook affords an extra protection to KB4) or with the KBP (when P–KB5 is no longer possible). If White plays KP×KBP, then Black must retake with a piece and try later on to eliminate White's QP and then follow up with . . . P–K4. He should not retake with the KNP since this almost always leaves the castled king's position very weak.

3) Instead of . . . P–KB3, . . . P–KB4 is another idea which can often be considered, since if White does not play KP×KBPep the pawn will effectively block a K-side attack and Black can continue with his plans in the centre and Q-side.

The player who keeps these ideas in mind and formulates his plans accordingly, when playing the French Defence for either side, will always be able to hold his own in the opening against any opponent of his own strength.

The 3 . . . N–KB3 Variation

1 P–K4	P–K3
2 P–Q4	P–Q4
3 N–QB3	

The move we recommend for White.

3 . . .	N–KB3

For the Winawer Variation, 3 . . . B–N5!, see below.

    4 B–N5

4 P–K5 KN–Q2 5 P–B4 P–QB4 6 P×P N–QB3 7 N–KB3 B×P 8 B–Q3 N–N5! 9 P–QR3 N×B+ 10 Q×N P–B3! is safe enough for Black.

    4 B–N5

Black has two main ideas now:

4 . . . B–K2 – Classical
4 . . . B–N5!? – MacCutcheon

Burn's Variation, 4 . . . P×P 5 N×P B–K2, is not to be recommended, since White obtains good attacking chances, e.g. 6 B×N B×B 7 N–KB3 N–Q2 8 P–B3 P–QN3 9 B–Q3 B–N2 10 Q–B2 0–0 11 0–0–0 Q–K2 12 P–KR4.

Classical Variation

4 . . .	B–K2
5 P–K5	

Anderssen's move 5 B×N only gives an attack if Black defends carelessly. With proper play, Black's two bishops begin to count, e.g. 5 . . . B×B 6 P–K5 B–K2 7 Q–N4 0–0 8 0–0–0 P×B4 9 Q–R3 P–B4 10 P×P N–B3 11 P–B4 Q–R4 12 K–N1 P–QN3 with counterplay.

5 . . .	KN–Q2

White's choice is between:
6 B×B – Main Line
6 P–KR4!? – Albin-Chatard

Main Line

6 B×B	Q×B(*82*)

This is the Classical Variation, which shows in very clear form the pros and cons of the ideas outlined in the introduction. Before proceeding to specific variations, some typical positions of the line are worthy of study.

A Good Position for White
Nielsen-Stahlberg, Herning 1938

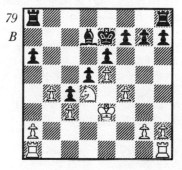

79
B

White has achieved a won ending, by exchanging his QP for Black's original QBP, trading off pieces and reaching a thematic knight against bad bishop situation. Now he will advance his K-side pawns, open files for the rooks, and attack the black pawns from the rear.

A Good Position for Black
Israel-Yanofsky, Ilford 1952

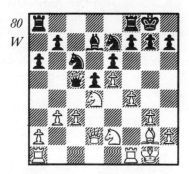

80
W

White has developed slowly and created pawn weaknesses. Black has pressure on the QB-file. This position is a particular warning against superficial assessments, for at first sight White's centre might have appeared impressive.

An Even Position
Bernstein-Lasker, Zürich 1934

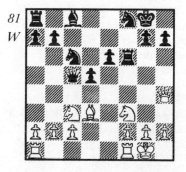

81
W

White has attacking chances, but Black's pieces have freedom, and his centre pawns some prospect of advancing.

The typical positions of the Classical Variation show the plans of each side. White aims at controlling K5 and Q4, keeping the black pawns static, and aiming at a long-term policy at a favourable knight versus bad bishop endgame. Black hopes to get free play for his pieces, in particular the QB, and to force weaknesses among White's Q-side pawns.

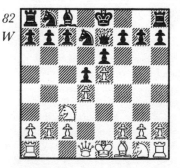

82
W

7 P–B4

Others:

a) 7 B–Q3 Q–N5 8 N–B3 (*8 KN–K2 P–QB4!*) 8 . . . Q×NP 9 N–K2 P–QB4 10 P–B3 Q–N3 and White should not have enough for his pawn.

b) 7 Q–N4 0–0 8 B–Q3 P–QB4 9 N–B3 P–B4 10 P×Pep R×P (The knight is best reserved for controlling K4, while the queen may find favourable play on the Q-side.) 11 Q–R4 N–B1 12 P×P Q×P 13 0–0 N–B3= see diagram 81.

c) 7 Q–Q2 0–0 see below.

7 . . .   0–0!

Not so good is 7 . . . P–QR3 8 N–B3 P–QB4 9 P×P (*9 N–K2 P×P 10 N2×P Q–N5+*) 9 . . . N–QB3 (*9 . . . Q×P 10 Q–Q4!* heading for the knight v. bishop ending) 10 P–QR3 Q×P 11 Q–Q2 P–QN4 12 Q–B2! B–N2 13 Q×Q N×Q 14 N–K2 P–B3; So far Boleslavsky-Guimard, Groningen 1946. White should now have played 15 P×P! P×P 16 N2–Q4 when Black has a bad bishop and weak centre pawns, the result of paying insufficient attention to the black squares.

8 N–B3

Or 8 Q–Q2 P–QB4 9 N–B3 N–QB3:

a) 10 P–KN3 is slow, e.g. 10 . . . P–QR3 11 B–N2 N–N3 12 P–N3 B–Q2 13 N–K2 P×P 14 N3×P Q–B4 15 P–B3 N–B1 16 0–0 N1–K2 reaching diagram 80.

b) 10 0–0–0 P–B3 (*10 . . . P–B5? 11 P–B5! R–N1 12 Q–N5!*) 11 KP×P N×BP 12 P×P Q×P 13 P–KN3= White has a grip on the centre, but when Black completes his development he will have attacking chances on the Q-side.

8 . . .   P–QB4

White gets an edge from 8 . . . P–KB3 9 P×P R×P (*9 . . . N×P!?*) 10 Q–Q2 P–B4 11 B–Q3 N–B3 12· P×P Bronstein-Yanofsky, Stockholm 1948.

9 P–KN3

We shall follow the game O. Penrose-Yanofsky, Oxford ˙1952. White is hoping to safeguard the base of his pawn-chain at KB4 and, by putting pressure on Q5, prevent any later . . . P–K4 by Black. But the move seriously weakens his QB4 and Black takes advantage of this. Better probably is 9 B–Q3 P–B4 10 P×Pep transposing to the previous note.

9 . . .   P×P

10 Q×P

A further loss of time; 10 KN×P is better.

10 . . .   N–QB3
11 Q–Q2   P–QR3
12 B–N2   N–N3

Threatening 13 . . . N–B5 14 Q–B1 Q–N5 and thus forcing White to retract his previous move.

13 B–B1   B–Q2
14 B–Q3   Q–B4
15 P–KN4!?

The strategically correct move here is 15 Q–B2, in order to exchange queens and gradually steer the game towards White's objective of a knight versus bad bishop ending. However, because of White's previous loss of time, the move fails tactically to 15 . . . Q–N5. Thus White decides to 'mix things' on the K-side. Although he fails, the principle is right: if you have been strategically outplayed and think you will lose by passive defence, then try to stir up tactical complications.

The game went on 15 . . . N–B5 16 B×N Q×B 17 0–0–0 P–QN4 18 K–N1 QR–Q1 19 KR–N1 P–B3 20 P×P R×P 21 P–B5 (This loses a pawn, but it was already difficult to find a satisfactory counter to the coming . . . QR–KB1.) 21 . . . P–N5 22 N–K2 P×P 23 P×P B×P 24 N2–Q4 N×N 25 N×N B–N3 26

QR–K1 QR–KB1 27 R–N2 B–K5 28 R2–K2 P–QR4 29 R–N1. White here over-stepped the time-limit, but Black wins anyway: 29 ... R–B8+ 30 R–K1 (*30 R×R R×R+ 31 R–K1 R×R+* wins a piece.) 30 ... R1–B7 31 Q–N5 Q×N.

Note, in this game, that Black's counter-attack takes place on both sides of the board simultaneously. First he gets ready to break through on the Q-side (moves 15–17), then he attacks on the KB-file (moves 19–20); then he puts pressure on the QB7 square (move 25) and finally he breaks through on the KB-file, so that the focal point of the two attacks (QB7) is menaced from several directions at once. This principle of alternating attacks was discovered by Nimzowitsch. One weakness in a position is not usually enough for victory, since the enemy pieces can cover it; but attack delivered simultaneously at different parts of the board will usually lead to the defence cracking somewhere.

Albin-Chatard-Alekhine Attack

6 P–KR4!?(*83*)

This move of Alekhine's is often adopted by attacking players to avoid the straightforward positional play of the main line. The offer of a pawn places great difficulties in the way of Black's castling. If he accepts the pawn, Black must face White's pressure down the KR-file; if he declines, White has both Q–N4 and R–R3 available as powerful attacking moves. On the other hand, 6 P–KR4 does not solve the problem of the centre, and so Black will look to the traditional counters of . . . P–QB4 and . . . P–KB3 for his defensive resources. However, the current state of theory offers Black no clear equalizing line against the Alekhine Attack, which

is one reason why Black nowadays normally prefers 3 . . . B–N5 to 3 . . . N–KB3.

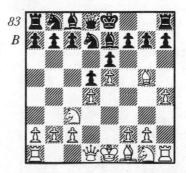

83
B

Black can try:

a) 6 . . . B×B 7 P×B Q×P 8 N–R3 Q–K2 9 N–B4 P–QR3 10 Q–N4 K–B1 (*10 . . . P–KN3 11 Q–N3!?*) 11 Q–B3! K–N1 12 B–Q3 with a tremendous attack, e.g. 12 . . . P–QB4 13 B×P+!! R×B 14 R×R K×R 15 0–0–0 winning Keres-Wade, London 1954.

b) 6 . . . P–QR3 7 Q–N4 P–KB4 8 Q–R5+ P–N3 9 Q–R6 B×B 10 P×B K–B2 11 KN–K2 when White's knight occupies the fine square KB4.

c) 6 . . . P–KR3 7 B–K3 P–QB4 8 Q–N4 K–B1 9 N–B3 N–QB3 10 0–0–0 Dubinin-Rabinovich, Leningrad 1934; Black has driven away the white QB, but he is unable to castle and White's KR will come very strongly into the attack via KR3–KN3.

d) 6 . . . P–KB3 7 Q–R5+ K–B1 (*7 . . . P–N3 8 P×P! P×Q 9 P×B*) 8 P×P N×P 9 Q–K2 and Black's backward KP will be a lasting weakness. A game Spassky-Guimard, Göteborg 1955, continued 9 . . . P–QB4 10 P×P N–R3 11 N–B3 N×P 12 0–0–0 P–QN4 and now 13 N–K5, with a strong grip, was best.

e) 6 . . . P–QB4 7 B×B K×B (The exchange sacrifice *7 . . . Q×B 8 N–N5*

0–0 9 N–B7 is not quite sound.) 8 P–B4!
Q–N3 (*8 ... N–QB3* is sounder.) 9
N–B3 Q×NP 10 N–QN5 P–QR3 11
N–B7 Q–N5+ 12 K–B2 R–R2 13 P–B4!
with a ferocious attack -Keres.

MacCutcheon Variation

4 ...	B–N5!?
5 P–K5	P–KR3(*84*)

This is the double-edged
MacCutcheon Variation, in which
Black tries to take advantage of the
weakness of White's QB3. Experience
has shown that Black can saddle White
with doubled QBPs, but that the first
player has at least adequate
compensation in the open QN-file and
a strengthened hold on the black
squares. The MacCutcheon is playable,
especially in postal games, but you are
warned to study it carefully before
trying it out.

6 B–Q2

Others worth considering:
a) 6 P×N P×B 7 P×P R–N1 8 N–B3 (*8
P–KR4 P×P 9 Q–N4 Q–B3=*) 8 ...
Q–B3 9 P–KR4 P×P (*9 ... B×N+!?*)
10 R×P Q×NP 11 Q–Q3! (Basman-
Hayes, Ilford 1973) is a line needing
more tests.
b) 6 B–K3 N–K5 7 Q–N4 K–B1 8 B–Q3
(or *8 P–QR3*) 8 ... N×N 9 P–QR3
B–R4! (*9 ... N–R7+* fails to disrupt

White's pawns.) 10 B–Q2 P–QB4 11
B×N B×B+ 12 P×B Q–R4 13 K–Q2
N–B3 14 N–B3 N×QP=

6 ...	B×N
7 P×B	N–K5

Now if 8 B–Q3 Black equalizes by 8
... N×B 9 Q×N P–QB4 10 N–B3 P–B5
11 B–K2 N–B3.

8 Q–N4   P–KN3

8 ... K–B1 is dubious, e.g. 9 P–KR4
P–KB4!? 10 Q–B3; Young-Sutton,
corres 1969.

9 B–B1

This is the main line of play, yet
White gets no clear plus. 9 B–Q3 is not
quite satisfactory either, since the king
becomes exposed in the centre: 9 ...
N×B 10 K×N P–QB4 11 Q–B4 (This
attempt to take control of the black
squares is more consistent than *11
P–KR4*.) 11 ... P×P 12 P×P Q–R4+!
13 P–B3 Q–R6 14 N–K2 N–Q2
(stopping Q–B6) and White's king
position is definitely shaky.

9 ...	N×QBP
10 B–Q3	P–QB4
11 P×P	Q–R4!?

The latest resource to be discovered
for Black. Another feasible line for
Black is 11 ... N–Q2 12 N–B3 Q–B2
but 13 0–0 N×BP 14 R–K1 ought to be
a bit better for White.

12 B–Q2	Q–R5
13 P–KR3	P–KR4!
14 Q×Q	N×Q=

Analysis by Keres; White's pawn
weaknesses are balanced by his two
bishops.

The Winawer Variation

1 P–K4	P–K3
2 P–Q4	P–Q4
3 N–QB3	B–N5!

This move leads to positions very
different from those following 3 ...

N–KB3, and the reason is simple. Black has in view the creation of a definite target for attack in the form of doubled QBPs, which White cannot avoid unless he cares to play a risky gambit (4 B–Q2) or allow easy equality (5 B–Q2). The target once created, Black can put pressure on the whole white Q-side by ... P–QB4, followed by ... P×P or ... P–B5 as appropriate, and by ... Q–R4–R5 and the action of his QR on the QB-file. Alternatively, he can try to exchange white-squared bishops, with the object of placing a knight or rook on the weakened white square ... QB5.

The other side of the coin, is that chances are created for White on the K-side, by the removal of the KB from the defence of the point KN2. So Q–N4 at any time will be a definite threat, which Black is wont to counter nowadays by offering the KNP as a gambit. If instead ... P–KN3 becomes necessary, then White will have the advantage because the black squares will be very weak and can be exploited by:

1) the advance of the KRP;
2) the action of the QB on the diagonals QR3–KB8 or KR4–Q8,
3) the posting of the knight on KN5, which in combination with the queen at KB4 would set up serious threats to KB6 and KB7.

Even without a weakness created by ... P–KN3, White can often find sufficient chances in the advance of his K-side pawns, even if Black does not castle KR. With a knowledge of those basic principles, we can proceed to some typical positions, and then to a study of the variations.

Favourable Positions for White
Hartston-Markland, Hastings 1971–2

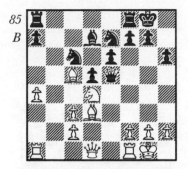

White has an unshakeable grip on the black squares.

Geller-Sokolsky, 18th USSR Ch 1950

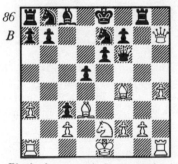

Black has unwisely wasted time capturing the KP, instead of preparing to castle Q-side. White won rapidly by advancing his KRP to the 8th rank, in conjunction with threats to the black king and queen.

Favourable Positions for Black
Phillips-Clarke, Chester 1952

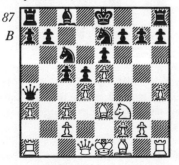

Black has energetically countered a premature K-side advance. He has control of the Q-side white squares, and consolidated his advantage with 11 . . . P–QN3 12 B–Q3 B–QR3.

Estrin-Hasin, corres 1970

88
W

White's attempt to break up the centre by 'energetic' advances of his doubled QBPs has only resulted in backward development and weaknesses.

A Balanced Position
R. Byrne-Uhlmann, Monaco 1968

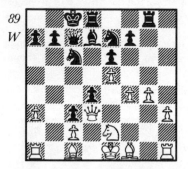

89
W

White counts on his passed KRP to tie down Black's pieces, after first playing B–KN2 to control the long diagonal. Black's chances lie in the relative security of his king, with blows like . . . P–B3 or . . . N×KP in mind, to destroy the white centre at an auspicious moment. This is a good example of a sharp modern opening variation, where the verdict of 'theory' is still suspended.

After 1 P–K4 P–K3 2 P–Q4 P–Q4 3 N–QB3 B–N5 White has:

4 B–Q2? – Variation 1
4 B–Q3!? – Variation 2
4 P–QR3!? – Variation 3
4 P–K5 – Variation 4

Variation 1
   4 B–Q2?
   This move had its introduction into master play as the result of a fingerslip by Alekhine against Flohr, at Nottingham in 1936. He had intended 4 P–K5 P–QB4 5 B–Q2, but played the moves in the wrong order.
   4 . . .   P×P
   5 Q–N4   Q×P
By 5 . . . N–KB3 6 Q×NP R–N1 7 Q–R6 R–N3 8 Q–R4 (*8 Q–K3* is also level.) 8 . . . N–B3 9 0–0–0 B×N 10 B×B Q–Q4 11 P–QN3 N–K2 12 P–B3 (trying to open up lines for attack) 12 . . . B–Q2 13 B–N2 (so far Keres-Botvinnik, Moscow 1948) 13 . . . 0–0–0 Black secures a satisfactory game. White's two bishops are balanced by his slightly shaky king's position and under-developed K-side.
   6 0–0–0   P–KB4
   7 Q–N3   B–Q3
8 B–KB4 B×B+ 9 Q×B Q–B4 10 P–B3 N–KB3! Keres analysed only 10 . . . N–K2, in White's favour. The text move was suggested by a Yugoslav player, Vukčevič; White now has insufficient compensation for a pawn.

Variation 2
   4 B–Q3!?
   This is a little-known line of play which aims, after the almost inevitable

exchanges in the centre, at establishing the white KB on KB3, thus obtaining the advantages of a fianchetto without having wasted time on P–KN3. Combinative players might find this move suits them.

    4 ...   P–QB4

Probably superior is 4 ... P×P 5 B×P N–KB3 6 B–B3 0–0 (*6 ... N–B3!?*) 7 N K2 QN–Q2 8 B–KB4 N–Q4 blockading the important diagonal; Pilnik-Petrosian, Belgrade 1954.

    5 KP×P   Q×P
    6 B–Q2

A better gambit than the last; White gets two bishops in an open position.

    6 ...   B×N
    7 B×B   P×P

8 B×QP Q×NP 9 Q–B3 Q×Q 10 N×Q P–KB3 11 R–KN1 K–B2 12 N–Q2! N–B3 13 B–QB5 White's hold on Q6 and better development sufficiently compensate for the pawn. A game Eisinger-Schmid, Nuremberg 1955, concluded 13 ... KN–K2 14 N–B4 R–Q1 15 N–Q6+ K–N1 16 0–0–0 N–Q4 17 B–B4 N–K4 18 R×N! N×B! (not *18 ... P×R? 19 B×QP+ K–R1 20 P–KB4*) 19 N–B5 R×R 20 N–R6+ Drawn by perpetual check.

Variation 3

    4 P–QR3!?

This is a very complicated variation in which the better combinative player usually wins.

    4 ...   B×N+
    5 P×B   P×P
    6 Q–N4   N–KB3
    7 Q×NP   R–N1
    8 Q–R6   R–N3

The simplest; 8 ... P–B4 is more commital, e.g. 9 N–K2 R–N3 10 Q–Q2 QN–Q2 11 B–N2 P–QN3 (Smyslov-

Botvinnik, 21st match game 1954) 12 N–B4 R–KN1 13 B–N5 favouring White – Bronstein.

    9 Q–Q2

Trying to transpose into the previous note

    9 ...   N–B3!
    10 B–N2   N–K2=

Black's knights are both well placed to occupy centre squares; Keres-Boleslavsky, Moscow 1940.

Variation 4

    4 P–K5   P–QB4

The main line of the Winawer

    5 P–QR3

Against 5 B–Q2, a safe equalizing line is 5 ... N–QB3 6 N–N5 B×B+ 7 Q×B N×QP 8 N×N P×N 9 N–B3 N–K2 10 Q×P 0–0 11 B–Q3 N–B3.

    5 ...   B×N+

5 ... B–R4!? is very risky on account of 6 P–QN4! P×QP (*6 ... P×NP 7 N–N5*) 7 Q–N4 N–K2 8 P×B P×N 9 Q×NP R–N1 10 Q×P N1–B3 11 N–B3 Q–B2 12 B–QN5! B–Q2 13 0–0 0–0–0 (Fischer-Tal, Leipzig 1960) 14 B×N! – Fischer.

    6 P×B   N–K2(*90*)

Reserving the option of developing the queen at QR4 or QB2. (Some players even go 4 ... N–K2, but then after 5 P–QR3 B×N+ etc. the same

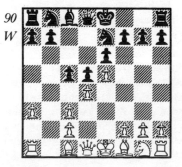

90
W

position as in the diagram should arise.)

Also possible is 6 . . . Q–B2 7 N–B3 (*7 Q–N4 P–B3!*) 7 . . . N–K2: see below.

The issue here is between:

7 Q–N4 – 'Poisoned Pawn'
7 N–B3 – Positional

The 'Poisoned Pawn'

7 Q–N4	Q–B2

This (or *7 . . . P×P* transposing) is almost invariably played nowadays. Only this pawn sacrifice appears to be adequate:

a) 7 . . . 0–0 8 N–B3 N1–B3 9 B–Q3 P–B4 10 P×Pep R×P 11 B–KN5 with an edge.

b) 7 . . . N–B4 8 B–Q3 P–KR4 9 Q–B4 P×P 10 P×P Q–R5 (Bogoljubow-Flohr, Nottingham 1936) 11 Q×Q N×Q 12 B–KN5! N–B4 13 N–K2 N–B3 14 P–QB3 B–Q2 is also better for White.

8 Q×NP	R–N1
9 Q×RP	P×P
10 N–K2	

Also critical is 10 K–Q1 N1–B3 (*10 . . . N–Q2!?*) 11 N–B3 P×P.

10 . . .	N1–B3
11 P–B4	B–Q2
12 Q–Q3	

Or 12 P–KR3 P×P 13 P–N4 0–0–0 14 Q–Q3 P–Q5 reaching diagram 89.

12 . . .	P×P
13 P–KR4	

Chances are balanced also after 13 N×P or 13 R–QN1.

13 . . .	N–B4

Vasyukov-Doroshkevich, Moscow 1967; White's KRP can get to R7 but, after Black's long castling, it will be blockaded and the outcome remains unclear. This is a line that offers plenty of winning chances to both White and Black.

The Positional Line

7 N–B3

A more conservative continuation, which gives Black two options:

7 . . . N1–B3 – Variation 1
7 . . . Q–B2 – Variation 2

Variation 1

7 . . .	N1–B3

The immediate 7 . . . Q–R4 is suspect, on account of 8 Q–Q2 P–QN3 (or *8 . . . N1–B3 9 B–K2*) 9 P×P! (not 9 P–B4 Q–R5! leading to diagram 88) 9 . . . P×P 10 P–B4! – Uhlmann.

8 P–QR4

Smyslov's finesse, designed to keep the black queen out of QR4; if Black plays too quietly the QB can go to QR3 and dominate the black squares.

8 . . .	Q–R4
9 B–Q2	

If 9 Q–Q2 Black hits back with 9 . . . P–B3.

9 . . .	P–B5
10 N–N5	

Or 10 P–N3 B–Q2 11 B–N2 0–0–0 12 0–0 P–B4 (to gain manoeuvring room on the K-side) 13 P×Pep P×P 14 KR–K1 N–N3 15 B–R6 R–KN1 and Black's pressure on the QBP balances White's in the centre; Boleslavsky-Barcza, Bucharest 1953.

10 . . .	P–KR3
11 N–R3	N–N3

12 Q–B3 (Uhlmann suggests 12 B–K2, intending 13 B–R5) 12 . . . B–Q2 13 N–B4 N×N 14 Q×N N–K2! 15 P–R4 B×P Black has won a pawn, and can weather White's attack; Smyslov-Botvinnik, 13th USSR Ch 1944.

Variation 2

7 . . .	Q–B2
8 P–QR4	P–QN3

Black hopes to exchange off his bad

bishop by ... B–R3, but an idea of Fischer's enables White to avoid this at the cost of a tempo.

    9 B–QN5+!   B–Q2
   10 B–Q3   N1–B3
11 0–0 P–KR3 (Not 11 ... 0–0? 12 B×P+ etc. winning.) 12 B–R3 N–R4 13 N–Q2 0–0 (13 ... B×P allows 14 P×P P×P 15 Q–N4 forking Black's QB and KNP.) 14 P×P P×P 15 N–N3 N×N (15 ... N4–B3? 16 B×P Q×P 17 N–Q4 reaches diagram 85.) 16 P×N Williams-Keene, British Ch 1973; Black's chances ought to be adequate. White has eliminated his own doubled pawns and opened up the position for the bishop pair, to some extent; yet Black's position remains compact and White's scattered pawns are targets. 16 ... P–B3 is probably best now.

The Tarrasch Variation

    1 P–K4   P–K3
    2 P–Q4   P–Q4
    3 N–Q2(*96*)

A move which not only avoids the pin by ... B–N5, but also has in view a more satisfactory defence of the pawn chain Q4+K5 than is possible in the 3 N–QB3 lines. With the knight at Q2, White does not have to waste another move before he can guard the base of the chain with P–QB3. The Tarrasch became popular in the early 1970s, but eventually grandmasters like Korchnoi and Uhlmann proved the soundness of Black's game. Let us consider some typical positions from the Tarrasch.

Favourable Positions for White
Karpov–Uhlmann, Madrid 1973

White's bishop is greatly superior to that of his opponent after 1 P–KN4! followed by P–B3, which also cleared the way for White's rooks to reach the seventh rank.

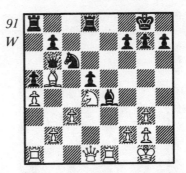

Radulov-Qinteros, Amsterdam 1973

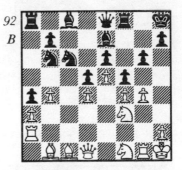

White's space advantage and better communications between wings are evident. The breakthrough on the KN file and QN1–KR7 is only a matter of time.

Favourable Positions for Black
Minić-Korchnoi, Belgrade 1964

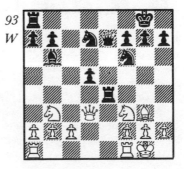

Black has a firm hold on the only open file, while most of White's pieces can only look on from the sidelines.

Hutchings-Keene, Nice 1974

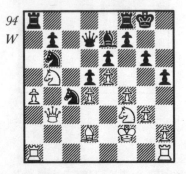

White's K-side 'attack' has got nowhere, while Black has a strongly-placed knight and pressure against the QRP.

An Even Position
Averbakh-Botvinnik, 19th USSR Ch 1951

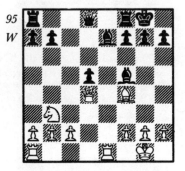

Black's two bishops are sufficient compensation for the isolated QP.

Black's main lines against the Tarrasch are:

3 ... P–QB4 – Open
3 ... N–KB3 – Closed
3 ... P×P – Rubinstein

Guimard's 3 ... N–QB3 is very difficult even for masters to play.

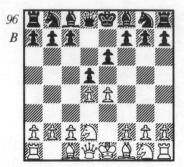

Open Tarrasch

3 ...   P–QB4

Favoured by Korchnoi in his 1974 Candidates' Final match against Karpov.

4 KP×P

The other critical line is 4 N–KB3 N–QB3 5 B–N5. Black's safest reply is 5 ... QP×P 6 N×P B–Q2 7 B–N5 Q–R4+ 8 N–QB3 P×P 9 N×P B–K2 10 Q–Q2 N–B3= – Tal.

4 ...   KP×P

4 ... Q×P (to avoid the IQP) is rarely played nowadays, although after 5 N–KB3 P×P 6 B–B4 ·Q–QB4 Black may be alright, e.g. 7 0–0 N–QB3 8 Q–K2 Q–N3 9 N–N3 B–K2 10 R–Q1 B–B3 11 B–QN5 KN–K2 12 QN×P 0–0= Olafsson-Bronstein, Amsterdam 1954.

5 N–KB3!   N–QB3

5 ... P–B5 is not good, because of Bondarevsky's suggestion 6 P–QN3! P×P (*or 6 ... P–QN4 7 P–QR4 Q–R4 8 N–K5!*) 7 B–N5+ B–Q2 8 Q–K2+.

6 B–N5   B–Q3
7 P×P

Korchnoi coped comfortably with 7 0–0 P×P 8 N–N3 (not *8 N×P B×P+ 9 K×B Q–R5+)* 8 ... KN–K2 9 QN×P 0–0 10 P–B3 e.g. 10 ... B–KN5 11 Q–R4 Q–Q2 12 B–K3 P–QR3 13 B–K2 N×N 14 Q×N N–B3 15 Q–Q2 R–K1 16 QR–Q1 QR–Q1 (16th game). Note the typical indirect defence of the IQP. 17 Q×P would allow Black to force a drawish ending by 17 ... B×P+ 18 N×B Q×Q 19 R×Q B×B etc.

7 ...	B×BP
8 0–0	KN–K2
9 N–N3	B–Q3

The older move 9 ... B–N3 is well met by 10 R–K1!, e.g. 10 ... B–N5 11 B–N5 P–B3 12 B–K3 B×B 13 R×B and Black has pawn weaknesses; Geller-Matulović, Skopje 1968.

10 B–N5!

For 10 QN–Q4 0–0 11 P–B3 see the note to White's 7th move (with a tempo lost by each player).

10 ...	0–0
11 R–K1	

Karpov's earliest idea, 11 B–KR4, is well met by Gulko's 11 ... Q–N3! 12 B–Q3 P–QR4.

11 ...	Q–B2
12 P–B3	B–KN5

This position is perhaps somewhat in White's favour, but he could make no significant progress in the 18th Karpov-Korchnoi game: 13 P–KR3 B–R4 14 B–K2 P–KR3 15 B×N N×B 16 KN–Q4 B×B 17 Q×B P–R3 and the IQP was not hard to defend. Retaining the KB is the key to Korchnoi's handling of the black side of the Tarrasch.

Closed Tarrasch

3 ...   N–KB3

This move leads to a closed type of game in which it can become very hard for Black to do anything relevant with his Q-side pieces. By comparison with the Classical Variation, White's centre is practically unassailable, and by comparison with the Advance Variation (below) White has more time.

4 P–K5   KN–Q2(97)

5 B–Q3

White sometimes prefers the slower build-up by 5 P–KB4 P–QB4 6 P–B3 N–QB3 7 N2–B3 which can lead to ponderous but effective K-side attacks if Black fails to find counterplay. There can occur:

a) 7 ... P×P 8 P×P N–N3 9 B–Q3 B–Q2 10 N–K2 P–KR4 11 0–0 P–R4 (*11 ... R–B1!?*) 12 P–QR3 P–QR5 13 Q–K1 (Wade-Uhlmann, Skopje 1968) when 13 ... P–KN3! with a fairly solid position, was necessary; instead, after 13 ... N–R4? White launched the decisive breakthrough by 14 P–B5!

b) 7 ... Q–N3 8 P–KN3 P×P (*8 ... P–KR4!?*) 9 P×P B–N5+ 10 K–B2 P–B3 11 K–N2 and White continues with B–Q3 and N–K2, and after Black's ... P–KB4 he has the lever P–KR3 and P–KN4 to open lines.

5 ...	P–QB4
6 P–QB3	N–QB3

When this variation was first introduced, Black used to attempt to eliminate White's good bishop, but this costs too much time: 6 ... P–QN3 7 N–K2 B–R3 8 B×B N×B 9 0–0 B–K2 10 N–KN3 0–0 11 Q–N4 Kotov-Keres, Moscow 1948.

7 N–K2

At this point, White can make a very interesting pawn sacrifice by 7 N1–B3!? Q–N3 8 0–0 P×P 9 P×P N×QP 10

N×N Q×N 11 N–B3 Q–N3 12 Q–R4!
but after 12 . . . Q–N5! 13 Q–B2 Q–B4!,
if White wants more than a draw, he
must try Trifunovic's speculative line
14 Q–K2!? B–K2 15 B–K3 Q–R4 16
Q–B2.

    7 . . .   P×P
    8 P×P   Q–N3

Keene has been successful with 8 . . .
P–B3 9 P×P N×BP.

    9 N–KB3   P–B3

9 . . . B–N5+ is weak, since 10 B–Q2
B×B+ 11 Q×B Q–N5 12 R–QB1
Q×Q+ 13 K×Q leaves White with
much more space.

    10 P×P

10 N–B4!? backfires after 10 . . . P×P
11 P×P B–N5+! 12 K–B1 N2×P 13
N×N N×N 14 Q–R5+ N–B2 15 B×P
Q–Q5! 16 B–K3 Q×P! – Schmid.

    10 . . .   N×BP
    11 0–0   B–Q3

This is a critical position in which,
over the years, White has tried a good
many moves, without any definite
conclusion having been arrived at. In
such a case, the underlying principles of
the various moves must be
remembered.

White is trying:
1) to consolidate his grip on the black
squares;
2) to safeguard his QNP.

Black is trying:
1) to force . . . P–K4;
2) to get his king into safety.

Some examples of play:
a) 12 N–B4 (the sharpest move) 12 . . .
0–0 13 R–K1 B–Q2! 14 N×KP KR–K1
15 B–B5 N–QR4! and Black regains his
pawn with equality, owing to the twin
threats of 16 . . . B×P+ and 16 . . .
B–N5; Ljundqvist-Schmid, 2nd World
Corres Ch 1956–8.
b) 12 B–KB4 B×B 13 N×B Q×NP! 14

R–K1 (*14 R–N1 Q×RP!*) 14 . . . 0–0 15
N×KP B×N 16 R×B QR–K1 = Platz-
Uhlmann, E. Germany 1962.
c) 12 N–B3! 0–0 (Uhlmann suggests *12
. . . B–Q2 13 B–KN5 0–0–0* with an
unclear position.) 13 B–K3 B–Q2 14
P–QR3! Q–Q1! 15 P–R3 R–B1 with
possibly a slight edge for White; Geller-
Uhlmann, Skopje 1968.

Rubinstein Variation

    3 . . .   P×P

This old move of Rubinstein's can
also be played against 3 N–QB3; it leads
to a simplified game where White is
inclined to over-estimate his attacking
chances.

    4 N×P   B–K2

The original idea, 4 . . . N–Q2, gives
White insistent pressure after 5 N–KB3
N1–B3 6 N×N+ N×N 7 N–K5! –
Capablanca's move.

    5 N–KB3   N–KB3
    6 B–Q3

After 6 N×N+ B×N! there is little
hope for an advantage for White, since
B–KN5 will be impossible and Black
keeps an eye on e5. White can only get
attacking positions by waiting for Black
to exchange pieces and accepting the
disadvantage of an IQP.

    6 . . .   N×N
    7 B×N   N–Q2
    8 0–0

In the game Keres-Pavey, New York
1954, White played 8 Q–K2. Black's
best continuation would have been to
delay . . . P–QB4, and play instead 8
. . . 0–0 9 B–K3 N–B3 10 B–Q3 P–QN3.

    8 . . .   P–QB4(*98*)

8 . . . N–B3 9 B–Q3 P–B4 10 P×P!,
forcing recapture with the bishop,
would not be so good.

    9 P–QB3   P×P

Not 9 . . . 0–0 10 Q–K2:

98
W

a) 10 ... N–B3? 11 B–B2 P–QN3 12 B–N5 (Toran-Trott, Beverwijk 1953) favours White.

b) 10 ... Q–B2 11 B–N5! B×B 12 N×B P–KR3 13 N–B3 N–B3 14 P×P! Q×BP 15 KR–Q1 Q–N3 16 R–Q2 and White has control of the only open file; Heidenfeld-Trott, Beverwijk 1953.

10 P×P N–B3
11 B–B2 0–0

12 Q–Q3 Q–Q3 13 B–N5 P–KN3 (So far analysis by the Australian former world correspondence champion Purdy, who now considered 14 QR–B1.) 14 N–K5! N–Q4 15 B×B Q×B 16 B–N3. White can aim, by an eventual B×N, at reaching an ending with knight against bad bishop. This type of strategem is little-known, even to strong amateurs, who generally assume that positions where White has an IQP must be handled as middle game attacks. Exchanging the blockading knight on Q4, however, does enable White to face an ending with confidence.

The Advance Variation

1 P–K4 P–K3
2 P–Q4 P–K5
3 P–K5

A logical move, which found particular favour with Nimzowitsch. White intends to stabilize his pawn chain and then make use of his advantage in space. Nowadays it finds few advocates, because Black has a much wider choice of good plans than his opponent.

3 ... P–QB4

Immediately challenging the white centre. If 3 ... P–QN3 4 P–QB3 Q–Q2 (*4 ... B–R3? 5 B×B N×B 6 Q–R4+* is a well-known trap.) 5 P–QR4 P–QR4 6 P–KB4 is theoretically a slight edge for White, but an experienced French Defence player knows that what really counts in such positions is the relative skill of the players at manoeuvring.

4 P–B3(*99*)

The most promising alternative is 4 N–KB3 P×P (by *4 ... N–QB3* Black can force *5 P–B3* with a return to the text) 5 B–Q3 N–QB3 6 0–0 P–B3 7 B–QN5 B–Q2 8 B×N P×B 9 Q×P Q–N3 10 Q–KB4 and now Keres suggests 10 ... P–B4 with an unclear position.

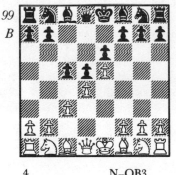

99
B

4 ... N–QB3

Other lines are less known:
a) 4 ... Q–N3 5 N–B3 B–Q2 6 P–QR3 (*6 B–Q3 B–N4 7 B–B2!?* has been suggested) 6 ... B–N4! 7 B–Q3 B×B 8 Q×B Q–R3! and Black can use the QB-file for his rooks in the ending.
b) 4 ... N–K2 5 N–B3 N2–B3!? followed by ... P×P, ... P–QN3 and

... B–R3 is a bizarre idea, worth further experimentation – Moles.

    5 N–B3   Q–N3

5 ... KN–K2 6 B–Q3! retains a slight but real plus for White after:

a) 6 ... N–B4 7 B×N! P×B 8 P×P! Basman-Keene, British Ch 1968.

b) 6 ... P×P 7 P×P N–B4 8 B–K3! – Moles; the capture ... N×B will strengthen White's centre and leave Black's K-side rather bare.

    6 B–Q3!?

The move most often played; but 6 P–QR3 is also seen for the ensuing gambit (devised by the British master Milner-Barry) can be offered with greater confidence after 6 ... P–QR4 7 B–Q3 etc. Against 6 P–QR3, Black might also play 6 ... P–B5 7 P–KN3 N–R4 8 QN–Q2 B–Q2 9 B–R3! P–B4 10 P×Pep P×P 11 0–0 0–0–0 12 R–K1 B–N2 13 R–N1 R–K1 14 P–N3 when White has the edge; Prakhov-Makarov, USSR 1962. However, Whiteley has tried 6 ... P×P 7 P×P B–Q2 8 N–B3 R–B1 and there are doubtless other untested improvements for Black.

    6 ...   P×P

If 6 ... B–Q2?! Nimzowitsch demonstrated the strength of 7 P×P B×P 8 0–0 P–B3 9 P–QN4 B–K2 10 B–KB4 followed by his famous plan of 'over-protecting' K5, first seen in his game against Salwe, Carlsbad 1911.

    7 P×P   B–Q2

Not, of course, 7 ... N×QP?? 8 N×N Q×N 9 B–N5+ winning the queen.

    8 0–0   N×QP

    9 N×N   Q×N

    10 N–B3   P–QR3!

Probably too risky is 10 ... Q×KP 11 R–K1 Q–N1 (or *11 ... Q–Q3!? 12 N–N5 B×N 13 B×B+ K–Q1 14 Q–B3* with an obscure position) 12 N×P B–Q3 13 Q–N4! K–B1 14 B–Q2 when

White's attack is certainly worth the pawn.

    11 Q–K2   N–K2

    12 R–Q1

If 12 K–R1 N–B3 13 P–B4 N–N5 14 B–N1 Q–QB5! is good for Black.

    12 ...   N–B3

    13 B×QRP!?

White will have to find something better than this, if he can (perhaps *13 B–QN5!?*), for now a well-known forced line runs: 13 ... Q×KP 14 Q×Q N×Q 15 B×P R–QN1! 16 B×P (*16 B–QR6 is* not very hopeful either.) 16 ... P×B 17 R–K1 P–B3 18 P–B4 B–QB4+ 19 K–R1 0–0 20 P×N P×P 21 N×P. White has won a pawn, but after 21 ... B–Q5 he has problems both with his Q-side development and with his king.

The Exchange Variation

    1 P–K4   P–K3

    2 P–Q4   P–Q4

    3 P×P   P×P

This variation usually implies peaceful intentions on White's part. Indeed it is one of the chief drawbacks of the French, that White can in this way secure a draw against even relatively strong opponents.

    4 B–Q3   B–Q3

    5 P–QB3

Simplest is 5 N–KB3. Not so good are 5 N–K2 Q–R5, or 5 Q–B3 N–QB3 6 P–QB3 N–B3 7 P–KR3 N–K5!

    5 ...   N–QB3

    6 Q–B2

A plan, devised by Markland, which aims at putting pressure on Black's K-side after 6 ... P–KR3 or 6 ... P–KN3, or 6 ... N–B3 7 B–KN5. However, it seems that Black can probably ignore this threat:

    6 ...   B–KN5!

For if 7 B×P!? now, Black has (inter

alia) 7 . . . Q–K2+, denying White the right to castle and creating obscure complications; another idea at Black's disposal is . . . Q–R5. White's safest line is 7 N–K2 and a draw should soon follow: 7 . . . N1–K2 8 B–KN5 Q–Q2 9 N–Q2 P–KR3 10 B–R4 0–0 11 B–N3 KR–K1 12 0–0 B–KB4 and Black finally manages to exchange his problem bishop; Harding-Vogel, Reserve Masters, Wijk aan Zee 1973.

The King's Indian Attack

1 P–K4	P–K3
2 P–Q3	P–Q4
3 N–Q2	

This method is quite often employed against the French nowadays; White turns the opening into a kind of King's Indian with reversed colours. A fuller discussion of this can be found in the *Guardian Chess Book*. Black has a wide choice of set-ups, but if he is satisfied with a draw there is one very simple method of equalizing.

3 . . .	P–QB4

As usually played, but the drawing method is 3 . . . N–KB3 4 N1–B3 N–B3 5 P–KN3 (As soon as White commits himself to the fianchetto, Black exchanges.) 5 . . . P×P 6 P×P P–K4! 7 B–N2 B–QB4 8 0–0 0–0= e.g. Klein-Moles, Essex–Oxfordshire 1972.

4 N1–B3	N–QB3
5 P–KN3	N–B3

Black can also try 5 . . . B–Q3 6 B–N2 KN–K2 7 0–0 0–0 8 N–R4 B–Q2 9 P–KB4 P–B4! with a sharp and unclear position; Harding-Penrose, Oxon–Essex 1972.

6 B–N2	B–K2
7 0–0	0–0
8 R–K1	P–QN4

Black must be active: he throws forward his Q-side pawns to break up

White's left flank and then infiltrate the knights. Even so, White's attacks can be very dangerous.

9 P–K5(*100*)

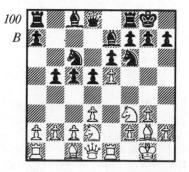

9 . . .	N–K1

The alternative is 9 . . . N–Q2, with different squares accessible to the knight, but little basic difference in procedure for White.

10 N–B1	P–QR4
11 P–KR4	

A thematic advance, which can prepare B–R3 (putting pressure on K6 to inhibit . . . P–KB3 by Black) or, as in the game, P–KR5–6 to weaken Black's king position.

11 . . .	P–R5
12 B–B4	P–R6
13 P–N3	B–N2

We are following the game Tringov-Lee, The Hague 1966.

14 N1–R2	P–Q5
15 P–R5	N–B2

16 P–R6 P–N3 17 Q–Q2 N–Q4 18 B–N5 (White has achieved the first stage of his programme.) 18 . . . N3–N5 19 B×B Q×B 20 N–N5! K–R1 21 N–K4 R–R2 22 N–N4 B–R1 23 R.K1–QB1 (If White can exchange knights and then penetrate with rooks on the QB-file, Black will always be in danger of getting checkmated.) 23 . . . R–B2 24

N.N4–B6 R–Q1 25 B–B1 N×N 26 N×N
N–Q4 27 N×N B×N 28 P–QB3! P×P
29 R×P P–N5 30 R–B2 P–B4 31 R1–B1
P–N4 32 P–Q4 B–R1 33 B–N2 B×B 34
K×B R2–Q2 (*34 . . . R×P? 35 Q×R*) 35 R×P R×P 36 Q–K3 P–B5 37 Q–B3
P×P 38 R–B7 R5–Q2 39 R×R R×R
(or *39 . . . Q×R 40 R–Q1! Q–K2 41
R×R+ Q×R 42 Q–B7!*) 40 R–B8+
R–Q1 41 Q–R8 Black Resigned.

6 OTHER DEFENCES TO 1 P–K4

In this chapter, we shall consider the following defences, all from the point of view of White, who is looking for a promising reply to each, based on sound principles but not necessitating too much rote learning of variations:

Alekhine's Defence 1 P–K4 N–KB3
Caro-Kann Defence 1 P–K4 P–QB3
Pirc Defence 1 P–K4 P–Q3
Modern Defence 1 P–KR P–KN3

There will also be a brief note on the other moves which are seen from time to time, namely 1 ... P–Q4, 1 ... N–QB3 and 1 ... P–QN3.

Alekhine's Defence

The basic idea of this defence is to lure the white pawns into advancing, in the expectation that they will later on become weak. White can either fall in with Black's plans (advance his centre and bishops' pawns, and hope that he will be able to maintain them by aggressive use of the extra space temporarily presented to him) or he can accept a more modest spatial advantage and try to keep Black cramped. If he can carry out this plan successfully, it will be Black who will have to create pawn weaknesses, later on in the game.

A Favourable Position for White
Banas-Kneževič, Luhačovice 1973

Black has been stifled, and can only

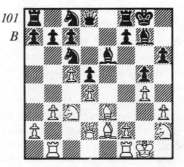

101
B

wait passively for White to prepare the advance either of his QNP or KBP.

A Favourable Position for Black
Altshuler-Berliner, 5th World Corres Ch 1965–8

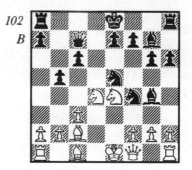

102
B

White has misplaced his queen, and will have difficulties in castling. Black will exchange a minor piece or two, and then advance decisively in the centre.

A Balanced Position
Kupreichik-Bagirov, Leningrad 1965

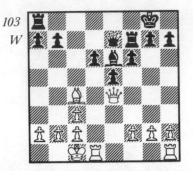

103
W

Black has coped fairly well with White's slight central initiative. In the forthcoming heavy piece game, a draw is probable.

In the subsequent analysis, we shall restrict ourselves to two of White's more promising ideas against Alekhine's Defence. Given best play by Black, there is no line to guarantee White an advantage anyway.

1 P–K4	N–KB3
2 P–K5	N–Q4

Now:

3 P–Q4 – to Exchange Variation
3 N–QB3 – Positional

3 P–QB4 N–N3 4 P–Q4 transposes.

Exchange Variation

3 P–Q4	P–Q3

It is essential to set about undermining the White centre without delay.

4 P–QB4	

Against the popular 4 N–KB3 Black has several possibilities, of which 4 . . . P–N3 is probably best and can cause White problems.

4 . . .	N–N3
5 P×P!	

With this move, White ensures that his centre will not be easily challenged, nor his development unduly disrupted. The sharp Four Pawns' Attack, 5 P–B4!?, has already been discussed in

the first chapter, in the section *How Openings Evolve*; the last word has not been said, but clearly only players who enjoy maniacal tactical adventures will feel at home in that line.

The text move already sets Black a tricky positional and psychological problem. If he recaptures with the KP, the symmetrical nature of the pawn structure leaves him no obvious way to challenge White's central control: see diagram 101 for a possible consequence. 5 . . . BP×P is a more fighting reply, in conjunction with a fianchetto of the KB, but then White's mobile Q-side pawn majority presents a danger; even if Black achieves the 'freeing' advance . . . P–K4, the result may only be that he is left with a weak QP.

We consider in turn:

5 . . . KP×P – Variation 1
5 . . . BP×P – Variation 2

Variation 1

5 . . .	KP×P
6 B–K2	B–K2
7 N–QB3	0–0
8 N–B3	

An idea worth trying is 8 P–KR3, to rule out Black's next.

8 . . .	B–N5
9 0–0	N–B3
10 P–QN3	

Necessary protection of the QBP.

10 . . .	B–B3
11 B–K3	P–Q4

This move, almost invariably played, fixes White's QP and prepares the manoeuvre N.N3–B1–K2–KB4, putting pressure on it. However, in Matanović-Hug, Berlin 1971, Black successfully executed a different plan: 11 . . . R–K1 12 P–KR3 B–R4 13 Q–Q2 P–KR3 (*13 . . . P–R4* is also interesting.) 14 R–B1 N–K2 15 P–KN4

B–N3 16 P–KR4 P–B4! 17 P×P P×P 18 Q×Q QR×Q 19 B×BP B×N 20 R×B N2–Q4!= and the position liquidated to an early draw.

    12 P–B5   N–B1

    13 P–KR3

No bishop move is wholly satisfactory here and White gets an advantage in each case:

a) 13 . . . B–K3 14 P–KN4 P–KR3 15 R–N1! (*15 Q–Q2 P–QN3!*) 15 . . . P–KN4 16 Q–Q2 B–N2 17 N–R2 reaching diagram 101.

b) 13 . . . B–R4 14 Q–Q2 B–N3 15 N–R2.

c) 13 . . . B–B4 14 Q–Q2 P–KR3 15 QR–Q1 N1–K2 16 P–KN4! Kurajica-Hort, Sombor 1968.

d) 13 . . . B×N 14 B×B N1–K2 15 Q–Q3 (*15 P–KN4!? P–KN3 16 R–B1!*) 15 . . . P–KN3 16 QR–Q1 – Boleslavsky.

Variation 2

    5 . . .   BP×P

    6 N–QB3

6 N–KB3 returns to the 4 N–KB3 line, after 6 . . . P–N3 7 P–KR3 or 7 B–K2, with about equal chances. White's plan in the text prevents Black from developing his QB effectively.

    6 . . .   P–N3

    7 B–K3   B–N2

    8 B–Q3   0–0

    9 KN–K2   N–B3

    10 0–0(*104*)

A critical position for Alekhine's Defence.

    10 . . .   P–K4?!

The usual move here, but results suggest that Black should look for a new plan. Eales and Williams, in their book on the defence, suggest that 10 . . . B–N5!? 11 P–B3 B–B4 may be best, while 10 . . . N–N5!? and 10 . . . P–K3 are other ideas.

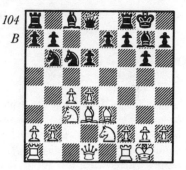

    11 P–Q5   N–K2

We are following the game Fischer-Berliner, USA Ch 1960–1. A subsequent game between the same players went 11 . . . N–N5 12 P–QN3 N×B 13 Q×N N–Q2 14 Q–Q2 P–B4 15 P–B4! and White won in the end.

    12 P–QN3   N–Q2

If 12 . . . P–B4 13 P–B5! P–B5 14 P×P White is ensured of a strong passed QP.

    13 N–K4   N–KB4

    14 B–N5   P–B3

15 B–Q2 N–B4 16 N×N P×N 17 B×N B×B 18 P–B4 P×P 19 N×P Q–Q3 (Black appears to have stabilized the situation, with two bishops to compensate for the passed pawn. But White keeps the ideas flowing:) 20 N–R5! QR–K1 (20 . . . B–R1 21 B–B4 is also embarrassing.) 21 N×B K×N 22 B–B4 Q–Q2 23 Q–Q2 R–B2 (Black cannot count on the bishops of opposite colour, for in case of an attack on his king his own bishop will only be a bystander, with the chief threats coming on black squares.) 24 B–R6+ K–N1 25 QR–K1 R2–K2 26 R×R Q×R 27 P–KR3 Q–K5 28 Q–KB2 Q–K2 29 P–KN4 B–Q6 30 R–Q1 B–K5 31 P–Q6 Q–K4 32 B–B4 Q–B6 33 P–Q7 R–Q1 34 Q–K2 Q–B6 35 Q×Q B×Q 36 B–B7 Black resigned. The necessity to both defend his KBP

and blockade the passed pawn was bound to be too much in the end.

The Positional Line

3 N–QB3   N×N
4 QP×N

This appears to infringe the 'rule' that pawn captures ought to be made towards, not away from, the centre, but in this case White gets more effective pressure there with his queen and minor pieces than he could with 4 NP×N. In that case, Black would reply 4 . . . P–Q4 5 P–Q4 (*5 B–R3!? N–Q2*) 5 . . . P–QB4 6 N–B3 N–B3 with a rather improved form of the French Defence.

4 . . .   P–Q3

4 . . . P–Q4!? 5 P–QB4 is also interesting, but hardly played.

5 N–B3(*105*)

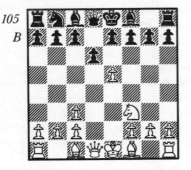

105
B

5 . . .   N–B3

Black can also try:

a) 5 . . . P×P 6 Q×Q+ K×Q 7 N×P K–K1 when the question is, does White's piece play compensate for his weakened pawn structure; in practice, White does well. There can follow 8 B–K3 P–KB3 9 N–Q3 P–K4 (*9 . . . N–B3? 10 P–KB4!*) 10 0–0–0 followed by P–KB4 with some chances for the initiative.

b) 5 . . . P–KN3 6 B–QB4 B–N2 7 B–B4

N–B3 8 N–N5!? with interesting complications.

6 B–QN5   B–Q2
7 Q–K2   N×P

7 . . . P–QR3 8 B–QB4 P–K3 9 B–B4 P×P 10 N×P B–Q3 11 B–KN3, followed by 0–0–0, is also fairly good for White.

8 N×N   P×N
9 Q×P   P–KB3!

9 . . . P–QB3 failed to equalize in the game Keres-Schmid, Zurich 1961, after 10 B–QB4 Q–N1 11 Q–K4 P–K3 12 B–KN5 P–KR3 13 B–R4 B–Q3 14 0–0–0 etc.

10 Q–R5+

Similar play, but without this zwischenzug, led to diagram 103.

10 . . .   P–KN3
11 Q–K2   P–K4
12 B–K3   B–Q3
13 0–0–0

White has the freer game, with chances of a big advantage should Black put a foot wrong; Markland-Korchnoi, European Team Ch, Bath 1973.

The Caro-Kann Defence

This defence has the same basic features as the French, with the difference that Black hopes to avoid the difficulties in the development of the QB, which are inherent in so many variations of the French. On the other hand, there is the disadvantage that the QP is supported not with another centre pawn, but with a side pawn. Hence one feature of the Caro-Kann is a·strong hold on the centre by White in the early stages.

Experience shows that the Caro-Kann gives Black fewer chances of winning than the French, though rather more of drawing. But if White finds the most exact moves against the Caro-Kann, Black is permanently on the defensive and struggling to equalize – something not true of the French.

A Favourable Position for White
Smyslov–Golombek, Venice 1950

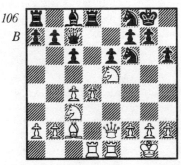

106
B

Black has failed to solve the problem of his QB.

A Favourable Position for Black
Broadbent-Golombek,   Nottingham 1946

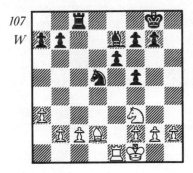

107
W

An ending arising from the Caro-Kann often enables Black to establish his knight on Q4, and use it as a support for a Q-side minority attack.

An Even Position
Matanović-Markland, Bath 1973

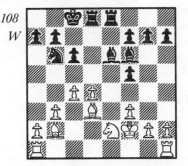

108
W

Against sensible play, White has no prospect of turning his superior pawn structure to account.

    1 P–K4   P–QB3

We shall look at just two lines:

2 N–QB3 – Two Knights'
2 P–Q4 – Main Line

2 P–QB4, leading to the Panov-Botvinnik isolated queen pawn attack, is discussed in the *Guardian Chess Book* (p. 117).

Two Knights' Variation

    2 N–QB3   P–Q4
    3 N–B3   P×P
    4 N×P   B–N5

A trap which often works in club games is 4 . . . B–B4? 5 N–N3 B–N3 6 P–KR4 P–KR3 7 N–K5 B–R2 8 Q–R5 P–KN3 9 B–QB4! P–K3 10 Q–K2 and Black's K-side pawns are ruined. If now 10 . . . N–Q2? 11 N×BP! wins.

    5 P–Q4

This pawn sacrifice offers the best chance of initiative.

    5 . . .   P–K3
    6 P–KR3   B×N

7 Q×B Q×P 8 B–Q3 QN–Q2 9 B–K3 Q–Q4 10 R–Q1 N–K4 11 Q–B4 P–KB4 12 N–N3 (In the game Bronstein-Golombek, USSR–Great Britain 1954, White chose to sacrifice a piece by 12 0–0!? N×B 13 R×N Q×N 14 Q–B7, but after 14 . . . B–K2! White has

insufficient compensation for the lost material.) 12 ... B–Q3 13 Q–QR4 0–0–0 14 0–0 N×B 15 R×N Griffiths-Clarke, Nottingham 1954; White stands very well.

The Main Line

2 P–Q4	P–Q4
3 N–QB3	

Other moves give no more than equality.

3 ...	P×P
4 N×P(*109*)	

A position commonly reached in Caro-Kann games. Black will seek exchanges to neutralize White's slight spatial advantage.

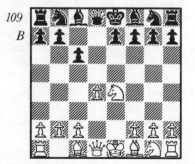

109
B

You may meet:

4 ... N–Q2 – Variation 1
4 ... N–B3 – Variation 2
4 ... B–B4 – Variation 3

Variation 1

4 ...	N–Q2
5 B–QB4	N1–B3

Or 5 ... P–K3 6 N–KB3 N1–B3 7 N×N+ N×N 8 0–0 B–K2 9 B–N3 0–0 10 Q–K2 Q–B2 11 B–N5 N–Q4 12 P–B4 and Black has trouble with his QB, Tylor-Golombek, Paignton 1953.

6 N–N5	P–K3
7 Q–K2	N–N3

8 B–Q3 P–KR3 9 N5–B3 P–QB4 10

P×P B×P 11 N–K5 Matanović-Pfleger, Tel Aviv 1964, White has a spatial advantage.

Variation 2

4 ...	N–B3
5 N×N+	KP×N

Sharper is 5 ... NP×N!? 6 N–B3 B–N5 7 B–K2 Q–B2 8 P–KR3! B–R4 9 0–0 N–Q2 10 P–Q5! Smyslov-Pachman, Amsterdam 1954.

6 B–QB4	Q–K2+!?
7 Q–K2	B–N5
8 Q×Q+	B×Q

White's Q-side majority gives him the better prospects, but Black is not really in danger: 9 N–K2 N–Q2 10 B–Q3 N–N3 11 P–QB4 0–0–0 12 P–B3 B–K3 13 P–QN3 KR–K1 14 B–N2 P–KB4 15 K–B2 B–B3 reaching diagram 108.

Variation 3

4 ...	B–B4
5 N–N3	B–N3
6 B–QB4	

This leads to interesting tactical play, and little-known positions. A very-much-analysed alternative is 6 P–KR4 P–KR3 7 P–R5 B–R2 8 N–B3 N–Q2 9 B–Q3 B×B 10 Q×B Q–B2 11 B–Q2 P–K3 12 Q–K2 followed by 0–0–0 and N–K5 with a slight edge to White. In practice, Caro-Kann defenders know all about this line and rarely lose in it!

6 ...   P–K3

Not 6 ... N–Q2 7 N1–K2 P–K4 8 0–0!

7 N1–K2   N–B3

7 ... B–Q3 is met by 8 P–KR4 P–KR3 9 N–B4 B×N 10 B×B N–B3 11 P–R5!

8 0–0   B–Q3
9 P–B4

White's aim is to play P–B5, and

Black can try to thwart this in various ways.

    9 ...   Q–B2

Others:

a) 9 ... 0–0 10 P–B5 P×P 11 N×P with an attack.

b) 9 ... N–K5 10 P–B5! B×N 11 N×B N×N 12 P×B! N×R 13 P×BP+.

c) 9 ... Q–Q2 10 B–Q3 B×B 11 Q×B P–KN3 and Black may eventually ease his way to equality; nonetheless White's plan based on 12 P–N3 is interesting.

    10 P–B5!

White plays this, notwithstanding the loss of his KRP! We are following the game Keres-Golombek, Moscow 1956.

    10 ...   P×P
    11 N×P   B×P+

Possible, but not likely to refute White's idea, is 11 ... B×N 12 R×B QN–Q2.

    12 K–R1   0–0

Interesting complications could result from 12 ... B×N 13 R×B B–Q3 14 B–KR6!? N–N5!

    13 P–KN3!   B×N

Or 13 ... N–N5 (*13 ... Q–Q2 14 Q–Q3 N–N5 15 Q–K4!*) 14 R–B4! B×N (*14 ... B–R4 15 Q–B1*) 15 R×B B×P 16 Q–N1 N–B7+ 17 K–N2 N–K5 18 Q–K3 – Keres.

    14 R×B   B×P
    15 R×N!?   Q–K2!

16 Q–B1! Q–K5+ 17 Q–B3 Q–R5+ 18 K–N2 Q–R7+ 19 K–B1 Q–R6+ 20 Q–N2 Q×Q+ 21 K×Q P×R 22 N×B White judged correctly that in this position, Black's K-side pawns being ruined, two bishops would easily overcome rook and two pawns. The remaining moves were: 22 ... N–Q2 23 B–KR6 KR–K1 24 K–B3 K–R1 25 N–R5 R–KN1 26 B×P R–N3 27 B×R P×B 28 N–N3 R–K1 29 B–B4 K–N2 30

N–K4 P–KN4 31 N–Q6 R–K3 32 B–N3 P–N3 33 R–K1 R×R 34 B×R K–N3 35 N–B8 P–QB4 36 P×P N×P 37 N×RP P–B4 38 B–B2 N–Q2 39 B–Q4 K–R4 40 N–B8 N–B1 41 N–K7 P–B5 42 N–B5 N–N3 43 N–N7+ K–R3 44 K–N4 N–B1 45 N–B5+ Black resigned.

The Pirc and Modern Defences

When Black meets 1 P–K4 by 1 ... P–Q3 or 1 ... P–KN3, he enters a complex of counter-attacking variations which have become extremely important in recent years. As in the Sicilian, Black aims for asymmetrical positions where his main chances will lie on the Q-side, or in the undermining of White's centre (like in the King's Indian). Black's fianchettoed KB clearly is the lynchpin of both these plans. White has to reckon with ... P–QB4, ... P–K4 or with ... P–QB3 (even ... P–QR3) followed by ... P–QN4-5 to undermine the white KP. If that pawn goes on to K5, then ... P–KB3 becomes an important possibility. As with the Alekhine's, White must decide whether to proceed modestly, or to try to annex as much central territory as possible with his pawns; also he has to make a decision about whether to castle on the K-side or the Q-side.

Favourable Positions for White
Fischer-Mednis, USA 1958

See diagram 110
page 92

White's king is secure and his P–KB4 has put Black in a dilemma. If 1 ... P×P then his KB2 is weak, while if 1 ... N×B (or *1 ... P–N5*) 2 P×N P–N5 White gets a strong initiative by 3 P–K5.

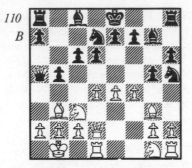

110
B

Borwell-M. Clarke, British Corres
Ch 1971–2

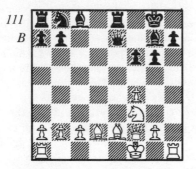

111
B

Black has defended inaccurately
against an all-out attack. Having
recaptured with the wrong pawn on
KN3, he is faced with ideas like B–B4+,
R–K1 and P–B5, before he can
complete his development.

Favourable Positions for Black
Tal-Kots, Leningrad 1962

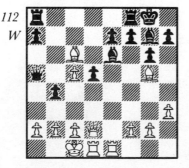

112
W

Black's exchange offer seizes the
initiative, since the threat of . . . B–B6
heralds a mating attack.

Klein-Keene, London 1973

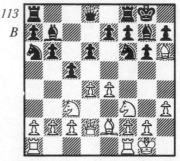

113
B

White has wasted time with P–KR3,
allowing Black a smooth mobilization.
Black should now play 1 . . . B×B 2
Q×B P×P 3 N×P N–B4 4 P–B3 P–K4 5
N–N3 N–K3 and N–B5.

A Balanced Position
Escott-Keene, Ilford 1974

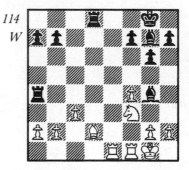

114
W

Black's pawn sacrifice has brought
him the total destruction of White's
centre, plus the two bishops and active
rooks. With care by White, a drawn
ending resulted.

In the available space, we can only
outline three main lines for White.
Bearing in mind possibilities of
transposition between the two, we
consider:

1 . . . P–Q3 – Pirc
1 . . . P–KN3 – Modern

The Pirc Defence

    1 . . .   P–Q3
    2 P–Q4   N–KB3

White is forced to defend his KP, ·
since 3 P–K5? loses a pawn after 3 . . .
P×P Q×Q+ 5 K×Q N–N5. 2 . . .
P–KN3, allowing White more options,
is discussed under the Modern.

    3 N–QB3

3 P–KB3 can transpose to the
Sämisch Variation of the King's
Indian, and 3 B–Q3 to the Modern –
but Black can also take an independent
course with moves like 3 . . . P–B4!? or 3
. . . P–K4!?

    3 . . .   P–KN3

We shall now look at one all-out
attack line and one positional system
against the Pirc Defence:

4 P–B4 – Austrian
4 B–KN5 – Byrne

The Austrian Attack

    4 P–B4   B–N2
    5 N–B3

For 5 P–K5 KN–Q2 6 N–B3 see the
next note. If 5 B–B4 Black can enter
favourable complications by 5 . . .
P–B4.

    5 . . .   0–0

Also possible is 5 . . . P–B4, as played
by Fischer against Spassky in 1972.
White can either:
a) Go for broke with 6 P–K5 KN–Q2
7 KP×P 0–0! (Recapturing is
positionally undesirable.) 8 P×BP or 8
B–K3 Q–N3 9 P×KP R–K1 10 Q–Q2
with a totally obscure situation.
b) Choose a positional game by 6 P×P
Q–R4 7 B–Q3 Q×BP 8 Q–K2 B–N5 9
B–K3 Q–R4 10 0–0 0–0 11 P–KR3
B×N 12 Q×B N–B3 (*12 . . . QN–Q2!?*)
13 P–R3 or 13 QR–Q1 with a sort of 6

P–B4 Najdorf Sicilian; the better player
will probably win this sort of position
whichever colour he has.

    6 P–K5!?

This leads to a violent assault, which
will overwhelm many opponents. The
usual move is 6 B–Q3; you can take it
that Black will be well-prepared for
that.

    6 . . .   KN–Q2

If Black is afraid of the
complications, he may prefer 6 . . . P×P
7 QP×P! Q×Q+ 8 K×Q R–Q1+ (*8
. . . N–R4!?*) 9 B–Q2! N–K1 (*9 . . .
N–Q4 10 N×N R×N 11 B–B4* favours
White somewhat) but then he will be
left with the problem of reviving his
KB, before White can exchange into an
ending. White's ideal deployment is
B–Q3–K4, N.QB3–K2, P–B3, K–B2
and rooks placed according to Black's
reply.

    7 P–KR4!?

Other wild lines:
a) 7 P–K6 P×P 8 P–KR4 (*8 N–KN5
N–KB3 9 B–B4 P–Q4*) 8 . . . N–KB3! 9
B–Q3 N–B3 10 P–R5 P×P 11 P–R3
B–Q2! is good for Black.
b) 7 N–KN5!? N–N3 8 B–Q3 N–B3 or 8
. . . P×P!? is unclear.
c) 7 B–B4 is positionally best, but 7 . . .
N–N3 should equalize.

    7 . . .   P–QB4

Black must react in the centre
without delay.

    8 P–R5

Or 8 P–K6!? P×KP 9 P–R5 P×RP
10 R×P (*10 P×P!? N–KB3*) 10 . . .
N–KB3 11 R–R4 P×P 12 N×P P–K4 13
B–B4+ P–Q4 14 N×P N×N 15 Q–R5
P×N! 16 B×N+ P–K3 17 Q×P K–B2
and White's attack will eventually
peter out – Botterill. In practice,
though, Black could easily go wrong in
this line.

8 ...   BP×P

9 Q×P

White can play 9 RP×P!? with murderous intent, but it founders on 9 ... P×N 10 P×BP+ R×P when:

a) 11 N–N5? N×P 12 P×N Q–R4! and Black wins.

b) 11 P–K6 P×P! 12 P×R+ K–B1 13 B×P B×B 14 B–B4 Q–R4+ 15 K–B1 N–KB3 16 R–QN1 (*16 N–N5 B–B4!*) 16 ... Q–B6! winning.

c) 11 B–B4 P–K3! 12 N–N5 (*12 P–B5 N×P 13 P×P R–K2 14 N×N Q–R4!*) 12 ... N×P (or *12 ... N–B1*) 13 P×N? (*13 Q–R5 P–KR3 and Black should win in the ending.*) 13 ... P×NP 14 Q–R5 Q×N and again Black wins.

9 ...   QP×P

The casual 9 ... N–QB3?! should lose after 10 Q–B2 etc.

10 Q–B2

Also possible is 10 Q–N1!? with a similar continuation, the point being that White will put his king on B2; but objectively speaking, the text move is superior.

10 ...   P–K5!

A strong line for White is 10 ... P×BP 11 P×P RP×P 12 B×P N–KB3 13 Q–R4 Q–R4 14 N–KN5 B–N5 15 B–Q3 QN–Q2 16 0–0! e.g. 16 ... B–R4 17 QR–K1 P–K4 18 B–Q2 Q–B4+ 19 B–K3 Q–B3 20 B–N5 Q–B2 21 B–K2 B×B 22 R×B KR–B1 23 N.B3–K4 K–B1 24 N×N N×N 25 R×N B×R 26 N–R7+ Black resigned.

Bronstein-Palmiotto, Munich 1958.

11 N×P

Others:

a) 11 N–KN5 N–KB3 12 P×P RP×P **13 Q–R4?** Q–Q5! Padevsky-Matanović, Havana 1966.

b) **13 B–B4** B–N5 or 13 ... N–B3 14 Q–R4 Q–Q5!

c) **13 N.B3**×**P** N×N 14 N×N Q–Q5 = – Botterill and Keene.

11 ...   N–KB3!

Dubious is 11 ... Q–N3 12 Q–R4 Q–R4+ on account of 13 B–Q2 Q×KRP 14 Q×Q P×Q 15 0–0–0 – Botterill.

12 N×N+   P×N

13 P×P   R–K1+

14 B–K2!   BP×P?

Probably the losing error. Critical is 14 ... RP×P 15 B–Q2 Q–K2 16 K–B1 (or *16 B–B3!? N–Q2!*) 16 ... B–B4 17 N–Q4 (Borwell) 17 ... B–K5 18 B–B3 N–B3 19 N×N P×N! with complications.

15 B–Q2!   Q–K2

16 K–B1!

Reaching diagram 111. The Borwell-Clarke game continued 16 ... B–K3 17 R–K1 Q–Q2 18 B–B3 P–KR4 19 B–Q3 B–B2 20 R×R+ Q×R 21 P–KN4! N–B3 22 P×P P×P 23 R–N1 Q–K3! 24 Q–N2 Q–N5 25 Q–R1! Q–K3 26 N–N5! Q–K6 (*26 ... P×N 27 R×P*) 27 N×B Q×P+ 28 K–K2 (to go to the Q-side if Black continues checking) 28 ... K×N 29 Q×P+ K–B1 30 R–KB1! R–K1+ (*30 ... Q–Q3 31 B×P B×B 32 Q–R8+*) 31 Q×R+ Black resigned.

The Byrne Variation

4 B–KN5(*115*)

White envisages Q–Q2 and B–R6, to

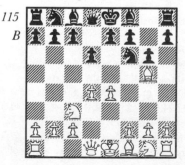

115
B

exchange Black's KB, whilst the idea of P–B4 and P–K5 is not altogether ruled out either. Black is also kept guessing as to which side White will castle. This move was favoured by the American grandmaster, Robert Byrne.

We shall consider Black's four main replies:

4 . . . P–KR3 – Variation 1
4 . . . B–N2 – Variation 2
4 . . . QN–Q2 – Variation 3
4 . . . P–B3 – Variation 4

Variation 1

4 . . .	P–KR3

Black hopes for B×N, when he will have the two bishops, half-open K-file and a solid game, which will be freed in due time by . . . P–KB4.

5 B–K3!	N–N5

Or 5 . . . B–N2 6 Q–B1! when Black cannot castle, unless he weakens his K-side by . . . P–KN4.

6 B–B1	

Also good is 6 B–KB4 B–N2 7 N–B3 N–QB3 8 B–N3 P–K4 9 P×P Juarez-Savon, Mar del Plata 1971.

6 . . .	B–N2

6 . . . P–K4!? might be better – Keene and Botterill.

7 P–B3	N–KB3
8 B–K3	

Schöneberg-Liberzon, Zinnowitz 1967, White has the better game.

Variation 2

4 . . .	B–N2

This encourages White to proceed with the plan of exchanging the black-squared bishops.

5 Q–Q2	P–KR3

For 5 . . . P–B3 see Variation 4, while 5 . . . 0–0 6 0–0–0 is a double-edged line where White's attack is likely to get in first.

6 B–KB4	P–KN4
7 B–N3	N–R4
8 B–QB4!	P–QB3

8 . . . N–QB3 9 KN–K2 with ideas of P–KR4!? is fine for White.

9 0–0–0	Q–R4

Not 9 . . . P–QN4? (Botterill suggests *9 . . . N–Q2.*) because of 10 N×P! N×B 11 RP×N P–Q4 12 B–N3 Mureil–Glotov, Moscow 1965.

10 B–N3	P–QN4
11 K–N1	N–Q2
12 P–B4!	– Diagram 110.

Variation 3

4 . . .	QN–Q2
5 P–B4	P–B3

A risky chance is 5 . . . P–KR3 6 B–R4 N–R4!? 7 KN–K2 or 7 P–B5.

6 P–K5	N–Q4
7 N×N	P×N

8 N–B3 Q–N3 9 B–Q3 B–N2 10 Q–K2 White has a life-long central superiority, e.g. 10 . . . P–B3 11 P×BP N×P 12 B–N5+ B–Q2 13 B×N B.N2×B 14 B×B+ K×B 15 0–0–0 Udovčić-Pirc, Yugoslav Ch 1952.

Variation 4

4 . . .	P–B3

Black prepares Q-side expansion and hopes that White will castle into his attack.

5 Q–Q2	P–QN4
6 B–Q3	B–KN2

Playable now that 7 B–R6 B×B 8 Q×B Q–N3 is equal, but Black can also experiment with 6 . . . P–KR3, 6 . . . P–N5 or 6 . . . QN–Q2.

7 P–B4	0–0

8 N–B3 QN–Q2 (Perhaps a better try is 8 . . . B–N5 9 P–B5 P–N5 10 N–K2 QN–Q2 11 0–0 P–B4 as in Browne-Hort, Madrid 1973.) 9 0–0 P–N5 (Or 9 . . . N–N3 10 P–K5 P–N5 11 N–K2

N.B3–Q4 12 P–B5! P–B4 13 B–KR6 as in Soltis-Botterill, Student Olympiad, Graz 1972, favouring White.) 10 N–K2! Q–N3 11 N–N3 P–K4 12 P–B3 P–B4!? (Since 12. . . NP×P 13 NP×P Q–R4 14 BP×P P×P 15 N×P N×N 16 B×N is good for White) 13 QP×KP QP×P (13 . . . P–B5+ ought to be tried, though 14 K–R1 P×B 15 P×N N×P may ultimately favour White – Botterill.) 14 B–B4! Black is under too much pressure, e.g. 14 . . . NP×P 15 NP×P R–N1 16 N×P N×N 17 P×N N–N5 18 B–K7 Mestel-Botterill, British Ch 1974.

The Modern Defence

1 . . .   P–KN3

Black can avoid the brunt of the B–KN5 variation by deferring the development of his KN, but White also gets new chances.

2 P–Q4   B–N2

2 . . . P–Q3 is also possible, to meet 3 P–KR4!? by 3. . . N–KB3 instead of 3 . . . P–KR4. In most cases, the order of moves makes no difference.

3 P–QB3

This is White's main try to 'punish' Black for not attacking the KP. Other moves:

a) 3 P–QB4 P–Q3 4 N–QB3 when Black can experiment with 4 . . . N–Q2 or transpose into the King's Indian Defence by 4 . . . N–KB3.

b) 3 P–KB4 P–QB4! e.g.:

b1) 4 P–QB3 P×P 5 P×P Q–N3!? 6 N–KB3 N–QB3 7 P–K5 (*7 N–B3 N–R3!*) 7 . . . N–R3 8 N–B3 0–0 9 P–Q5 N–QN5 10 P–QR3 N–R3 11 B–Q3 P–Q3 12 Q–K2 N–QB4 13 B–B4 B–N5 14 B–K3 B×N (Caro-Keene, Camaguey 1974) favours Black.

b2) 4 N–KB3 P×P 5 N×P N–QB3 and White has an unfavourable Sicilian Dragon.

b3) 4 P–Q5 P–Q3 5 N–KB3 (*5 P–B4* King's Indian Defence) 5 . . . N–KB3 6 B–N5+ QN–Q2! = .

3 . . .   P–Q3

Against 3 . . . P–QN3 White does best with 4 B–Q3 B–N2 5 N–B3 P–Q3 6 0–0 N–KB3 7 QN–Q2 0–0 8 R–K1 with a firm centre, and chances on the Q-side.

4 P–B4

4 N–B3, aiming to transpose into the previous note, is also possible – but Black is not here committed to a Q-fianchetto, and can equalize with care in other ways.

4 . . .   N–KB3

5 B–Q3(*116*)

R. Byrne-Botterill, Hastings 1971–2, went 5 P–K5 P×P 6 BP×P N–Q4 7 N–B3 0–0 8 B–QB4 P–QB4 9 P×P B–K3 with plenty of counterplay for Black.

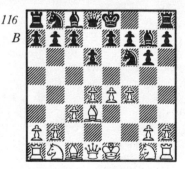

116
B

Black must now find a way to strike back in the centre.

5 . . .   0–0

6 N–B3   P–B4!?

After 6 . . . P–K4!? (*6 . . . QN–Q2 7 0–0 P–B4 8 P–K5!*) 7 0–0 P×BP (*7 . . . QN–Q2 8 Q–K1!*) 8 B×P P–B4 9 K–R1 White's centre is still intact.

7 P×P

7 0–0 P×P 8 P×P N–B3 9 N–B3 should not give much. However the text

move allows Black to make an interesting pawn offer.

    7 . . .   QN–Q2!

    7 . . . P×P 8 0–0 (*8 P–K5!?*) 8 . . . N–B3 9 P–K5 N–KN5 10 N–R3! P–B3 11 P–R3 is sharp, but good for White.

    8 P×P   P×P

    9 0–0

Better than 9 B–K3? R–K1 of Rodriguez-Keene, Skopje 1972.

    9 . . .   N–B4

    10 Q–B2   R–K1

    11 QN–Q2 N×B 12 Q×N N×P! 13 N×N B–B4 14 Q×P R×N 15 Q×Q+ R×Q 16 B–Q2 B–N5 17 QR–K1 R–R5 – diagram 114.

Other Defences

Scandinavian

    1 P–K4   P–Q4

    2 P×P   N–KB3

One rarely sees 2 . . . Q×P on account of 3 N–QB3 Q–QR4 (or *3 . . . Q–Q1 4 P–Q4 P–KN3 5 B–KB4 B–N2 6 Q–Q2!*) 4 P–Q4 N–KB3 5 N–B3 B–N5 6 P–K4 3 B×N 7 Q×P P–B3 8 B–Q2 QN–Q2 9 0–0–0 P–K3 10 B–QB4 with two bishops and the freer game for White.

    3 P–Q4   N×P

    4 N–KB3

White stands better, e.g.

a) 4 . . . P–KN3 5 P–KR3! B–N2 6 P–QB4 N–N3 7 B–K3 0–0 8 N–B3 N–B3 9 Q–Q2

b) 4 . . . B–N5 5 P–KR3 B–R4 6 P–KN4 B–N3 7 N–K5 N–Q2 8 N×B RP×N 9 B–N2

Nimzowitsch Defence

    1 P–K4   N–QB3

This is a somewhat anti-positional defence, but it can unsettle White if he is not prepared for it. There are two principal lines after 2 P–Q4:

a) 2 . . . P–Q4 3 N–QB3 P×P 4 P–Q5 N–K4 (or *4 . . . N–N1 5 B–KB4 N–KB3 6 B–B4* with an attacking position) 5 B–KB4 (*5 P–B3!? P–K3!* and *5 Q–Q4 N–N3* are also critical.) 5 . . . N–N3 6 B–N3 P–QR3 7 B–QB4 P–KB4 and White has active pieces to compensate for Black's extra pawn.

b) 2 . . . P–K4 3 P×P N×P 4 N–KB3 Q–B3 5 N×N Q×N 6 B–Q3 B–N5+ 7 N–Q2 N–B3 8 0–0 P–Q3 9 N–B4 Q–K2 10 P–QB3 B–B4 11 P–QN4 B–N3 12 P–QR4 with some initiative to White; Zagorovsky-Wade, Le Havre 1966.

Queen's Fianchetto Defence

    1 P–K4   P–QN3

A 19th Century favourite, revived by some London players in 1974.

    2 N–KB3!?

White can also play 2 P–Q4 B–N2 3 N–QB3 P–K3 4 B–Q3 B–N5 (*4 . . . N–KB3* is not bad.) 5 KN–K2 when, by comparison with the Modern Defence, it is not so easy for Black to undermine the centre. Nevertheless, White must beware being provoked into premature attacks.

    2 . . .   B–N2

    3 B–B4   P–K3

Avoiding the trap 3 . . . B×P? 4 B×P+ K×B 5 N–N5+ etc.

    4 Q–K2   B–K2

    5 0–0   P–Q4!?

    6 P×P   P×P

    7 B–N3   N–KB3

    8 R–K1

It is not easy for Black to castle, but otherwise his position is quite sound.

7 THE QUEEN'S GAMBIT DECLINED

Just as in KP openings White's objective is to get two pawns abreast in the centre by P–Q4, so in QP openings the idea is to set up this formation by P–Q4. In all QP openings, much of the play is taken up with White's attempts to force this advance and Black's to stop it, or at least to neutralize its effects. The force of the Queen's Gambit, the oldest of the Q-side openings, lies in the fact that there is an immediate threat to control the centre by 3 P×P Q×P 4 N–QB3 followed by P–K4.

In the Orthodox Defence (2 ... P–K3) and the Slav Defence (2 ... P–QB3), Black hopes to maintain a strongpoint at Q4. Later on, when he is further developed, he will try to liberate himself and obtain good squares for his problem child, the QB, by ... P–QB4 or ... P–K4. The Queen's Gambit Accepted (2 ... P×P) will be discussed separately in chapter 8.

The Orthodox Defence

1 P–Q4	P–Q4
2 P–QB4	P–K3
3 N–QB3	

Now we shall examine:

3 ... N–KB3 – to Exchange Var.

3 ... P–QB4 – Tarrasch

An unusual move is 3 ... B–K2, obliging the white QB to go to KB4 instead of the normal KN5; Petrosian experimented with this line in his 1963 World Championship match against Botvinnik. After 4 P×P P×P 5 B–B4 P–QB3 6 P–K3 B–KB4 interesting complications follow 7 P–KN4!? B–N3 8 N–B3 and P–KR4.

The Exchange Variation

3 ...   N–KB3

This, the Orthodox Defence, has tended to fall out of favour, mainly because of the Exchange Variation, which we shall be discussing. Against the Exchange Variation, it is more than usually difficult for Black to obtain more than a draw. White's aim in the positional (B–KN5) lines is to obtain the types of position shown in diagrams 117 and 118. White wants to advance P–QN5, leaving his opponent with a weak Q-side pawn, whatever the reply. If Black allows P×BP, then his QBP is backward on an open file; if he plays ... BP×NP, then after R×P both his QNP and QP are under pressure. If he tries ... P–QB4, White replies QP×P and has a fine square at Q4 for his knight, blockading the isolated QP. Finally, if Black plays ... P–QR3, White continues with the Q-side attack by means of P–QR4. This procedure is known as the 'minority attack', because three pawns advance to do battle with four; opportunities for carrying out this plan sometimes arise from other openings.

Black has a great number of defensive set-ups to choose between, depending upon whether he tries to exchange off

only the white QB (by . . . N–KR4 or
. . . N–B1–K3) or two pairs of minor
pieces (by . . . N–K5), and on his
timing of moves like . . . P–KR3. We
have simplified the variations as much
as possible. The reader will easily
understand them if he keeps in mind the
basic ideas: White is trying to set up the
minority attack and Black tries to stop it
before it gets going, exchanges off
enough pieces so it no longer has any
sting, or seeks counter-attacking
chances against the white K-side. Let us
look at some typical positions.

Favourable Positions for White
Kramer-van Scheltinga, Beverwijk
1950

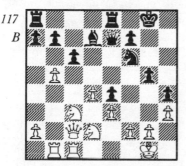

A typical minority attack in which
White is ready to break through on the
QN- or QB-file with his heavy pieces,
which are massed behind the QNP. In

contrast, Black's bishop is entirely
passive and his K-side gesture with
pawns is too lacking in support to be
dangerous.

Botvinnik-Keres, 20th USSR Ch
1952 (*118*)

Here White has chosen to prepare a
break in the centre as well as a minority
attack. Black has defended badly and
now cannot prevent the powerful
P–K4.

Favourable Positions for Black
Castillo-Guimard, Buenos Aires 1954

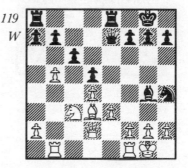

In this case, the build-up of Black's
pieces against the white king, together
with the pressure on the K-file which
prevents natural defensive moves like
P–B3 or P–B4, makes Black's
counterplay very dangerous.

Portisch-Letzelter, Monte Carlo
1968

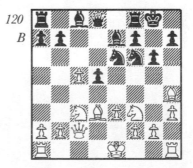

White has failed to meet Black's . . .
P–QB4 counter-thrust in an organized
way. Now 1 . . . P–Q5! opens up the
centre lines against the king.

An Even Position
Pachman-Averbakh,   Saltsjöbaden
1952

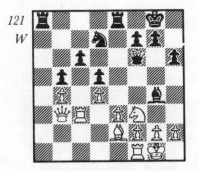

121
W

The minority attack has been
brought to a halt, and the apparent
weakness at QB3 will be protected by
. . . R–K3 and then completely
shielded by . . . N–N3–B5.

1 P–Q4	P–Q4
2 P–QB4	P–K3
3 N–QB3	N–KB3
4 P×P	

4 B–N5 is more common, but the text
move is just as good a way of reaching
the Exchange Variation. It also avoids
the tricky line 4 B–N5 P–B4!?

4 . . .   P×P

White has two interesting plans here:
5 N–B3 – Attacking
5 B–N5 – Positional

Attacking with B–B4

5 N–B3	P–B3
6 B–B4!	

Not:
a) 6 Q–B2? (Always a mistake before
Black develops his QN) 6 . . . P–KN3! 7
B–KN5 B–N2 8 P–K3 B–B4 9 B–Q3

B×B 10 Q×B 0–0 11 0–0 QN–Q2 12
KR–B1 Q–K2 13 QR–N1 Q–K3 14
N–Q2 KR–K1 = Pachman-Ragozin,
Saltsjobaden 1948. Black's extremely
well centralized position compensates
adequately for the forthcoming
minority attack.
b) 6 B–N5? (too late now) 6 . . . B–B4 7
P–K3 Q–N3! and Black takes the
initiative; Monostori-Benko, Hungarian Ch 1950.

6 . . .   B–K2

7 P–K3

7 Q–B2 P–KN3 8 P–K3 B–B4 solves
Black's QB problem for him.

7 . . .   QN–Q2
Others:
a) 7 . . . B–KB4 8 P–KR3! and White
gains ground by 9 P–KN4.
b) 7 . . . N–R4 (to exchange White's
irksome QB) fails to equalize after 8
B–N3 N×B 9 RP×N QN–Q2 10 B–Q3
N–B3 11 Q–B2 P–KR3 12 0–0–0 Q–R4
13 K–N1, Bogoljubow-Spielmann, 2nd
match game 1931.

8 Q–B2   N–B1

Or 8 . . . 0–0 9 B–Q3 R–K1 10
P–KN4! N–B1 (*10 . . . N×P 11 B×P+*
with an open KN-file for attack) 11
P–KR3:
a) 11 . . . B–Q3 12 B×B Q×B 13 0–0–0
and White has the stronger attack;
Barden-Sergeant, Nottingham 1954.
b) 11 . . . N–N3 12 0–0–0 P–B4 13 P×P
B–K3 14 K–N1 Q–R4 15 N–Q4! Geller-
Nora, Paris 1954.

9 B–Q3   N–K3

By 9 . . . N–N3, Black can achieve
the exchange of the white QB, but the
time expended allows White to launch
a favourable minority attack, after all:
10 B–N3 0–0 11 0–0 N–R4 12 QR–N1
N×B 13 RP×N B–Q3 14 P–QN4
Geller-Horowitz, USSR – USA 1954.

10 B–K5!

Thus the QB remains alive. We follow Petrosian-Stoltz, Saltsjobaden 1952:

10 ...	P–KN3
11 P–KR3	B–Q3
12 0–0–0	0–0

Normally, in cases of castling on opposite sides, the player castling QR has the greater dangers to surmount, due to the larger front that the king has to defend; but here White's attack is far more advanced than his opponent's.

| 13 K–N1 | N–N2 |
| 14 P–KN4 | |

Not only attacking, but preventing the simplifying . . . B–KB4.

| 14 ... | N.B3–K1 |
| 15 QR–N1 | P–B3 |

16 B×B N×B 17 N–K2 P–KB4 (Played both to establish a knight on K5 and to safeguard himself against the threat of P–R4–5.) 18 P–N5 N–K5 19 N–B4 N–K3 20 P–KR4 (with the idea of P–R5, P×P and R–R6) 20 ... P–B4 (Black is already sufficiently desperate to make this unsound pawn sacrifice.) 21 P×P Q–B2 22 N×N B×N 23 P–R5! B–B2 24 P×P B×P 25 N–Q4 Q–K4 26 P–B4 (Decisive) 26 ... Q–K2 27 B×N Q×B 28 Q×Q QP×Q 29 R–QB1 B–K1 30 R–R6 B–N3 31 P–B6 QR–B1 32 R–R2 P×P 33 R×BP R×R 34 N×R R–B2 35 R–Q2 R–B2 36 R–Q6 Black resigned.

Positional Line

| 5 B–N5 | QN–Q2 |

5 ... B–K2 should transpose.

6 P–K3

White cannot win a pawn by 6 N×P?? After 6 ... N×N 7 B×Q comes 7 ... B–N5+ and Black will end up with an extra piece.

| 6 ... | P–B3 |

Almost invariably played, although

diagram 120 was reached by 6 ... B–K2 7 B–Q3 N–B1 (*7 . . . 0–0 8 KN–K2* see Mariotti-Radulov, p. 11) 8 Q–B2 (*8 R–QB1!?*) 8 ... N–K3 9 B–R4 P–KN3 10 N–B3 0–0 11 P–KR3? (*11 0–0* was necessary.) 11 ... P–B4! 12 P×P etc.

| 7 B–Q3 | B–K2 |

7 ... B–Q3 is only good if White unthinkingly continues with his minority attack, in which case Black's bishop is better placed to assist his natural counterplay on the K-side. Correct in reply is 8 Q–B2 0–0 9 N–B3 R–K1 10 0–0 N–B1 11 KR–K1! B–KN5 12 N–Q2 B–K3 13 N–B1 as in Fine-Horowitz, New York 1948–9. White plays on the K-side himself and gets ready to attack by P–B4 or P–K4.

8 Q–B2 (*122*)

Note that White always plays this before developing his KN. If 8 N–B3 then 8 ... N–K5 equalizes at once.

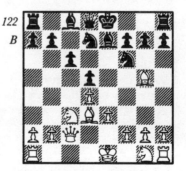

122
B

This is the main point of division for Black against the Minority Attack.

8 . . . N–R4 – Variation 1
8 . . . N–B1 – Variation 2
8 . . . P–KR3 – Variation 3
8 . . . 0–0 – Variation 4

Variation 1

| 8 ... | N–R4 |

To exchange bishops

9 B×B

9 P–KR4 is an interesting and little-played alternative:

a) 9 . . . P–B3? 10 P–KN4! Reshevsky-Guimard, New York 1951.

b) 9 . . . B×B 10 P×B Q×P 11 0–0–0 with good attacking chances.

c) 9 . . . P–KR3 10 B×B Q×B 11 KN–K2 0–0 12 P–KN4 N4–B3 13 R–KN1.

    9 . . .   Q×B
    10 0–0–0!

a) 10 . . . P–KN3 11 P–KN4! N–N2 12 N–KB3 N–B1 13 KR–N1 P–KR4 14 P–KR3 B–K3 15 N–K5 N–Q2 16 P–B4 (Euwe-Beni, Zurich 1954) favours White.

b) 10 . . . N–N3 11 N–B3 B–N5 12 QR–N1 B×N 13 P×B 0–0–0 14 N–R4 N×N 15 Q×N K–N1 16 K–N1 when 16 . . . Q–R5 (Neishtadt) should give Black sufficient counterplay against KB7 and KR7 to equalize.

Variation 2

    8 . . .   N–B1
    9 N–B3   N–K3
    10 B×N!?

This is somewhat premature, but enables us to illustrate the strategic idea of . . . P–QN4 by an actual game continuation.

Also possible:

a) 10 B–R4 P–KN3 11 P–KR3! N–N2 12 P–KN4! 0–0 13 0–0–0 N3–K1 14 B×B Q×B 15 QR–N1 N–Q3 16 P–KR4 with a powerful attack; Taimanov-Persitz, Hastings 1955–6.

b) 10 P–KR4!? P–KR3 11 B×N B×B 12 P–KN4! Q–R4 (*12 . . . N–B2 13 B–B5*) 13 0–0–0 B–Q2 14 P–N5 with a strong attack; Furman-Klaman, Leningrad 1950.

    10 . . .   B×B
    11 0–0   P–KN3

12 P–QN4 0–0 13 N–QR4 P–QR3 14 N–B5 Q–K2 15 QR–N1 N–N2 16 P–QR4 P–QN4 17 N–Q2 N–B4 18 N–N3 N–Q3 19 R–R1! (Filip-Jezek, Marianske Lazne 1951).

This is the right idea, and is applicable whether or not Black tries . . . P–QN4 before White's P–QR4. With the QN-file closed, the QR-file becomes the natural avenue of attack. Compare diagram 121, where . . . P–QN4 worked partly because Black controlled that file. But now after 19 . . . B–Q2 20 R–R2 N–B5 21 R1–R1 R–QN1 22 P×P RP×P 23 R–R7 White's invasion should eventually prove decisive.

Variation 3

    8 . . .   P–KR3

Often useful to create an escape-hole for the king.

    9 B–R4!   0–0
    10 N–B3   R–K1

11 0–0 N–K5 12 B×B Q×B 13 B×N (Not *13 QR–N1* because after *13 . . . N–Q3! 14 P–QN4 P–QN4!* Black posts his knight strongly at QB5.) 13 . . . P×B 14 N–Q2 N–B3 15 P–QN4! B–Q2 (*15 . . . P–QN3* followed by . . . B–R3, to control Q6, should equalize according to the Soviet theoretician Neishtadt; if White replies Q–R4, the bishop is developed at N2). 16 KR–B1 P–KR4 17 QR–N1 P–R5 18 P–KR3 P–KN4 19 P–N5 and White has the advantage, as almost always when he has carried through this advance; see diagram 117.

Variation 4

    8 . . .   0–0 (*123*)

With two lines:

9 KN–K2 – Flexible
9 N–B3 – Normal

The Flexible Line

    9 KN–K2

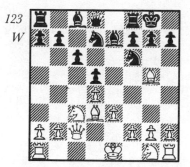

123
W

Less played, but not inferior to 9 N–B3. The white knights protect each other so that if the black KN comes to K5, White can go ahead with the minority attack without bothering to exchange off the knight. In addition, ... B–KN5 can now always be answered by P–KR3.

    9 ...   R–K1

Possibly better is 9 ... P–KR3, e.g. 10 B–R4 N–K1 11 B–N3 N2–B3 12 0–0 B–Q3 = .

    10 0–0

White can also play 10 0–0–0, with obvious intentions of K-side attack: 10 ... N–B1 11 N–N3 P–KR3 12 B×N B×B 13 N–R5 B–N4 14 P–KN3 Petrosian-Mikenas, 17th USSR Ch 1949.

    10 ...   N–B1

If 10 ... P–KR3 11 B–R4 N–R4 12 B×B 13 QR–K1 N–B1 14 N–B1 Q–N4 15 P–QN4 and White gets his attack going just the same; Taimanov-Beni, Vienna 1953.

    11 QR–N1

a) 11 ... B–Q3 12 K–R1! N–N3 (12 ... B×P 13 B×N) 13 P–B3! see diagram 118.

b) 11 ... N–K5 12 B×B Q̇×B 13 B×N (13 P–QN4 and 13 P–B3 are also good.) 13 ... P×B 14 N–N3 P–KB4 15 P–B3 with good prospects.

c) 11 ... N–N5 12 B×B Q×B 13 P–KR3 N–B3 and White must watch the weakness of his KN3 square–Neishtadt.

Normal Line

    9 N–B3   R–K1
    10 0–0   P–KR3?!

10 ... N–B1 is probably better, and White should then prepare his minority attack by 11 QR–N1, e.g.:

a) 11 ... N–K5 12 B×B Q×B 13 P–QN4 N–N3 (13 ... P–QR3!?) 14 P–N5 B–N5 15 B×N P×B 16 N–Q2 P–KB4 17 P×P P×P 18 P KR3 B–R4 19 Q–N3+ K–R1 20 Q–N7 and the weakened Black Q-side is under heavy attack.

b) 11 ... P–KN3 12 P–QN4 P–QR3 13 P–QR4 N–K3 14 B–R4 N–N2 15 P–N5 RP×P 16 P×P B–KB4 17 P×P P×P 18 N–K5! Van den Berg-Kramer, Amsterdam 1950.

    11 B–KB4!

If 11 B–R4 Black equalizes by 11 ... N–K5! as in Geller-Jimenez, Palma 1970.

    11 ...   N–B1

11 ... N–R4? loses a pawn to 12 N×P! (12 ... P×N?? 13 B–B7).

    12 QR–N1   P–QR4
    13 P–QR3   N–R4

We are following the game Reshevsky-Jimenez, Palma 1970.

    14 B–K5   B–KN5
    15 N–Q2   P–B3

Black is defending in unorthodox fashion. He hopes to complicate the game, but Reshevsky, a great exponent of the Exchange Variation, is not to be confused.

    16 B–N3   N×B
    17 RP×N   B–R4

18 N–QR4 B–Q3 19 KR–K1 N–K3 20 P–QN4 P×P 21 P×P P–QN4 22 N–B5 N×N 23 QP×N (An unusual pawn

structure. Although the QN- and QB-files are now sealed, the black QBP remains vulnerable to a knight on Q4.) 23 . . . B–B1 24 N–N3 Q–B2 25 R–R1 B–B2 26 N–Q4 Q–N2 27 B–N6! R–K2 28 B×B+ K×B 29 R–R2 P–N3 30 R1–R1 R×R 31 Q×R P–B4 32 Q–R6 B–N2 33 N×QBP! and in view of the threat of the N–Q8+, Black resigned

The Tarrasch Defence

1	P–Q4	P–Q4
2	P–QB4	P–K3
3	N–QB3	P–QB4

This defence, which is still quite controversial, gained a new lease of life in the 1960s through the discoveries of Spassky and other Soviet players, notably Lein and the Zaitsevs. Black can play 3 . . . P–QB4 with any one of three plans in mind. He may keep pawns at QB4 and Q4, in which case an eventual QP×QBP by White will lead to the isolation of the black QP. This was the original idea of Tarrasch, to which Spassky brought attention in his 1969 match against Petrosian. The second plan, introduced into master play by the Swedish team at the Folkestone Olympiad of 1933, is to advance the QBP to B5 and so to base Black's hopes on the Q-side pawn majority which is thereby created. The drawback to this scheme is that Black lags behind in development, so that White is able to strike vigorously at the pawn chain, either by P–QN3, blunting the spearhead, or by P–K4, undermining the base. The third possibility is to sacrifice the QP, in return for a couple of tempi which give Black compensation in terms of the more aggressive piece postings, which in turn can develop into a middle game attack.

4 BP×P

The symmetrical positions resulting from 4 P–K3 N–KB3 5 N–B3 N–B3 required delicate handling, though with best play Black should equalize. The text move is generally recommended; Black can reply:

4 . . . KP×P – Usual
4 . . . BP×P!? – Gambit

The Usual Form

4 . . .	KP×P
5 N–B3	N–QB3
6 P–KN3	

when:

6 . . . N–B3 – Spassky
6 . . . P–B5 – Swedish

Spassky's Line

6 . . .	N–B3
7 B–N2	B–K2
8 0–0	0–0
9 B–N5	

White defers isolating the black QP until a favourable moment presents itself. 9 P×P is best met by 9 . . . P–Q5 (*9 . . . B×P 10 N–QR4*) 10 N–QR4 B–B4 (*10 . . . P–KR3!? 11 P–N3 N–R2* is also good.) 11 B–B4 B–K5! and Black has compensation for the pawn.

9 . . .	P×P
10 N×P.4	P–KR3

Spassky's idea; 10 . . . N×N 11 Q×N Q–R4 may also equalize, according to advocates of the Tarrasch. Black's QP is of course very weak in any endgame that may arise, so Black, remembering our introduction to IQP positions in the first chapter (pp. 5–6), has to find active piece play.

11 B–K3	R–K1!

With this idea, Black managed to equalize in the 18th Petrosian-Spassky game, when 12 R–B1 was played. Games played more recently, with

Bronstein and Korchnoi handling the white pieces, indicate that 12 Q–N3 N–QR4 13 Q–B2 is the continuation most likely to give an edge.

The Swedish Variation

6 ...	P–B5
7 B–N2	B–QN5
8 0–0	KN–K2
9 P–K4	

The best way of instituting a counter-action against the Q-side majority. No reply is wholly satisfactory:

a) 9 ... P×P 10 N×P 0–0 11 Q–B2! Q–Q4 12 B–K3 N–N3 13 N–KR4! Q–QN4 (*13 ... N×P?* loses a pawn to *14 Q–Q1*.) 14 N×N RP×N 15 P–QR3 B–K2 16 P–Q5 N–QR4 17 P–Q6 Reshevsky-Stahlberg, Zürich 1953.

b) 9 ... 0–0 10 P×P N×P.4 11 B–N5! B–K2 (*11 ... N3–K2!?*) 12 N×N B×B 13 N×B Q×N.B4 14 N–K3!

The Hennig-Schara Gambit

| 4 ... | BP×P!? |

Recommended in *The Guardian Chess Book*, where more detail can be found.

5 Q–R4+

Or 5 Q×P N–QB3 6 Q–Q1 P×P 7 Q×P B–Q2 transposing.

5 ...	B–Q2
6 Q×QP	P×P
7 Q×QP	N–QB3 (*124*)

| 8 N–B3 | N–B3 |
| 9. Q–Q1 | |

The safest retreat for the queen.

9 ...	B–QB4
10 P–K3	Q–K2
11 B–K2	

Black must now either content himself with a slight initiative, and a fairly safe draw but no more, or throw everything into a double-edged K-side attack:

a) 11 ... 0–0 12 0–0 KR–Q1 13 P–QR3 B–B4 14 Q–R4 N–KN5 15 P–R3 N5–K4= Vladimirov-Ravinsky, USSR 1955.

b) 11 ... 0–0–0!? 12 0–0 P–KN4 with sharp play. After 13 P–QN4!? Black can play 13 ... B×NP 14 Q–N3 KR–N1! 15 R–N1 B–KB4 16 R–N2 B–K3! e.g. 17 B–B4 B×B 18 Q×B Q–B4!= (not 19 Q×P? R–Q2).

The Slav Defence

| 1 P–Q4 | P–Q4 |
| 2 P–QB4 | P–QB3 |

The Slav attempts to maintain Black's centre pawn while permitting, unlike the Orthodox Defence, the free development of the QB. Further, when Black plays ... N–KB3, B N5 will lack a point since it will no longer be a pin. To compensate for these advantages, the Slav has two disadvantages not present in the Orthodox: the absence of the QB weakens Black's Q-side, so that it may come under early attack (particularly by Q–N3), and it is easier for White to advance P–K4 effectively, since the natural counter ... P–QB4 wastes a tempo (Black's QBP is already committed to QB3!).

Since the war the Slav has been extensively analysed, and played by grandmasters like Smyslov and Petrosian. We examine it from White's point of view, recommending the Exchange Variation to positional players, and the exciting Tolush-Geller Gambit to those of combinative disposition. We shall also look at the Meran Variation, a favourite of Larsen's, which is a hybrid of the Orthodox and Slav Defences.

After 2 ... P–QB3 we therefore examine:

3 P×P – Exchange
3 N–KB3 – Main

Exchange Variation

3 P×P	P×P
4 N–KB3	N–KB3
5 N–B3	N–B3

5 ... B–B4? is bad because of 6 Q–N3!

6 B–B4(*125*)

The Exchange Slav is more dangerous to Black than most other symmetrical opening variations. Alert defence should be able to neutralize White's pressure eventually, but it is very pleasant for the first player to know that he is the only one with winning chances.

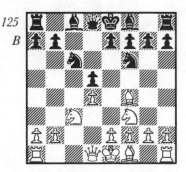

125
B

The main replies are:
6 ... B–B4 – Variation 1
6 ... P–K3 – Variation 2

Keres experimented with 6 ... Q–R4!? but after 7 P–K3 N–K5 (*7 ... B–B4!?*) 8 Q–N3 P–K3 9 B–Q3 B–N5

10 QR–B1, as once played by Botvinnik, White has the edge.

Variation 1

6 ...	B–B4

Black continues to 'follow the leader', not wishing to have his QB shut in by the pawn chain after all.

7 P–K3	P–K3

7 ... P–QR3 has been tried, to prevent the B–QN5 pin. But this gives White a tempo to execute his other main idea: 8 N–K5 e.g. 8 ... R–B1 9 P–KN4! B–Q2 10 P–B3! P–K3 11 B–Q3.

8 B–QN5

Botvinnik-Trifunovic, Moscow 1947 was agreed drawn after 8 Q–N3!? B–QN5! (*8 ... Q–N3 9 Q×Q P×Q 10 P–QR3!* favours White) 9 B–QN5 (Unwise would be *9 P–QR3 B×N+ 10 P×B 0–0 11 Q×NP* because of *11 ... Q–R4! 12 Q–N3 QR–N1!*) 9 ... 0–0 10 0–0 B×N 11 B×N B×NP 12 B×NP B×R 13 R×B Q–N3 14 B×R R×B.

8 ...	N–Q2!

This is the only satisfactory move. 8 ... B–QN5 is met by 9 N–K5! Q–R4 10 B×N+ P×B 11 0–0 B×N 12 P×B e.g.:
a) 12 ... Q×BP 13 Q–B1! Q×Q 14 KR×Q 0–0 15 P–B3 P–KR3 16 N×QBP KR–K1 17 P–QR4 N–Q2 18 B–Q6 Botvinnik-Tal, 11th game, World Championship match 1961.
b) 12 ... R–QB1 13 P–B4 0–0 14 P–KN4! B–N3 15 P–B5 N–K5 16 P–B3 Botvinnik-Pomar, Amsterdam 1966.

9 0–0

Now that N–K5 has been prevented, White cannot increase his pressure, e.g. 9 Q–R4?! Q–N3 10 0–0 B–K2 11 QR–B1 0–0 12 P–QR3 KR–B1 with a good game for Black.

9 ...	B–K2
10 R–B1	0–0
11 P–KR3	R–B1 =

Spassky-Larsen, 1st game, Candidates' match 1968.

Variation 2

6 ...   P-K3

Maybe not best, but necessary if Black wishes to unbalance the game. The Slav Exchange is particularly useful for White against players who want to win at any cost.

7 P-K3   B-Q3

Black must show his hand now. Also possible:

a) 7 ... N-KR4!? 8 B-KN5 (Taimanov suggests that *8 B-K5* and *8 B-QN5* should be looked into.) 8 ... Q-N3 9 P-QR3 P-KR3 10 B-R4 P-KN4 11 B-N3 N×B 12 RP×N B-N2 was played in some games by Botvinnik. Now 13 B-N5, suggested by Whiteley, should easily lead to a drawish position after minor piece exchanges.

b) 7 ... B-K2 8 B-Q3 0-0 9 0-0 (*9 P-KR3!?*) 9 ... N-KR4 (*9 ... B-Q2 10 N-K5!* leaves Black somewhat cramped.) 10. B-K5!? P-B3 may be best, as 11 N-N5 is now known to be unsound.

8 B-N3   0-0

Not so good are:

a) 8 ... B×B 9 RP×B P-QR3 10 B-Q3 Q-Q3 11 Q-K2 B-Q2 12 0-0-0 P-QN4 (*12 ... 0-0-0? 13 B×QRP!*) 13 P-K4! Petrosian-Smyslov, Moscow 1967.

b) 8 ... N-K5 9 N×N P×N 10 N-Q2 P-B4 11 B-N5 0-0 12 B×N P×B 13 Q-R4 B×B 14 RP×B Q-N3 15 N-B4 Gheorghiu-Pomar, Skopjc 1972.

9 B-Q3   P-QN3

Too quiet. Black should try 9 ... R-K1, threatening to gain freedom by ... P-K4, at the risk of an IQP. Then 10 0-0 may be best, for if 10 N-K5 B×N 11 P×B N-Q2 12 P-B4 N-B4!

equalizes-Taimanov.

10 R-B1   B-N2
11 B-R4

We are following the game Bobotsov-Pomar, Skopje 1972; White has enduring pressure, but in view of the symmetrical pawn structure the game requires delicate handling.

11 ...   B-K2
12 0-0   R-B1
13 B-N1

So that 13 ... N-K5 would fail to 14 B×B N×B 15 N×N P×N 16 N-N5!

13 ...   P-KR3
14 Q-K2

Intending KR-Q1 and N-K5 with good piece co-ordination.

14 ...   N-R2
15 B-N3   N-B3

15 ... P-B4 16 N-K5 N-B3 17 P-B3 preparing an eventual P-K4 breakthrough.

16 N-K5   N×N
17 B×N   B-Q3
18 N-N5!

Mounting a definite assault at last.

18 ...   B×B
19 P×B   N-K5
20 P-B3

White avoids the trap 20 N×RP? losing all his advantage, after 20 ... R×R 21 R×R Q-N1 22 N-N5 Q×P.

20 ...   N-B4
21 P-QN4   N-Q2
22 N-Q6   R-B2
23 Q-Q3   P-B4
24 P-B4

With an unshakable grip on the centre and black squares. The game continued 24 ... B-R1 25 Q-Q2 N-B3 26 R×R Q×R 27 R-B1 Q-Q2 28 B-Q3 (All White's pieces now control important squares, like QN5 and QB8.) 28 ... N-K5 29 B×N QP×B 30 P-N5 B-Q4 31 P-KR4 (preventing ...

P–KN4 desperadoes and giving the king a safe square) 31 ... R–R1 32 P–QR3 (intending Q–B3) 32 ... P–R3 33 P×P R×P 34 R–B8+ K–R2 35 Q–B1 P–QN4 36 R–B7 Q–Q1.

The ingenious defensive try 36 ... R–B3!? would narrowly fail to the line given by Bobotsov: 37 R×Q R×Q+ 38 K–R2 R–B6 39 N×BP! P×N 40 R×B R×KP 41 P–R5 R×P 42 P–K6 R–R2 43 R×BP R–K2 44 R–K5 P–N5 45 P–B5 and White's passed pawns are superior.

The text move also lost nicely. The Bulgarian grandmaster played 37 P–R5 Q–R5 38 N–K8! R–B3 39 N–B6+! Q×N (*39 ... K–R1 40 R–B8+* mates) 40 P×Q R×Q+ 41 R×R P×P 42 R–B5 B–B5 43 P–R4 Black resigned.

Main Line Slav

1 P–Q4	P–Q4
2 P–QB4	P–QB3
3 N–KB3	N–B3
4 N–B3	

Now Black has:

4 ... P×P – to Gambit
4 ... P–K3 – Semi-Slav

Tolush-Geller Gambit

4 ...	P×P
5 P–K4!?	

This move inaugurates the Tolush-Geller Gambit, which we recommend against the Slav for combinative players. Quieter moves like 5 P–K3 and 5 P–QR4 make sure of regaining the pawn, but do not really make it hard for Black to equalize. For the pawn sacrificed, White gains in space and development, and Black has to watch out constantly for tactical ideas that threaten to destroy his position.

5 ...	P–QN4

Since White has grabbed the centre,

Black must try to hold the extra pawn as compensation.

6 P–K5

6 Q–B2, playing more positionally behind the broad centre, allows Black to develop with less interruption, and the game is about level; e.g. 6 ... P–K3 (*6 ... N–R3!? 7 B–K2 P–N3 8 B–N5 B–KN2 9 0–0*) 7 B–K2 B–N2 8 0–0 QN–Q2 9 B–N5 P–KR3 10 B–R4 Q–N3 11 KR–Q1 but not now 11 ... P–N4?! 12 B–N3 N–R4 13 P–QR4 N×B 14 RP×N P–R3 15 P–Q5 with a dangerous attack for White, Geller-Florian, Helsinki 1952.

6 ...	N–Q4
7 P–QR4	

The usual move, played to break up the black Q-side phalanx, but there is a case for 7 N–N5!? too. There can follow:
a) 7 ... P–K3 8 Q–R5 Q–Q2 (*8 ... P–N3 9 Q–B3* and *10 N5–K4*) 9 N×RP K–Q1 10 N×B: an odd position!
b) 7 ... P–KR3 8 N5–K4 P–K3 9 P–QR4 P–N5 (Euwe recommended *9 ... Q–N3.*) 10 N–N1 B–R3 11 Q–N4 P–N6 12 B–Q2 N–N5 13 N–R3 was good for White in Spassky-Mnatsakanian, Moscow 1959.
c) 7 ... B–B4 might be met by 8 P–K6!? P×P (*8 ... B×P 9 N×B P×N 10 Q–R5+ K–Q2* is also unclear.) 9 P–KN4 P–KR3 10 P×B P×N 11 P×KP etc.

7 ...	P–K3

Experience has shown that other moves are inferior:
a) 7 ... B–B4 (*7 ... B–K3 8 N–N5!*) 8 P×P N×N (Or *8 ... N–N5 9 B×P! N–B7+ 10 K–K2 N×R 11 Q–R4! B–B7! 13 Q×N*-Lilienthal) 9 P×N P×P 10 N–N5! P–K3 11 P–N4! Szabo-Burstein, Tel Aviv 1958.
b) 7 ... B–N2 8 P–K6! P–B3 (*8 ... P×P 9 N–K5*) 9 P–KN3 Q–Q3 10 B–R3

N–R3 11 0–0 Najdorf–Ojanen, Helsinki 1952.

8 P×P	N×N
9 P×N	P×P
10 N–N5	B–N2
11 Q–R5(*126*)	

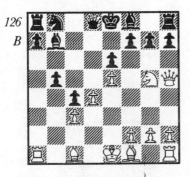

126
B

Black must now decide how to defend his KBP.

11 ...   P–N3

After 11 ... Q–Q2, White should not play 12 N×RP?! because of 12 ... N–B3! 13 N–B6+ P×N 14 Q×R P×P! and Black has a strong counter-attack in return for the exchange. Simply 12 B–K2! is correct, e.g. 12 ... B×P 13 R–KN1 B–Q4 14 N×RP! N–B3 15 N–B6+ P×N 16 Q×R 0–0–0 17 R–N8.

12 Q–N4	B–K2
13 B–K2	N–Q2
14 B–B3!	

This is a great improvement upon Geller's original idea 14 P–R4 when 14 ... P–KR4 15 Q–N3 N–N3 16 0–0 P–R4! commences thematic counter-play on the Q-side. The best practical chance then is 17 P–Q5!?, as in Petrosian–Smyslov, 19th USSR Ch 1951, when Black should have played 17 ... B×P.

14 ...   Q–B2?!

Correct is Petrosian's 14 ... Q–B1!, but this is not an easy move to find; the point is that then 15 N–K4 can be met by 15 ... 0–0 16 B–R6 P–B4 17 P×Pep N×P as the KP is protected by the queen. Nor is 15 B–R3 good enough, in view of 15 ... B.N2×B! 16 N×B Q–R3!, but Panov's 15 P–KR4, discouraging Black from castling, leaves the position unclear.

15 N–K4   N–N3

Grandmaster Flohr suggested 15 ... P–KR4!?

16 B–R6   R–KN1

Pachman's suggestion, 16 ... B×N 17 B×B 0–0–0 is not very promising, but now Black really suffers from his inability to castle. We are following the game Geller–Unzicker, Stockholm 1952.

17 B–N5	B×N
18 B.B3×B	N–Q4
19 B×N!	

White correctly judges that he will have plenty of targets in the ensuing game without minor pieces.

19 ...   P×B

20 B×B   Q×B

21 0–0 K–B1 22 KR–N1 P–QR3 23 Q–B3 Q–K3? (The last chance was to return the extra pawn, by 23 ... *K–N2 24 Q×QP R.N1–Q1* with still some chances of making a draw; the move played meets with an elegant refutation.) 24 Q–B6!! (Now the black KR is definitely cut out of play. If 24 ... Q×Q 25 P×Q, White threatens 26 R×NP and the roof caves in.) 24 ... Q–B1 25 P–B4 Q–N2 26 R–R5 K–K1 27 R1–R1 P–N5 28 P×P Q×P 29 R×QP Q–N2 30 P–K6 Black resigned, because he could not face 30 ... P×P 31 Q×KP+ K–B1 32 R–Q7. Although the Tolush–Geller Gambit is rarely seen nowadays, few club players know how to meet it–and it is anyway unclear that there is any refutation.

The Semi-Slav

1	P–Q4	P–Q4
2	P–QB4	P–QB3
3	N–KB3	N–KB3
4	N–B3	P–K3

This is the Semi-Slav Defence, which is favoured by Larsen and other masters. As 5 B–N5 P×P, though sharp, is not unfavourable to Black, White should continue quietly:

5	P–K3	QN–Q2

As we shall see below, Black's main idea is to exchange his QP for the white QBP, and then advance his Q-side pawns with gain of tempo. This, the Meran Variation and its offshoots, leads to tense play in which White is often provoked into an unsound sacrifice. We shall look at:

6 N–K5 – Rubinstein
6 B–Q3 – Meran

Rubinstein Variation

6 N–K5

We recommend this to the player who wants to avoid well-analysed lines.

6	...	N×N
7	P×N	N–Q2
8	P–B4	P–KB4?

A better defence is 8 ... B–B4 9 P–QR3 Q–K2 10 P–QN4 B–N3 (Spielmann-Lokvenc, Vienna 1936), but White always has some attacking chances, because of his aggressive pawn formation on the K-side.

9	KP×Pep	Q×P
10	B–K2	B–B4
11	0–0	0–0

A good example of the force of 6 N–K5 is the game Tartakower-Ravn, Southsea 1951, which continued from this point 12 K–R1 P–QR3 13 Q–B2 P–QN4 14 P×NP BP×P 15 B–Q3 Q–R5 16 B–Q2 N–B3 17 B–K1 Q–R3 18 R–B3 N–N5 19 R–R3 N×KP 20

Q–K2! Q–B3 21 B×P+ K–B2 22 B–R4 Black resigned.

Meran Lines

6	B–Q3	P×P

An alternative to the Meran is 6 ... B–Q3 7 P–K4 P×KP 8 N×P N×N 9 B×N 0–0 10 0–0 P–QB4!? 11 B–B2 Q–B2 12 Q–Q3 P–B4!= as revived by Larsen against Portisch at Teesside 1972.

7	B×BP	P–QN4
8	B–Q3(*127*)	

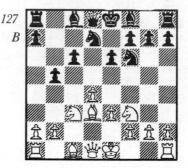

127
B

At the parting of the ways:

8 ... P–N5 – Neo-Meran
8 ... B–N2 – Wade
8 ... P–QR3 – Blumenfeld

The Neo-Meran

8	...	P–N5
9	N–K4	N×N

White gets very active play after 9 ... B–K2 10 N×N+ N×N 11 Q–R4! B–N2 12 B–Q2 P–QR4 13 P–K4! The game Portisch-Johannessen, Havana 1966, continued 13 ... 0–0 14 P–K5 N–Q2?! 15 Q–B2 P–R3 16 P–KR4! P–QB4 17 R–R3! B×N and now came the brilliant finish 18 B×RP!! B×RP 19 P×B P×B 20 K–K2! N×P 21 P×N Q–Q5 22 R×B! Q×R 23 R–KN1+ K–R1 24 Q–B1! P–B3 25 R–N6! Black resigned.

10 B×N   B–N2
11 0–0
Or 11 Q–R4 Q–N3! but 11 B–Q2
B–K2 12 P–QR3 may be better.
11 . . .   B–K2 =
Also after 11 . . . B–Q3, Black's game
is satisfactory.

Wade Variation
8 . . .   B–N2
The most elastic move, which we
shall illustrate with the game
Uhlmann-Larsen, 6th Candidates'
match game 1971.
9 P–K4
Black easily equalizes after 9 0–0
P–N5 10 N–K4 B–K2 11 N×N+ N×N
12 P–K4 0–0 as in Polugayevsky-
Larsen, Palma 1970.
9 . . .   P–N5!
10 N–R4   P–B4
11 P–K5   N–Q4
12 N×P
Critical is 12 0–0 (*12 P×P? Q–R4 13
0–0 B×P!*) when Larsen suggests 12 . . .
P–QR3 13 B–KN5 (*13 R–K1!?*) 13 . . .
B–K2 14 B×B Q×B 15 R–B1 P×P 16
R–K1 0–0 with complex play and
balanced chances.
12 . . .   N×N!
Improving upon his former preference 12 . . . B×N 13 P×B N×BP
when 14 B–QN5+ K–B1 15 0–0 gives
White some chances.
13 P×N   B×P!
Formerly, it was not realized that the
ensuing check was innocuous.
14 B–QN5+   K–K2
15 0–0 (Or *15 B–N5+ P–B3 16 B–KR4
Q–R4!*) 15 . . . Q–N3 16 B–Q3
(Possibly 16 Q–K2 is superior.) 16 . . .
P–KR3 17 Q–K2 KR–Q1 (Now Black
is fully mobilized and has pressure in
the centre and on the Q-side.) 18 B–Q2
K–B1 19 QR–B1 (According to Larsen,

19 P–QR3 was better, challenging
Black's supremacy.) 19 . . . QR–B1 20
R–B2 P–QR4 21 R1–B1 K–N1 22
P–KR3 N–K2 23 N–K1 (Perhaps *23
B–K1*, defending KB2 and maintaining
control of Q4, might have made it
harder for Black to demonstrate his
advantage.) 23 . . . B–Q5 24 R×R
R×R 25 R×R N×R and with the rooks
gone, White is left with weaknesses at
QN2, KB2 and K5. Larsen gives 26
N–B3 as relatively the best defence.
Instead the game continued 26
P–QN3? N–K2 27 N–B3 B–B4 28 B–K1
N–B4 29 K–B1 (*29 B–K4 N–N6!*) 29 . . .
Q–B3! 30 B–N5 Q–B2 31 B–Q3 N–Q5
32 N×N B×N 33 P–B4? (*33 B–K4 B–B1*
was preferable.) 33 . . . Q–B8 34 Q–Q2
Q–R8 35 Q–QB2 B–QB6 36 Q–N1
B–R3! White resigned.

Blumenfeld/Reynolds Variation
8 . . .   P–QR3
9 P–K4   P–B4(*128*)
The Meran proper, which is pretty
rare nowadays.

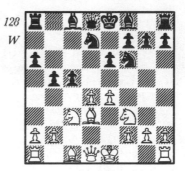

128
W

10 P–Q5
The Reynolds Variation, which is
probably better for White than the
older lines based upon 10 P–K5!? P×P
11 N×NP, on which the last word has
still to be spoken.
10 . . .₁   P–K4

Other critical lines:
a) 10 . . . P×P 11 P–K5! N–N5 12 B–N5! is a pawn sacrifice for a dangerous White attack.
b) 10 . . . P–B5 11 P×P! P×P 12 B–B2 B–N2 13 0–0 Q–B2 14 Q–K2 B–Q3 15 N–N5! N–B4 16 P–B4 P–K4 17 P–QR4! with a strong initiative, for if 17 . . . P–N5 18 N–Q5!; Uhlmann-Fuchs, East German Ch 1963.
c) 10 . . . N–N3 11 P×P! B×P 12 Q–K2 B–K2 13 0–0 P–N5 14 N–Q1 P–B5 15 B–B2 B–B4 16 N–K3 and White's pieces have good squares.

11 P–QN3!

A critical line, but probably one that is good for White.

11 . . .   B–Q3

Or 11 . . . P–B5!? 12 P×P when:
a) 12 . . . P×P 13 B×P B–N5 14 Q–N3 R–QN1 15 0–0 B×N 16 Q×B N×KP 17 Q–K3 or 17 Q–R3–Taimanov.
b) 12 . . . B–N5 13 B–Q2 P×P (*13 . . . . N–B4 14 Q–K2!*) 14 B×P B×N (*14 . . . Q–B2 15 Q–N3*) 15 B×B N×KP 16 Q–B2 again with better chances for White.

12 0–0   0–0
13 P–QR4   P–B5!?

Quiet play like 13 . . . P–N5 14 N–N1 followed by N–Q2 and N–B4 leaves White with positional advantage.

14 NP×P   P–N5
15 N–K2   N–B4
16 N–N3   Q–B2

Or 16 . . . P–QR4!?–Simagin

17 B–K3

In practice, Black has done well with this positional sacrifice of Simagin's. However, exact play may refute it, e.g. after the text play may go 17 . . . P–N3 18 B×N! B×B 19 N–Q2 P–QR4 20 N–N3 and Taimanov considers that White stands slightly better.

Irregular Defences

1 P–Q4   P–Q4
2 P–QB4

From time to time, you may have to meet one of these unorthodox replies to the Queen's Gambit:

2 . . . *N–KB3* – Marshall
2 . . . *P–QB4* – Symmetrical
2 . . . *P–K4* – Albin
2 . . . *N–QB3* – Chigorin

Marshall Defence

2 . . .   N–KB3

Often played by beginners but very weak.

3 P×P   N×P
4 N–KB3!

Surprisingly, 4 P–K4 is not so good. Black goes 4 . . . N–KB3 5 Q–B3 (or *5 N–QB3*) 5 . . . P–K4! 6 P×P N–N5 7 N–KB3 N–QB3 8 B–KN5 (*8 B–KB4??* loses to *8 . . . N–N5*) 8 . . . B–K2 9 B×B Q×B 10 N–B3 N3×P 11 N×N N×N=.

4 . . .   B–B4

Or 4 . . . P–KN3 with an unusual form of the Grünfeld Defence.

5 Q–N3!   N–QB3

6 QN–Q2 (Not *6 Q×P? N4–N5*) 6 . . . N–N3 7 P–K4 B–N3 8 P–Q5 N–N1 9 P–QR4 P–QR4 10 N–K5 QN–Q2 11 B–N5 and Black has a dreadful position; Takacs-Havasi, Budapest 1926.

The Symmetrical Defence

2 . . .   P–QB4

This conceals a trick or two.

3 BP×P

3 N–KB3 transposes to the English Opening, and 3 QP×P P–Q5! 4 N–KB3 N–QB3 5 P–K3 P–K4 is level.

3 . . .   N–KB3!

Rubinstein's move, which is not easy to refute.

4 P×P

The only reasonable alternative is 4
N–QB3 (*4 P–K4 N×KP 5 P×P
N×QBP! 6 N–QB3 P–K4=*) 4 . . . N×P
5 P–K4 N×N 6 P×N P–KN3 with a
Grünfeld position.

    4 . . .   Q×P
    5 Q×Q

5 B–Q2 N–K5 6 N–KB3 has been
suggested.

    5 . . .   N×Q
    6 B–Q2

White should probably play Hans
Müller's line 6 P–K4 N–N5 7 N–QR3
P–K4!? (*7 . . . P–K3* favours White
slightly.) 8 B–Q2! B×P 9 R–B1. If here
8 B–K3 Black's best is probably 8 . . .
P–B3!–O'Kelly.

    6 . . .   P–K4(*129*)

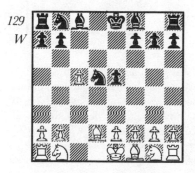

129
W

    7 N–QR3   N–QR3!
    8 P–K4   N4–N5

9 R–B1 B–Q2! 10 B×N N×B 11 P–QN4
P–QN3! 12 P–B6 B–K3 13 N–N5
B×NP! with a tense struggle that ended
in a draw; O'Kelly-Estrin, corres
1959–60.

Albin Counter-Gambit
    2 . . .   P–K4
    3 QP×P   P–Q5

Black gives up a pawn for rapid
development. White should follow the
usual formula in such cases: be ready to

give back the pawn for positional
advantage at the right moment.

    4 N–KB3   N–QB3
    5 P–QR3

If 5 QN–Q2 immediately, 5 . . .
Q–K2 regains the pawn with little
disadvantage for Black, e.g. 6 N–N3
B–N5 (threatening *7 . . . 0–0–0*) or 6
P–KN3 B–N5 7 B–N2 0–0–0 followed
by . . . N×P, or finally 6 P–QR3 N×P
and 7 N×P?? is impossible because of 7
. . . N–Q6 mate.

    · 5 . . .   B–N5(*130*)

Instead:

a) 5 . . . P–QR4 6 Q–Q3! (Ulvestad-
Adams, West Orange 1954) allows
White to play QN–Q2 without
breaking the pressure of his queen on
Black's QP.

b) 5 . . . B–K3 6 QN–Q2 Q–Q2 7
P–KN3 KN–K2 8 B–N2 B–K2 9 0–0
0–0 10 P–QN4 and Black will only
capture the KP at the cost of his own
QNP; Pirc-Kostić, Zagreb 1947.

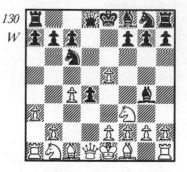

130
W

    6 P–QN4

6 QN–Q2 is also good.

    6 . . .   Q–K2
    7 Q–R4   0–0–0

8 B–B4 B×N 9 NP×B K–N1 10 N–Q2
N×KP 11 Q–N3 N–N3 12 B–N3
Petrosian-Porreca, Belgrade 1954;
Black has regained the pawn but White
retains a lasting advantage because of

the two bishops and his chances of attack on the Q-side.

Chigorin Defence

   2 ...   N–QB3

This defence used to be played exclusively by the great Russian master of the 19th Century, Chigorin, even in his world championship matches against Steinitz. Black hopes to develop a counter-attack by rapid development of the pieces. Although with correct play. White has the better central position, some players may find this defence suits their style.

   3 N–QB3!

Stronger than:

a) 3 P×P Q×P 4 N–KB3 P–K4! 5 N–B3 B–QN5 6 B–Q2 B×N 7 B×B P–K5 8 N–K5 P–K6! 9 P×P N×N 10 P×N B–K3 gives Black a tremendous advantage in development at the cost of a pawn which is, anyway, troubled.

b) 3 N–KB3 gives Black a target: 3 ... B–N5 4 Q–R4 (or *4 P×P B×N*) 4 ... B×N 5 KP×B P–K3 6 N–B3 KN–K2 7 B–K3 P–KN3! (Füster-Bronstein, Moscow 1949) and suddenly White's QP has become weak. Or 7 P×P P P×P 8 B–QN5 P–QR3 9 B×N+ N×B 10 0–0 Q–Q2 and 11 ... 0–0–0 with a good game.

   3 ...   P×P

Others:

a) 3 ... N–B3 4 N–B3 B–N5 5 P×P KN×P 6 P–K4 B×N 7 P×B N–N3 8 P–Q5 N–N1 9 B–KB4 and White has full control of the centre; Keres-Terpugov, 19th USSR Ch 1951.

b) 3 ... P–K3 4 N–B3 B–N5 5 B–N5! P–B3 6 B–Q2 KN–K2 7 P–K3 0–0 8 P–QR3 (Bondarevsky-Terpugov, 19th USSR Ch 1951) gradually shows up the defect of this defence–Black has in the long run restricted his counter-

attacking possibilities by denying himself ... P–QB4.

   4 N–B3!   B–N5?

This turns out badly. 4 ... N–B3 is correct, e.g. 5 P–K4 (*5 P–Q5 N–QR4 6 Q–R4+ P–B3*) 5 ... B–N5 6 B–K3 P–K3! 7 B×P B–N5 with pressure against the white pawn centre.

   5 P–Q5   B×N

   6 KP×B   N–K4(*131*)

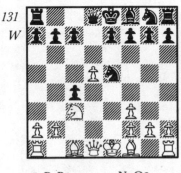

   7 B–B4   N–Q2

We are following the game Donner-Keene, Holland-England 1971. Black thought 20 minutes on this, in view of the obvious danger he was already in. Worse would be:

a) 7 ... N–Q6+ 8 B×N P×B 9 N–N5 and White gains the advantage in all the elements of space, time and material.

b) 7 ... N–N3 8 B×P.4!! N×B 9 B–N5+ P–QB3 10 P×P! wins at once (for if 10 ... P–QR3 11 P–B7+).

   8 B×P.4   P–QR3

Not 8 ... N1–B3? 9 N–N5.

   9 0–0   N1–B3

10 R–K1 N–R4 11 B–K3 (More exact, according to Donner, was *11 B–K5 N×B 12 R×N P–KN3 13 Q–N3*.) 11 ... P–KN3 12 P–Q6! (White has a lead in development, so to exploit that factor he needs open lines.) 12 ... BP×P 13 Q–N3 P–K3 14 B–Q4 B–N2 15 B×KP!

0–0 (White wins after *15 . . . P×B 16 Q×KP+ K–B1 17 Q×QP+ K–B2 18 Q–K6+ K–B1 19 QR–Q1 B×B 20 R×B N4–B3 21 Q–Q6+* and *22 N–Q5.*) 16 B×B N–B4! (*16 . . . K×B 17 B×N* and *18 N–Q5* would be horrible.) 17 Q–R3 K×B 18 B–Q5 Q–N4 19 QR–Q1 and the Dutch grandmaster's positional advantage steadily tells. The sequel was 19 . . . QR–K1 20 R×R R×R 21 P–KN3 Q–K2 (*21 . . . N–B5 22 N–K4*) 22 P–QN4 N–K3 23 N–K4 P–B4 24 Q–B3+ K–R3 25 B×N P×N 26 B–Q5 N–B3 27 B×KP N×B 28 P×N Q×P 29 Q–Q2+ K–N2 30 Q×P R–K2 31 P–KR4 Q–K7 32 Q–Q4+ K–R3 33 Q–B4+ K–N2 34 R–Q2 Q–K8+ 35 K–N2 R–KB2 36 Q–Q4+ K–N1 37 R–B2 Q–K3 38 P–R4 Q–B4 39 R–B5 Q–B6+ 40 K–N1 R–B1 41 R–B7 Black resigned, since he is quite lost after 41 . . . R–B2 42 R–B8+ R–B1 43 R×R+ Q×R (*43 . . . K×R 44 Q–R8+*) 44 Q–Q5+.

8   THE QUEEN'S GAMBIT ACCEPTED

In the Gambit Accepted, Black cedes the centre temporarily in order to get free play for his pieces. He believes that once all his pieces are developed on good squares, counterplay in the centre can follow in due course. White aims to dislocate this plan by a vigorous advance in the centre (involving P–K4 and if possible P–Q5), and by P–QR4, which is aimed at Black's proposed Q-side pawn advances. He must also be prepared to accept an isolated QP; for the general ideas concerning such positions, look again at the relevant section of chapter 1, beginning on page 5.

1 P–Q4   P–Q4
2 P–QB4   P×P
3 N–KB3

It is not advantageous for White to play P–K4 at this very early stage, for his lack of development allows Black to hit back against the centre. Bogoljubow analysed 3 P–K4?! P–QB4! 4 P–Q5 (Safer is *4 N–KB3 P×P 5 Q×P Q×Q=*.) 4 ... P–K3 5 N–KB3 P×P 6 P×P N–KB3 7 B×P B–Q3 8 0–0 0–0 9 N–B3 P–QR3 10 P–QR4 B–N5 11 B–KN5 QN–Q2 12 N–K4 B–K4 when White's passed pawn is blocked, and Black holds the initiative.

After 3 N–KB3 Black can play:
3 ... P–QN4?! – Ericson
3 ... P–QR3 – Alekhine
3 ... N–KB3 – Normal
The latter is by far the most usual.

Ericson's Line
3 ...   P–QN4?!
Because Black cannot safely hold the pawn in this way, the Queen's Gambit is not a true gambit like the King's, but its name is very ancient.

4 P–QR4   P–QB3
5 P–K3   P–K3
Or 5 ... B–N2 6 P×P P×P 7 P–QN3 breaks up the Q-side, with the better game for White.

6 P×P!
Black's play would be justified after 6 P–QN3? P–QR4 7 NP×P P–N5 and the supported passed pawn is valuable; Rokhlin-Ericson, 5th World Corres. Ch 1965–8.

6 ...   P×P
7 P–QN3   P–QR4
8 P×P   P–N5
9 N–K5   N–KB3
10 B–Q3   B–K2
11 0–0 0–0 12 N–Q2 B–N2 13 P–B4 Hybl-Ericson, 5th World Corres. Ch. By contrast with the previous note, White has play against Black's backward QRP as well as a very strong centre and mobile passed QBP.

Alekhine's Variation
3 ...   P–QR3
Black intends to advance on the Q-side in conjunction with ... B–KN5 (not *3 ... B–KN5 4 N–K5!*). The line experienced a brief revival in the 1950s

after Smyslov had played it several times against Botvinnik.

4 P–K4!?(*132*)

This sacrifice is little-known, the normal reply being 4 P–K3 B–N5 5 B×P P–K3 etc., but it offers good chances of attack. Moreover, it is well suited to club play where any opponent who adopts Alekhine's Variation is likely only to know the main line.

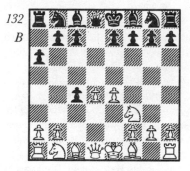

132
B

4 ...   P–QB4

Others:

a) 4 ... N–KB3 5 P–K5 N–Q4 6 B×P (Geller-Nilsson, USSR-Sweden 1954) gives White a space advantage without difficulty.

b) 4 ... B–N5? 5 B×P P–K3 (*5 ... N–KB3?? 6 B×P+ K×B 7 N–K5+*) 6 0–0 N–Q2 7 N–B3 P–QB4 8 P–Q5 P–K4 9 P–QR4 and White has a useful spatial advantage; Borisenko-Flohr, 18th USSR Ch 1950.

c) 4 ... P–QN4, to hold the pawn, is logical. Then we recommend 5 P–QR4 B–N2 6 P×P P×P 7 R×R B×R 8 N–B3 P–QB3 (*8 ... P–N5? 9 Q–R4+*) 9 B–B4 when White has control of the centre and much the better development in return for the sacrificed pawn. Naturally, this does not constitute a won game, but the variation is worth trying, especially in view of its surprise value.

5 B×P   P×P
6 N×P   P–K4

6 ... P–K3 is safer, but leaves White clearly freer.

7 Q–R4+!   Q–Q2

The Soviet master Borisenko also analysed in White's favour:

a) 7 ... B–Q2 8 Q–N3 Q–K2 9 0–0! P×N 10 Q×P N–QB3 11 Q×R+ Q–Q1 12 B×P+.

b) 7 ... N–Q2 8 N–B5 P–KN3 9 B×P+ K×B 10 Q–N3+ K–B3 11 P–KR4.

c) 7 ... P–QN4 8 B×NP+ P×B 9 Q×R Q×N 10 Q×N.

8 B–QN5!   P×B
9 Q×R   Q×N

10 Q×N B–QN5+ 11 N–B3 and now:

a) 11 ... Q×P+ 12 B–K3 Borisenko-Grechkin, corres 1955; Black's pawns are weak so he has no real compensation for the exchange.

b) 11 ... B×N+ 12 P×B Q×QBP+ 13 K–B1 and if 13 ... Q×R 14 Q×B+ K–K2 15 B–R3+ wins the queen.

Normal Q.G.A.

3 ...   N–KB3
4 P–K3(*133*)

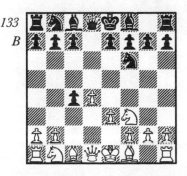

133
B

4 ...   P–K3

Rarely played moves are:

a) 4 ... B–K3 5 N–B3 (or *5 N–R3!?*) 5 ... P–B3 (*5 ... B–Q4 6 N×B Q×N 7*

Q–B2 P–K3 8 B×P B–N5+ 9 K–K2) 6 P–QR4 P–KN3 7 P–K4 B–N2 8 N–K5 and White regains the pawn with a good position – Pachman.

b) 4 . . . P–KN3 5 B×P B–N2 6 0–0 0–0 7 N–B3 with a type of Grünfeld Defence in which Black has been a little hasty in playing . . .. QP×QBP. Symslov used to play 7 . . . KN–Q2!? now (*7 . . . P–B4* is a little better.) but after 8 Q–K2! N–N3 9 B–N3 P–QR4 10 P–QR3! White's KB stays on its good diagonal.

c) 4 . . . B–N5 5 B×P P–K3 6 P–KR3 (If *6 Q–N3* Black plays Larsen's gambit *6 . . . B×N 7 P×B QN–Q2 8 Q×P P–B4*.) 6 . . . B–R4 7 N–B3! P–QR3 (*7 . . . QN–Q2 8 0–0 B–Q3 9 P–K4*) 8 P–KN4 B–N3 9 N–K5 QN–Q2 10 N×B RP×N 11 B–K2 or 11 P–N5. The possession of the two bishops gives White the edge.

    5 B×P   P–B4
    6 0–0   P–QR3(*134*)

This remains the main line of the Q.G.A.

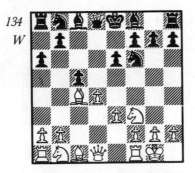

134
W

Black intends to play . . . P–QN4 in conjunction with . . . QN–B3 or, better, . . . QN–Q2. If thwarted in this intention, he can exchange centre pawns and try to exploit the white IQP. A lot depends upon which move White chooses here:

7 Q–K2 – Variation 1

7 N–B3 – Variation 2
7 P–QR4 – Variation 3

Variation 1
    7 Q–K2

Nowadays, this is reckoned to leave Black too free a hand.

    7 . . .   P–QN4

7 . . . P×P is also possible, and may transpose to Variation 3.

    8 B–N3

Usually better than retreating to Q3, for from here the bishop is better placed to support an eventual P–Q5.

    8 . . .   B–N2

8 . . . N–B3 is less constructive; after 9 N–B3 (*9 R–Q1? P–B5 10 B–B2 N–QN5*) Black has to choose between these unappetizing lines:

a) 9 . . . B–K2 10 P×P B×P 11 P–K4! P–N5 12 P–K5!

b) 9 . . . B–N2 10 R–Q1 Q–B2 11 P–Q5 P×P 12 P–K4! P–Q5 (to keep the centre closed) 13 N–Q5 Q–Q1 14 B–KB4 R–B1 15 P–QR4! with excellent attacking chances.

c) 9 . . . P–N5 10 P–Q5!

d) 9 . . . P–B5 10 B–B2 B–N2 11 P–QR4 P–N5 12 N–K4 N–QR4 13 N×N+ P×N 14 P–K4 Q–B2 15 B–K3 B–Q3 16 QR–B1 R–KN1 Gligoric-Troianescu, Sofia 1947. White has control of the centre, but he must proceed with great care since opening the position also exposes his own king.

    9 P–QR4

It is important for White to take some immediate action either in the centre or on the Q-side, lest Black emerge with an important pawn majority on that wing. The main alternative is 9 R–Q1 QN–Q2 10 N–B3 Q–B2 when:

a) 11 P–Q5 P–B5! 12 P×P P×P 13 B–B2 B–Q3 14 P–KR3 0–0 15 P–K4 N–B4 and Black has active positions for his

pieces to support his pawn majority.
b) 11 P–K4 P×P 12 N–Q5!? P×N 13
P×P+ K–Q1 14 N×P with a very
dangerous attack for the sacrificed
piece, since Black's king is very unsafe
in the centre.

9 ...	QN–Q2
10 RP×P	RP×P
11 R×R	Q×R
12 N–R3!	

Again White must continue sharply,
to prevent Black from consolidating his
pawn majority by ... P–B5. Note that
12 Q×P? B×N would merely enable
Black to regain the pawn with the
better game.

12 ...	P–N5
13 N–QN5	Q–R4
14 P–K4!	B–K2!

The slightest slip in this type of
position can lead to disaster in view of
the black king's situation in the centre.
This explains why the Queen's Gambit
Accepted is not recommended to the
ordinary club player: in practical play
under a fast time-limit, Black's
difficulties are very great, if
theoretically soluble. Here he dare not
take the pawn:
a) 14 ... N×P 15 N–N5! N×N 16 B×N
threatening 17 B×P.
b) 14 ... B×P 15 N–N5 B–N3 16 P–Q5!

15 P–K5	N–Q4
16 B–N5	B–R3
17 B×N	B×N

Maderna-Stahlberg, Mar del Plata
1947; Black should emerge from his
troubles with equality.

Variation 2

7 N–B3	P–QN4
8 B–Q3	

Better is 8 B–N3 B–N2 9 Q–K2
QN–Q2 10 R–Q1 transposing to
Variation 1, note to White's 9th move.

8 ...	P×P
9 P×P	B–N2
10 B–N5	B–K2
11 Q–K2	0–0
12 QR–Q1	QN–Q2
13 N–K5	N–Q4!

This is a strong simplifying
manoeuvre, which is carried out before
White can get in the attacking thrust
P–B4. Best now is 14 B×B Q×B 15
N3×N B×N 16 B–K4=.

14 B–B1? is too artificial. The
instructive game Em. Lasker–
Reshevsky, Nottingham 1936, con-
tinued 14 ... N4×N 15 P×N N–B3 16
P–QR4!? Q–Q4! (*16 ... P×P? 17
P–QB4* controlling Q5) 17 N–B3
KR–B1! (assuming the initiative) 18
B–N2 N–K5! 19 R–B1 N–N4! 20 P×P
P×P 21 B×P (*21 N–K1* also loses
eventually, to *21 ... N–R6+ 22 K–R1
N–B5* etc.) 21 ... N×N+ 22 P×N
Q–N4+ White resigned. (*23 K–R1
Q–N5*).

Variation 3

7 P–QR4(*135*)

White rules out the ... P–QN4 ideas,
and in effect elects for an IQP game.

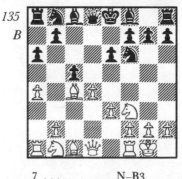

135
B

7 ...	N–B3

Also possible is the immediate 7 ...
P×P 8 P×P N–B3 9 N–B3 B–K2 with
the white queen temporarily tied to the

defence of the QP, although 10 B–K3 and 10 R–K1 both offer White chances of an initiative. The text move is more usual, the reasoning behind it being that K2 is not a specially good square for the white queen to exploit the positive sides of his IQP.

8 Q–K2   P×P

8 . . . B–K2 will transpose after 9 R–Q1 P×P 10 P×P, but in two games of the 1963 world championship match, Botvinnik chose instead 9 P×P B×P 10 P–K4 N–KN5 and the critical line, played in the 8th game, was thought to be 11 P–K5! N–Q5 12 N×N Q×N 13 N–R3! with great complications that should favour White, according to most commentators on the match. Note however that, 8 years later, Petrosian (White this time!) rejects Botvinnik's idea in favour of the usual IQP plan.

9 R–Q1   B–K2
10 P×P   0–0
11 N–B3

The 2nd Botvinnik-Petrosian match game had gone 11 B–KN5 N–Q4 (*11 . . . N–QN5!?*) 12 B×B N3×B 13 N–K5 (*13 R–R3!?*) and now 13 . . . P–QN3 followed by . . . B–N2 would probably have equalized.

11 . . .   N–Q4(*136*)

A critical moment, since Black might also try 11 . . . N–QN5, with the same idea of preventing the P–Q5 thrust; that would probably be no better than the text. After 11 . . . N–QN5 play might go:
a) 12 N–K5 B–Q2! 13 P–Q5 (otherwise . . . B–QB3 with a firm blockade) 13 . . . N3×P 14 N×N N×N 15 B×N P×B 16 R×P B–KN5! 17 Q–B4 Q×R 18 Q×Q QR–Q1 19 Q–N3 R–Q8+ with a drawn endgame.
b) 12 B–KN5 P–R3 (*12 . . . B–Q2 13 P–Q5!* was another Botvinnik-

Petrosian continuation.) 13 B–R4 R–R2 14 N–K5 P–QN3 (Gligoric-Korchnoi, Yugoslavia–USSR 1965) and now 15 N–R2! would have given White a great advantage; but perhaps some improvement for Black is possible at an earlier stage.

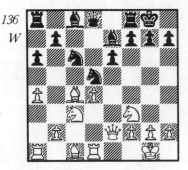

136
W

12 Q–K4!?

We shall follow the game Petrosian–Spassky, Moscow 1971. The text move was a novelty which Petrosian had prepared for use against Fischer in their match earlier in the same year, but the opportunity to play it had not arisen. Formerly 12 B–Q3 was thought best, e.g. 12 . . . N3–N5 13 B–N1 B–Q2 14 N–K5! (improving upon Botvinnik's *14 Q–K4*) 14 . . . B–B3 15 Q–N4! again with White standing better; Gligoric-Suetin, Yugoslavia–USSR 1963.

12 . . .   N3–N5

It might be sounder to play 12 . . . N–B3, when White could of course repeat the position and try the B–Q3 idea instead.

13 N–K5   R–R2

An odd-looking move, but it is not easy to suggest an improvement, since 13 . . . P–QN3 would meet with the startling refutation 14 N–B6!! (threatening to eliminate the valuable defender, the KB) 14 . . . N×N.B3 15

N×N P×N 16 B×QP winning a pawn, since the knight is pinned on to the QR.

14 B–N3	N–KB3
15 Q–R4	P–QN3
16 Q–N3	B–N2

16 . . . K–R1 would have avoided White's next.

| 17 B–R6 | N–K1 |

17 . . . N–R4? 18 Q–N4! would be most unpleasant.

| 18 QR–B1 | K–R1 |
| 19 P–Q5! | |

With many Black pieces in restricted positions, this thematic break-through is strong. 19 . . . P×B 20 P×P leads to a winning attack.

19 . . .	P×P
20 B–K3	R–R1
21 N–B4! (*137*)	

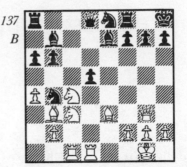

137
B

White regains the pawn and simplifies into an ending where Spassky wriggles hard, but without success. He pondered 40 minutes over his reply, only to find that his planned 21 . . . B–B4 is met by 22 N–R5! with complications favourable to White.

21 . . .	N–Q3
22 B×P	Q–N1
23 N–R5	N–B4
24 Q×Q	QR×Q

25 N×B R×N 26 P R5 B–N4 27 R–N1 P–Q5 28 N–Q5 N–B3 29 B–R4 R–QB1 30 P–B4 N3–K2 31 R.N1–B1! R.B1–QN1 32 P×B N×N 33 B–B6 R×B 34 P×R N.Q4–K6 35 P–N7 N×R 36 R×N P–N3 (*36 . . . N–Q3 37 R×P N×P 38 R–QN4*) 37 P–KN4 N–N2 38 R×P N–K3 39 R–Q7 Black resigned. If 39 . . . N–Q1 40 B–Q5 followed by R–QB7 and R–B8 wins.

9 THE NIMZO-INDIAN DEFENCE

1	P–Q4	N–KB3
2	P–QB4	P–K3
3	N–QB3	B–N5

This defence is particularly suitable as a reply to 1 P–Q4 for players who like a game where the strategic pattern is well-defined and there is much scope for positional manoeuvring. It is called the Nimzo-Indian for a somewhat tortuous reason. All QP games where Black plays 1 . . . N–KB3 and does not contest White's centre by direct means are known as Indian systems (this is not the place to argue why), and the particular form we are discussing here was pioneered and welded into a coherent defensive plan by Aron Nimzowitsch, the Latvian-born Danish grandmaster who was one of the strongest and most original players of the first third of this century.

The immediate effect of Black's third move, pinning the white knight, is that the first player is prevented from advancing P–K4. In the commonest variations, where White plays 4 P–K3 or 4 P–QR3, the bishop is usually exchanged, sooner or later, for the white knight; the effect of this exchange shapes the pattern of the following play.

Black has two possible plans that fit in with these factors. First he can, after giving White doubled QBPs by . . . B×N, fix the position of these pawns by . . . P–QB4, and then build up pressure on them with moves like . . . R–QB1,

. . . N–QR4, . . . B–QR3 and . . . Q–Q2 followed by . . . Q–QR5. This pressure is both offensive, in that it represents a direct attack on the front QBP, and defensive, in that the play against the QP and QBP is intended to divert White from gaining the upper hand in the centre by P–K4. In some modern variations of the Nimzo, Black intensifies the fight for White's K4 square by . . . P–QN3 and . . . B–N2, sometimes followed even by the occupation of that square by . . . N–K5 and . . . P–KB4.

The second possible plan for Black is to play . . . P–Q4 and . . . P–QB4 quite early on; however it is not appropriate in some circumstances where White has forced . . . B×N. For the debit side of the Nimzo is that White almost invariably obtains the two bishops, which become a real advantage if the position is opened up (in conjunction with P–KB3 and P–K4 by White in many cases) for an attack on Black's K-side, or if many simplifications bring about an endgame. In recent years, the West German grandmaster Hübner has often employed a plan of allowing White to attain his ostensible aims of P–K4 and the two bishops, countering with . . . N–QB3, . . . P–Q3 and . . . P–K4, setting up a blockade on black squares and getting play with his knights and QB. However, this rather advanced plan is not to be recommended to the average Nimzo-Indian club player.

We shall now illustrate these general remarks by considering some typical positions, and then proceed to the main lines and illustrative games.

Favourable Positions for White
Gligorić-Benko, Budapest 1948

This position arose by the sequence 1 P-Q4 N KB3 2 P-QB4 P-K3 3 N-QB3 B-N5 4 P-QR3 B×N+ 5 P×B 0-0 6 P-K3 P-Q4 7 P×P P×P (7 . . . *N×P* or 7 . . . *Q×P* enables White to obtain the upper hand in the centre by a speedy *P-K4*.) 8 B-Q3 P-B4 9 N-K2. It has been proved many times in master play that White stands better, for these factors are in his favour: he has the bishop pair, and he cannot be prevented from setting up a powerful central pawn steam-roller by P-B3 and P-K4. For instance, if Black tries to hold back P-K4 by doubling his rooks on the K-file, White can do the same on K2 and K1. The continuation of the Gligoric-Benko game is given in section A, below, note to Black's 5th.

Gheorghiu-Olafsson, Athens 1969

Here (*139*) we have a typical ending, where, with one white pawn blockading two black ones on the Q-side, White's bishop pair has every

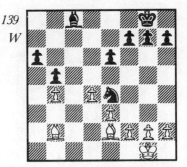

prospect of success. This position arose after 1 P-Q4 N-KB3 2 P-QB4 P-K3 3 N-QB3 B-N5 4 P-K3 0-0 5 B-Q3 P-B4 6 N-B3 P-Q4 7 0-0 QP×P 8 B×BP P-QN3 9 P-QR3! P×P 10 P×B P×N 11 Q×Q R×Q 12 P×P B-N2 13 B-N2 P-QR3 14 B-K2 N-B3 15 KR-Q1 N-K5! 16 R×R+ R×R 17 N-Q4! N×N 18 BP×N P-QN4 (No better is *18 . . . R-QB1 19 B×P B×B 20 R×B P-R3 21 P-B3 N-Q7 22 P-N5!*) 19 R-QB1 R-QB1 20 R×R+ B×R. This variation is particularly bad for Black because he must exchange rooks to prevent White penetrating via QB7, but even with a pair of rooks on the board, and even without a central pawn majority to contend with, such endings are often difficult to draw. In the present case, Gheorghiu-Olafsson concluded 21 P-B3 N-Q3 22 B-B3 B-N2 23 P-N4! P-B4 24 P-R3 K-B2 25 K-B2 B-Q4 26 B-Q3 B-N2 27 B-K1! B-Q4 28 K-N2 B-B5 29 B-QB2 B-Q4 30 P×P! P×P 31 B-KN3 N-B5 32 K-B2 N-Q7 33 B×P B×P 34 B-B8 B-Q4 35 K-K2 N-K5 36 B-K5 P-N4 37 B×P B-B5+ 38 K-B3 N-B3 39 B×N K×B 40 B-B8 B-Q4+ 41 P-K4 B-B2 42 P-K5+ Black resigned.

Favourable Positions for Black
Gligoric-Beni, Dubrovnik 1950 (*140*)

This is a typical case of Black's first

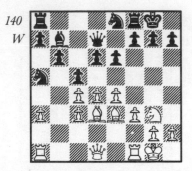

140
W

R.Q1–QB1 N–R5 2 K–Q3 R–Q1 3
P–KB4 N–B5 4 B×N R×B 5 R–B2
N×P White resigned.

A Balanced Position
Spassky-Fischer, 1st match game 1972

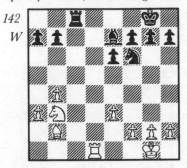

142
W

White has played unambitiously,
missing a chance to play P–K4, and his
white-squared bishop has now been
exchanged. With symmetrical pawns
and each player controlling an open
file, a draw would be the normal result.

1 P–Q4	N–KB3
2 P–QB4	P–K3
3 N–QB3	B–N5

We shall now consider:

4 P–QR3 – Sämisch
4 P–K3 – Rubinstein
4 Q–B2 – Classical
4 B–N5 – Spassky

Other fourth moves are virtually
never seen, but here is a brief resumé:
a) 4 Q–N3 is simply answered by 4 . . .
P–B4 5 P×P N–R3 e.g. 6 P–QR3 B×P 7
N–B3 P–QN3 8 B–N5 B–N2 9 P–K3
B–K2, followed by . . . N–B4 with equal
chances; Bronstein-Boleslavsky, Zürich
1953.
b) Against 4 N–B3, an enterprising plan
is 4 . . . P–QN3 (*4 . . . P–B4* is also
possible.) 5 Q–N3 Q–K2 6 P–KN3
B–N2 7 B–N2 N–B3! threatening both 8
. . . N×P and 8 . . . N–QR4.

plan working well against the 4 P–QR3
(Sämisch) Variation. White's apparently huge centre is immobile, his
QBP subject to attack, and there is little
likelihood of his being able to open up
or simplify the game for the two bishops
to gain in power. A typical
continuation from diagram 140 is 14
P–B4 P–B4 (to prevent White's
beginning an attack by P–B5) 15 Q–K2
P–N3 (safeguarding the pawn
structure) 16 KR–Q1 N–N2 17 R–R2?
Q–R5 18 B–B1 QR–B1 19 Q–B2 Q×Q
20 R×Q B–R3 and Black wins a pawn.
See also Sämisch, Variation 1, below.

Puc-Matanovic, Yugoslav Ch 1969

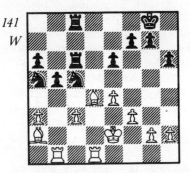

141
W

Despite obtaining two bishops
against two knights, White has a
hopeless position. Black is in complete
control of his QR5 and QB5, and the
white QBP is pitifully weak. White was
rapidly put out of his misery after 1

c) 4 P–KN3 hands over the initiative immediately: 4 . . . P–B4 5 P–Q5 N–K5 6 B–Q2 B×N 7 B×B 0–0 8 B–N2 N×B 9 P×N P–K4 Jauregui-Bolbochan, Mar del Plata 1953.

d) 4 P–B3 has affinities with the Sämisch Variation. Black can however reply 4 . . . P–Q4 (*4 . . . P–B4* is also sound.) 5 P–QR3 (Kieninger's *5 Q–R4+ N–B3 6 P–QR3* is very satisfactorily met by *6 . . . B×N+ 7 P×B B–Q2!*) 5 . . . B–K2 (probably best) 6 P–K4 (Else his fourth move is redundant.) 6 . . . P×KP 7 P×P P–K4! 8 P–Q5 B–QB4 (*8 . . . N–N5!?*) with play on the black squares, e.g. 9 B–N5 P–QR4 10 N–B3 Q–K2 11 B–Q3 QN–Q2 12 Q–K2 P–R3 with a good game for Black; Tal-Keres, Bled 1959.

The Sämisch Variation

    4 P–QR3   B×N+

    5 P×B

White is aiming for the kind of position shown in diagram 138, which he is able to do if Black plays . . . P–Q4 at an inappropriate moment. However, there are much better ways of defending.

    5 . . .   P–B4! (*143*)

The mistaken line is 5 . . . 0–0?! 6 P–K3 P–Q4? 7 P×P P×P 8 B–Q3 P–B4 9 N–K2 reaching diagram 138 on page 123. The Gligoric-Benko game went on 9 . . . P–QN3 10 0–0 B–R3 11 B×B N×B; Black has exchanged a pair of bishops, but White's remaining prelate will prove very strong on the black squares once the position is opened: 12 Q–Q3 P–B5 13. Q–B2 N–N1 14 P–B3 R–K1 15 N–N3 N–B3 16 Q–B2 Q–Q2 17 B–N2 R–K3 18 QR–K1 QR–K1 19 R–K2 P–N3 20 KR–K1 N–QR4 21 P–K4 Q–N2 22 P–K5 N–Q2 23 P–B4 P–B4 24 N–B1 P–QN4 25 N–K3 N–N3

26 P–N4 P×P 27 N×NP R–KB1 28 N–B6+ K–R1 29 Q–N2 N–B3 30 Q–R3 N–Q1 31 B–B1 N–B1 32 K–R1 R–R3 33 P–B5 P×P 34 B–R6 Black resigned. (If 34 . . . R–B2, 35 R–KN1 gives an easily winning attack.)

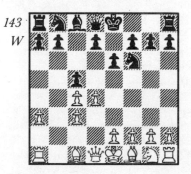

143
W

White may now play:
6 P–K3 – Variation 1
6 P–B3 – Variation 2

Variation 1

    6 P–K3   P–QN3

This marks the beginning of a system worked out by the Belgian grandmaster O'Kelly.

    7 B–Q3   B–N2

    8 P–B3

8 N–K2 B×P 9 R–KN1 B–K5 10 B×B (*10 R×P B–N3* traps the rook.) 10 . . . N×B 11 R×P N×KBP!, and 8 N–B3 N–K5 9 0–0 P–KB4 with good attacking chances, are also not to be feared by Black.

    8 . . .   N–B3

    9 N–K2   0–0

    10 P–K4   N–K1

White was hoping to be allowed 11 B–N5, with a nasty pin.

    11 B–K3

If 11 0–0, Black must be very careful how he replies:

a) 11 . . . P–Q3 would be a loss of tempo, answered by the storming break-through 12 P–B4 P–B4 13 P–Q5, e.g. 13 . . . N–QR4 14 N–N3 P–N3 15 QP×P BP×P 16 N×P N–N2 17 P–B5! P×P 18 B–N5 Q–B2 19 N–B6+ K–R1 20 Q–K1 N–B3 21 R–B3 N–K1 22 Q–R4 Q–N2 23 N–Q5 N–K4 24 R×P! N×B 25 R×R+ Q×R 26 R–KB1 Q–N1 27 R–B7 Q–N3 28 R–B8+ K–N2 29 B–R6+ Q×B 30 R–B7+ K–N3 31 N–K7 mate (a very pretty finish); Hooper-Trott, Ilford 1951.

b) 11 . . . R–B1 is the correct answer, since 12 N–N3? would now leave the white QP en prise. A likely continuation is 12 P–K5 P–KB4 13 P×Pep Q×P 14 B–K3 P×P 15 P×P N–Q3= Balanel-Voiculescu, Bucharest 1953.

11 . . .	P–Q3
12 0–0	N–R4!

Organizing active play against the weak doubled QBP.

13 N–N3	Q–Q2

Reaching diagram 140; Black keeps his central pawn information intact, prepares to meet the advance of White's KBP by . . . P–KB4 himself, and gets ready to increase the pressure on the doubled pawns by . . . Q–R5. Note carefully that, to avoid giving White targets for attack in the centre, Black has held back his two centre pawns for the moment. The advance . . . P–K4, for instance, is not usually to be recommended for Black, despite its attraction of fixing still more firmly White's static, weak, pawn formation. For it enables White to relieve the pressure on his doubled QBPs by himself beginning an attack.

An instructive example . of how White's position can then, after all, spring to life is the game Geller-Broadbent, USSR–Great Britain 1954. Black played 13 . . . R–B1 14 P–Q5

P–K4? (*14 . . . P–KN3!* preparing . . . *P–B4*) and after 15 P–B4 R–QB2 16 P–B5 was faced with the threat of 17 P–B6 N×P 18 B–N5 and N–R5. Broadbent tried 16 . . . P–B3 17 Q–K2 B–B1 (*17 . . . P–KR3* followed by *K–B2* and a king-march to the Q-side was a better chance.) 18 P–KR4 R–N2 19 R–B2 B–Q2 20 P–R4 N–B2 21 N–B1 Q–K1 22 B–B2 P–KR3 23 P–N4 K–B2 24 P–N5! and now White is in a position to break through before Black's king can escape to safety. With the king already at QB1, Black could take twice on his KN4 with equanimity, since the resulting open files would favour him at least as much as White; but alas . . .

Geller-Broadbent continued 24 . . . RP×P 25 P×P K–K2 26 R–KR2 R–R1 27 N–Q2 R–QN1 28 R×R Q×R 29 K–N2 R–KB1 30 R–R1 Q–N1 31 P–N6 (The point of White's play is that the KR-file, and the KR7 outpost in particular, will now be cleverly used to bring about the decisive irruption.) 31 . . . K–Q1 32 N–B1 R–K1 33 R–R7 Q–B1 34 N–N3 Q–K2 35 N–R5 R–N1 36 B–R6 N–K1 37 K–B2 Q–B1 38 B–Q3 B×RP (*38 . . . P×B* would lose to *39 R–B7.*) 39 Q–K3 B–Q8 40 N×NP! N×N 41 B×N Q–K1 (for if *41 . . . R×B 42 Q–R6 R–N1 43 Q×Q+ R×Q 44 P–N7 R–N1 45 R–R8*) 42 B×P+ K–B1 43 Q–R6 B–R5 44 R–K7 Black resigned.

14 P–B4	

This attack is harmless, but other methods also promise nothing to White. For instance, after 14 P–QR4 B–R3 15 Q–K2 P–B4 16 KP×P KP×P 17 B–KB2 P–N3 18 P–Q5 N–B3 Black holds the initiative; Milev-Olafsson, Amsterdam 1954.

14 . . .	P–B4
15 Q–K2	P–N3

16 KR–Q1 N–N2 17 P–K5 (17 R–R2 leads to the loss of a pawn, as we saw on page 124.) 17 ... BP×P 18 BP×P P×P 19 QP×P Q–B3 White is on the defensive, so the opening cannot be considered satisfactory for him (Gligoric–Beni).

Variation 2

6 P–B3(*144*)

6 ...   Q–R4!?

White's last move stated the intention of advancing P–K4 without loss of tempo (P–K3, P–B3, P–K4 in Variation 1), so Black must proceed vigorously. Other ideas are:

a) 6 ... P–QN3? is too slow in view of 7 P–K4.

b) 6 ... P–Q4 is playable here, and after 7 P–K3 (*7 BP×P N×P!* leaves White's position shaky.) 7 ... QP×P! 8 B×P N–B3 the freeing move ... P–K4 will soon follow castling, thanks to the pressure on White's centre pawns.

7 B–Q2

7 Q–Q2 is also possible, as in Cruz-Najdorf, Mar del Plata 1962; for the bishop inside the pawn chain is hardly a danger to Black.

7 ...	P–Q3
8 P–K4	N–B3
9 B–Q3	P–K4
10 N–K2	

We are following the game Del Corral–Larsen, Palma 1969. From what we have already seen, White should (as Larsen recommended later) play 10 P–Q5, with ideas similar to those in Geller–Broadbent. However, as Black has not castled K-side, his position would not be too bad.

| 10 ... | Q–B2 |
| 11 B–N5 | |

Larsen felt that 11 P×BP P×P 12 N–N3 B–K3 13 N–B1 0–0–0 14 B–K2 might have offered White a slight advantage.

| 11 ... | N–Q2 |
| 12 P–Q5 | N–R4 |

13 N–N3 P–KR3 14 B–Q2 P–KN3 15 · P–KR4 P–R4 16 N–B1 P–N3 17 N–K3 B–R3 18 Q–B2 0–0–0 (Black has a very pleasant position now. His king is where Broadbent's ought to have been; he has pressure on the weak QBP and the blocked centre favours the pair of knights.) 19 P–R4?! K–N1 20 0–0–0 (This looks like the safest place for the king. However, a more constructive plan was 20 Q–R2!?, relieving the guard, followed by N–QB2–QR3–N5.) 20 ... QR–KB1 21 P–N4 Q–Q1 22 B–K1 Q–B3 23 Q–K2 Q–K2 24 K–N2 N–KB3 25 B–N3 (*25 B–KB2,* though passive, was preferable.) 25 ... Q–Q2 (Now Black is attacking two weaknesses; his manoeuvring has borne fruit.) 26 R–R1 P×P 27 P×P(*145*)

(Now Black begins to dismantle the opponent's position.) 27 ... N×KP! 28 B×N P–B4 29 P×P P×P 30 B×BP (If the bishop moves, *30 ... P–B5* regains the piece with great advantage–which is why White's 25th move was mistaken.) 30 ... R×B 31 N×R Q×N (Black has given up the exchange, but is certain to win at least the front QBP, after which all his pieces will be strongly

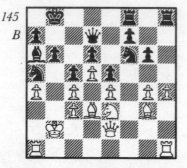

145
B

placed, while he also has a protected passed KP and the safer king. The game continued . . .) 32 KR–KB1 Q–N3 33 R–KN1 N×P+ 34 K–R2 Q–K1 35 Q–QB2 N–K6 36 Q–K4 N–B5 37 Q–B2 B–N2 (winning at least the QP) 38 QR–Q1 N–K6 39 Q–N3 B–R3 40 K–R3 B–B5 41 Q–N1 N×R 42 Q×N Q–B2 43 R–N2 R–N1 44 P–KR5 R–N4 45 P–R6 Q–R2 46 P–R5 P–N4 47 Q–B3 R–B4 48 Q–K4 Q×P! 49 K–N2 (*49 Q×R? Q–B8+ 50 R–QN2 Q–QR8+*) 49 . . . R–B8 50 B–K1 R–B5 51 R–N8+ K–N2 52 Q–N2 R–B2 53 B–Q2 (*53 Q–N4 R–B7+!*) 53 . . . Q–R4 54 R–N7 K–R3 55 R–N6 and, without waiting for his opponent's reply (55 . . . Q–Q8! 56 R×P+ K×P soon mating), White resigned.

The Rubinstein Variation

4 P–K3(*146*)

This is less committal than the Sämisch. White aims for more open positions in which his doubled QBP can be dissolved as soon as it arises and the two bishops will become effective. Black should fight against simplifications leading to endings of the diagram 146 type, and also against the advance P–K4. He can concentrate his pieces against the white QP, and also consider the advance . . . P–K4–5 (backed by . . . R–K1 and . . . Q–K2), for if the

white QB can be locked inside a pawn chain QB3+Q4+K3, then it is almost useless; if White plays QP×KP, he generally isolates his QBP thereby and allows Black's pieces fair play. In most cases, Black's counterplay is on the white squares, e.g. along the . . . QR1 / . . . KR8 diagonal with his QB, and on the Q-side at QB5, Q5 and QN6 with his knights–of which diagram 141 is an extremely successful example.

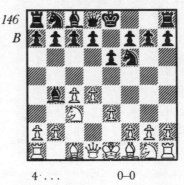

146
B

4 . . .   0–0

Others in brief:

a) 4 . . . P–B4 will usually transpose to B1.

b) 4 . . . P–Q4 5 P–QR3 B×N+ 6 P×B 0–0 7 P×P transposes to the Sämisch, note to Black's 5th move–a good line for White.

c) 4 . . . P–QN3 is sometimes played, in the hope of 5 B–Q3 B–N2 6 N–B3 N–K5 7 0–0 P–KB4 with counterchances. However, 5 KN–K2 is stronger.

d) The aforementioned Hübner Variation, 4 . . . B×N+!? 5 P×B P–QN3 6 B–Q3 B–N2 7 P–B3 P–Q3 8 N–K2 N–B3 9 P–K4 P–K4, does not really equalize after 10 0–0 Q–K2 11 P–B4 0–0–0 12 P–Q5 N–QR4 13 P×P P×P 14 B–N5!; Ivkov–Lombard, European Team Ch, Bath 1973.

5 B–Q3

Rubinstein's original idea was 5 KN–K2 (ready to capture on QB3 with the knight), but Black has nothing to fear if he plays carefully: 5 . . . P–Q4 6 P–QR3 B–K2 7 P×P N×P 8 N×N P×N 9 N–B4 P–QB3 10 B–Q3 N–Q2 11 0–0 P–QR4= D. Byrne-Reshevsky, New York 1954–5.

5 . . .   P–Q4

It is a good general rule in the 4 P–K3 system, that you should delay this move until White plays 5 B–Q3.

Black can also play 5 . . . P–QN3!? 6 N–B3 (*6 KN–K2 B–N2 7 0–0 P–Q4*) 6 . . . B–N2 7 0–0 P–B4 with reasonable prospects, e.g.:

a) 8 N QR4!? (once thought strong, because of the threat to Black's KB) 8 . . . P×P 9 P×P R–K1! 10 B–N5 P–KR3 11 B–R4 B×N 12 Q×B N–B3 Visier-Portisch, Las Palmas 1972.

b) 8 B–Q2 B5×N 9 B×B N–K5.

c) 8 P–QR3 B5×N 9 P×B B–K5 10 B–K2 N–B3 11 N–Q2 B–N3 12 N–N3 P–Q3 and Black can organize a rigorous blockade: Ivkov-Keene, European Team Ch, Bath 1973.

In the immediate post-war years and 1950s, Black tended to play the Nimzo in rather stereotyped fashion, reeling off instantaneously the first seven moves leading to the 'normal position'. Recent improvements in White's play in the old main lines, however, forced Black to look for more original treatments of the defence. The foregoing line is typical of modern thought-trends in the opening.

6 N–B3

Other plans for White:

a) 6 P×P P×P 7 P–QR3 when:

a1) 7 . . . B×N+? 8 P×B P–B4 9 N–K2 would bring us again to our old friend, diagram 138.

a2) Black should instead reply 7 . . . B–Q3! (P–B5 is no longer available to

White.) with a good game since his QB, in contrast to White's, is not blocked in by its own pawns.

b) 6 P–QR3 B×N+ 7 P×B P×P! (not 7 . . . 0–0? *8 N–K2* en route for diagram 138) 8 B×P P–B4 and now:

b1) 9 N–B3 Q–B2! 10 B K2 (*10 B–Q3? P×P 11 BP×P Q–B6+*) 10 . . . N–B3 11 0–0 R–Q1 and Black has an excellent position; Kottnauer-Szabo, Venice 1949.

b2) 9 N–K2 Q–B2 10 B–Q3 R–Q1 11 0–0 N–B3 12 Q–B2 P–K4 13 B–N2 B–K3! Donner-O'Kelly, Beverwijk 1952; if 14 P–K4? P–B5 wins a piece. 14 N–N3 is best.

c) 6 N–K2 P–B4 7 BP×P BP×P! (*7 . . . KP×P 8 P–QR3!* etc.) 8 P×P N×P is good for Black: White's IQP is weak in this position. It is weak because the advantage of an isolated pawn at Q4 is its control of the squares QB5 and K5, which become natural outposts for the pieces (particularly the knights) of the side with the IQP; but here White has already developed his knight at K2, whence, in contrast to KB3, it will not have an easy journey to K5. On the other hand, playing 6 N–B3, White gives up all attempts to secure the attacking formation of diagram 138.

6 . . .   P–B4
7 0–0(*147*)

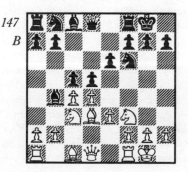

147
B

Black now plays:

7 . . . *N–B3* – Variation 1
7 . . . *QN–Q2* – Variation 2
7 . . . *QP×P* – Variation 3

Variation 1

7 . . .   N–B3
8 P–QR3

Although not as 'normal' as it once was, this position still quite often arises in practice.

8 . . .   B×N

The most consistent move. Others give White an edge:

a) 8 . . . QP×P 9 B×P (*9 P×B P×QP!*) 9 . . . B–R4 10 Q–Q3! (Since *10 B–Q3* allows *10 . . . P×P 11 P×P B–N3* with approximate equality.) 10 . . . P–QR3 (*10 . . . B–N3 11 R–Q1!*–Taimanov) 11 P×P! Q×Q 12 B×Q B×N 13 P×B N–Q2 14 P–QR4 N×P 15 B–B2 Alatortsev-Levenfish, match 1938.

b) 8 . . . BP×P 9 KP×P P×P 10 B×P B–K2 leads to a typical conflict between White's freer development and Black's pressure on the isolated QP. Here, however, the move 8 P–QR3 is a strengthening of White's position, since it enables the KB to be transferred via QR2 to QN1, where it helps in setting up a battery against KR7. See the discussion of diagram 7 in the first chapter for a further elaboration of the ideas in this type of position; an example of play is 11 R–K1 P–QN3 12 B–B4 B–N2 13 B–R2 R–B1 14 Q–Q3 Q–Q2 15 QR–Q1 N–Q4 16 B–N1! P–N3 17 B–R6 with a strong attack for White, as in Najdorf-Reshevsky, match 1953.

c) 8 . . . B–R4 (as in Spassky-Fischer) is perhaps due for a revival. One critical line is 9 BP×P (*9 P–R3!?*) 9 . . . KP×P 10 P×P B×N (Otherwise, White retains his extra pawn by P–QN4.) 11 P×B

B–N5! Panno-Averbakh, Argentina–USSR 1954.

9 P×B   QP×P

An inferior line is 9 . . . P–QN3 10 BP×P KP×P when:

a) 11 N–K5! gives White the advantage, since:

a1) 11 . . . N×N 12 P×N gives him a dangerous pawn-roller on the K-wing, and

a2) 11 . . . Q–B2 12 P–KB4 N–K2 13 P–B5 (Stahlberg-Sämisch, Dresden 1936) has similar dangers.

b) 11 N–Q2 B–K3 12 B–N2 P–B5 gives Black a Q-side majority, which will be useful in an ending. The game Euwe-Averbakh, Zürich 1953, continued 13 B–B2 P–QN4 14 P–B3 P–QR4 15 R–K1 (Pachman suggested *15 P–K4! P×P 16 N×KP!*) 15 . . . Q–N3 16 N–B1 P–N5 17 Q–Q2 P–N6 18 B–N1 P–R5 19 P–K4 N–K2 20 N–N3 K–R1 21 R–K2 N3–N1 22 N–R5 P–B4 23 Q–N5 R–B2 24 P×BP B×P 25 B×B N×B 26 QR–K1 Q–Q1 27 Q×Q R×Q 28 R–K8? (*28 B–B1* was a better chance.) 28 . . . R×R 29 R×R R–K2 30 R×R N1×R 31 K–B2 K–N1 32 P–N4 N–Q3 33 K–K3 N–N4 34 P–B4 N–B1 35 P–B5 N1–Q3 36 N–B4 N×RP! 37 B×N N–N4 38 B–B1 N×BP 39 N–K2 N–N8! White resigned. Although White's play was not above criticism, Black's Q-side majority was clearly always dangerous.

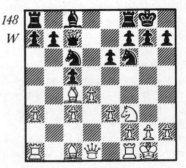

148
W

10 B×P   Q–B2(*148*)

This type of position occurs often in the Nimzo-Indian, and is important for an understanding of the defence; the reader should refer back to the chapter introduction at this point. White has a majority of pawns in the centre, which he must imbue with mobility so that his other potential plus (the bishop pair) may come to its full value. Black must, as we already observed, seek to prevent this by advancing his KP and keeping up piece pressure on the white centre.

11 B–Q3

The most direct method, and probably the best, of trying to force through P–K4. To players who wish to avoid these well-known lines, we can recommend 11 B–R2!?, after which play usually goes 11 . . . P–K4 12 P–R3! P–K5 13 N–R2 B–B4 (*13 . . . P×P!?* is critical.) 14 N–N4! N×N (or *14 . . . B×N 15 P×B P–KR3 16 P–QR4*) 15 P×N e.g. 15 . . . B–N3 16 Q–K2 N–R4 17 P–R4 P–N3 18 P×P! P×P 19 B–Q5! QR–Q1 20 P–QB4 and White controls the white squares and has a Q-side initiative; Yudovich-Strand, corres 1959.

11 . . .   P–K4

To prevent 12 P–K4 which 11 . . . P–QN3?, for instance, would permit.

12 Q–B2   R–K1

This currently considered strongest, although the alternatives 12 . . . Q–K2 and 12 . . . R–Q1 may also give Black adequate chances. An example of how deeply masters have studied this line is the game Gligorić-Janosević, Yugoslav Ch 1957, which continued 12 . . . R–Q1 13 R–K1 B–N5 14 N×P N×N 15 P×N Q×P 16 P–B3 B–K3 17 R–N1 P–B5 18 B–B1 N–Q4 19 B–Q2 Q–B2 20 P–K4! N–K2 21 B–K3 N–B3 (All this had been thought equal, after a game

Pachman-Rabar, Göteborg 1955.) 22 P–B4 P–B3 23 Q–R2! (Gligoric gains a tempo by diverting the knight.) 23 . . . N–R4 24 Q–KB2 N–N6 25 P–B5! B–B2 26 B–B4! Q–B4 27 P–K5! (offering a pawn for a dangerous attack) and White went on to win.

13 P–K4

Or 13 N×P N×N 14 P×N Q×P when 15 P–K4? (safer *15 P–B3 B–Q2 16. P–QR4 B–B3=*) would allow Black K-side chances after 15 . . . P–B5 16 B×P N–N5 17 P–N3 Q–KR4 etc.

13 . . .   P–B5!

After 13 . . . KP×P 14 P×P B–N5 15 Q×P KN×P 16 B×N R×B 17 N–N5 there are complications which may favour White; Bronstein-Euwe, Zürich 1953.

14 B×P   P×P

15 P×P (If *15 R–K1*, Black has *15 . . . B–N5!*–Pachman.) 15 . . . N–QR4! (Not *15 . . . R×P 16 B–Q3 R–K2 17 P–Q5!*) 16 B–Q3 Q×Q 17 B×Q N×P 18 KR–K1 B–B4 19 B–B4 N–Q3 20 B–R4 P–QN4 21 B×N P×B The simplifications have brought about a level position; Donner-Larsen, match 1958.

Variation 2

7 . . .   QN–Q2(*149*)

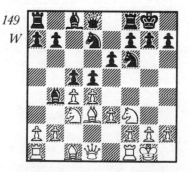

149
W

This is quite a reasonable alternative

to 7 ... N–B3. Black's object is to
accentuate the pressure on the QB-file,
and to allow an open line for the
fianchettod QB. The drawbacks are
that there is not the same pressure on
the white QP, and that ... N–QR4, the
thematic white-square manoeuvre, is
not possible.

8 P–QR3

There are two main alternatives:
a) 8 Q–K2 P–QR3 9 P–QR3 B–R4 10
R–Q1 QP×P 11 B×BP P–QN4 =
Szabo–Unzicker, Hastings 1954–5.
b) 8 BP×P KP×P 9 B–Q2 (*9 Q–N3
N–N3!* but first *9 P–QR3* and only after
9 ... B–R4 then *10 B–Q2*, as Euwe
suggests, may be more precise.) 9 ...
R–K1 10 P–QR3 B×N 11 B×B P–B5 12
B–K2 N–K5 13 B–K1 Bronstein-
Gligorić, Belgrade 1954; at any rate,
White has the two bishops, but careful
defence should keep the balance.

8 ...   QP×P

Or 8 ... B×N 9 P×B QP×P 10
B×BP Q–B2 11 Q–K2 P–K4 12 B–N2
P–K5 13 N–Q2 N–N3 14 B–N3 R–K1
15 P–R3 with a complicated game,
probably favouring White; Ragozin-
Szabo, Budapest 1949.

9 B×P

9 P×B leads to equality after 9 ...
P×QP! 10 B×P P×N 11 P×P Q–B2.

9 ...   P×P

10 Q×P

White gets nowhere with 10 P×P
B×N 11 P×B Q–B2 12 Q–K2 P–QN3
13 B–Q2 B–N2 14 B–Q3 N–Q4
Holmov-Averbakh, Dresden 1956.

10 ...   B–K2

Gligoric suggested 10 ... B–R4.

11 R–Q1   P–QN3
12 Q–B4   B–N2

13 P–K4 Q–B1 14 B–R2 N–B4 15 P–K5
White has a distinct central initiative;
Portisch-Unzicker, Tel Aviv 1964.

Variation 3

7 ...   QP×P
8 B×BP(*150*)

Black hopes that he can thus get
pressure against the white QP, but by
and large this idea does not work out
well. We follow the game Donner-
Mazzoni, The Hague 1966.

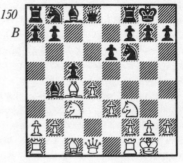

150
B

8 ...   QN–Q2

For 8 ... P–QN3 9 P–QR3! see the
comments to diagram 139, on page 123.
8 ... N–B3 9 B–Q3 P×P 10 P×P B–K2
is discussed in chapter one (diagram
7!). Finally, if 8 ... P×P 9 P×P P–QN3
Gligoric-Unzicker, Milan 1975, continued in White's favour 10 B–KN5
B–N2 11 R–K1 QN–Q2 12 B–Q3
B.N5×N (*12 ... R–B1!* was essential.)
13 P×B Q–B2 14 P–B4 Q–Q3? 15
N–K5!

9 Q–K2   P–QR3
10 P–QR3   B–R4

Possibly better is 10 ... P×P!? 11
P×P B–K2 with a slightly unusual IQP
position (compare diagram 7), in that
Black's QN is on Q2 and White's queen
is on K2: i.e. more like a Queen's
Gambit Accepted than a Nimzo-
Indian.

11 B–Q3!   P–QN4
12 N–K4   B–N3

13 P×P N×P 14 N×N.B5 B×N 15 P–K4
(White has a clear advantage, as his
pawn cannot be prevented from

reaching K5, driving away Black's defensive knight, after which all White's pieces can take up aggressive posts.) 15 . . . B–K2 16 P–K5 N–Q4 (Otherwise *17 Q–K4* will threaten the QR as well as checkmate.) 17 Q–K4 P–N3 18 B–R6 R–K1 19 P–KR4! B–N2 20 QR–Q1 Q–N3 (Guarding the QB, and so preparing to advance the knight with a discovered attack from the bishop on to the white queen. However, White's attack is already so strong that he can afford to ignore this.) 21 N–N5! (Threatening *22 N×RP! K×N 23 P–R5* and *24 P×P+* with certain victory.) 21 . . . B×N 22 B×B N–B6 23 Q–KB4 N×R 24 R×N QR–Q1! (Black offers back the exchange he has won, for after *25 B×R R×B* he should escape with a draw. He also sets a trap.)

25 R–QB1!!

Coolly and precisely played. 25 Q–B6 would be met by 25 . . . Q–B3, with a threat of mate on KN7, and if:
a) 26 B–KB1? R×R 27 B–R6 Q×P mate;
b) 26 P–B3 Q–B4+ 27 K–R2 Q–KB1 defends.

25 . . .   R–QB1

Forced, since there is no direct way of defending his KN2, now that the queen is denied squares on the QB-file.

26 R×R   R×R
27 Q–B6   R–B8+

A final fling: 28 B×R? Q–B3 draws. The immediate 27 . . . Q–B3 would be simply met by 28 B–KB1, for compared with note a to White's 25th move, the black rook is not able to come to the 8th rank.

28 K–R2   Q–B3
29 Q–Q8+   K–N2
30 B–B6+

Black resigned, as after 30 . . . K–KR3 31 Q–B8+ K–R4 32 B–K2+ there is no way out.

Classical Variation

4 Q–B2(*151*)

This, once popular, move does not receive much attention nowadays. White re-establishes control of his K4 square, and makes it possible to recapture at QB3 with his queen, avoiding the doubled pawn characteristic of other variations. On the other hand, he unguards his QP, allowing Black to obtain rapid counterplay based on . . . P–B4 or . . . N–B3. There is also a danger, as with all openings involving early queen moves, that White will fall behind on minor piece development.

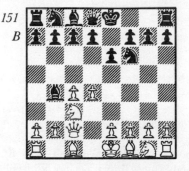

151
B

4 . . .   P–B4

The most logical and vigorous reply. Also possible are:
a) 4 . . . P–Q4 5 P×P (or *5 P–QR3 B×N+ 6 Q×B Q–K1!?* Dueball-Keene, Dortmund 1973) 5 . . . P×P 6 B–N5 with a complicated position, in which Black might try Pachman's idea 6 . . . P–B4 7 P×P P–KR3.
b) 4 . . . N–B3 5 N–B3 P–Q3 6 P–QR3 B×N+ 7 Q×B P–QR4 (preventing *P–QN4*) 8 P–QN3 (*8 B–N5!? P–R3 9 B–R4!*–Pachman) 8 . . . 0–0 9 B–N2 R–K1! (Black still wants to advance . . . *P–K4*) 10 R–Q1 Q–K2 11 P–Q5 N–N1 12 P×P P×P 13 P–N3 P–QN3 14 B–N2 B–N2 15 0–0 QN–Q2 16 N–K1 B×B 17

N×B N–B4 18 P–B3 with a slight edge to White; Donner-Reshevsky, Amsterdam 1950.

    5 P×P

5 P–K3 0–0 6 N–B3 P–QN3 gives Black no difficulties.

    5 ...   0–0!

This waiting move, recommended by Pirc, is best. Black can also consider:

a) 5 ... B×P 6 N–B3 P–Q4! and White's extra tempo is insignificant.

b) 5 ... N–R3 6 P–QR3 Q–R4! 7 B–Q2 N×P with sharp play, but not here 6 ... B×N because after 7 Q×B N×P 8 P–B3! P–Q3 9 P–K4 White has two bishops and a solid pawn centre.

    6 P–QR3

The latest attempt to make something of the opening for White is 6 B–B4 (or *6 B–K3 P–QN3! 7 P×P P–Q4!*–Bronstein) when:

a) 6 ... N–R3 7 B–Q6! R–K1 8 P–QR3 B×BP 9 B×B N×B 10 P–QN4 N–R3 11 P–K3 and White has the freer game–analysis by Pachman.

b) 6 ... B×P 7 N–B3 P–QN3 (or first 7 ... *N–B3*) 8 P–K3 B–N2 9 B–Q3 B–K2 and White's threats against KR7 only amount to slight pressure; Wade-Csom, European Team Ch, Bath 1973.

c) 6 ... Q–R4!? when Pachman's suggestion 7 P–K3 B×N+ 8 Q×B Q×Q+ 9 P×Q N–K5 10 P–B3 (hoping for *10 ... N×P.6? 11 P–QR4!* or *10 ... N×P.4? 11 B–Q6*) only leads to weak white pawns after 9 ... N–R3! 10 P–B3!? N–K1 11 B–Q6 N×B 12 P×N P–QN3 followed by ... B–N2 and ... KR–B1.

    6 ...   B×BP

7 N–B3 N–B3 8 P–QN4 (White's only reasonable plan is to steal space on the Q-side.) 8 ... B–K2 9 P–K3 P–QN3 10 B–N2 B–N2 11 B–Q3 R–B1 12 0–0

P–KR3 13 KR–Q1 P–QR4!(*152*)

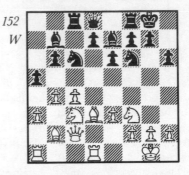

152
W

This advance is the positional refutation of White's system. Black is going to tie up the white pawns on the Q-side. For the results of the pawn formation QN5+QB4, now coming into existence, are very bad for White. Black gets the important central square QB4 at his disposal, the white QBP becomes weak, and it becomes very difficult for White to formulate a useful plan.

In a game Najdorf-Reshevsky, match 1952, there now followed 14 P–N5 N–N1 15 P–K4 Q–B2 16 Q–K2 P–Q3 17 N–QR4 QN–Q2 18 P–R3? B×P 19 B×B Q×BP winning a pawn, since White must relinquish either his QN or his KB. 18 QR–B1 would have been better, but with possibilities like 18 ... N–N5, followed by ... N–K4, in store, the chances are on Black's side.

Spassky's Variation

    4 B–N5(*153*)

A sharp move, favoured by Spassky and analysed a long time ago by his former trainer, Zak–and also by the English master Golombek! The variation is subject to fluctuations of fashion; in 1973 and 1974 it was seen quite often.

153
B

4 ...	P–KR3
5 B–R4	P–B4
6 P–Q5	P–QN4!

This enterprising pawn sacrifice makes vain White's hopes of an opening advantage. Also satisfactory for Black is the quieter line 6 ... P–Q3 7 P–K3 B×N+ 8 P×B P–K4 as seen in Williams-Karpov, Nice 1974.

7 QP×P

Or 7 P–K4?! KP×P 8 BP×P P–N4 9 P–K5 P×B! 10 P×N Q×P 11 B×P B–R3! with complications (Perez-Pachman, Havana 1965); White's only chance here is 12 Q–K2+ K–B1 13 R–B1!?–Botterill.

7 ...	BP×P
8 P×P	P–Q4
9 P–K3	0–0
10 B–Q3	

An improvement, this, upon 10 N–B3 Q–R4 11 B×N R×B 12 Q–Q2 P–QR3 13 P×P N–B3! of Spassky-Tal, Tallin 1973, when Black won a famous victory.

10 ...	P–Q5
11 P×P	P×P
12 P–QR3	B–R4

13 P–QN4 P×N 14 P×B B–N2 15 N–B3 Q×P 16 0–0 QN–Q2 17 Q–K2 B×N!= Spassky-Unzicker, European Team Ch, Bath 1973. The sharp play has been balanced, and a draw soon resulted.

1 P–Q4	N–KB3
2 P–QB4	P–K3
3 N–KB3	P–QN3

This is the sister opening to the Nimzo-Indian Defence 3 N–QB3 B–N5, since it arises from White's attempt at move three to avoid that defence, and Black's preference for a position where his strategical aims, in particular control of his K5 square, are akin to those in the Nimzo. For Black could, after 3 N–KB3, transpose into the Queen's Gambit Declined (page 98 by 3 . . . P–Q4; or into the Benoni (page 156) by 3 . . . P–B4; or into the Bogoljubow Variation (page 140) by 3 . . . B–N5+, which last we recommend as the safest and soundest way of taking the sting from 3 N–KB3.

We shall deal with 3 N–KB3 from two points of view: firstly, White's, when he decides to avoid the Nimzo-Indian. We shall recommend a line of play which avoids the drawish main variations of the Queen's Indian that commence with 4 P–KN3.

Secondly, we shall deal with 3 N–KB3 from Black's point of view, as that of a player foiled in his attempt to play the Nimzo-Indian. In this case, we recommend Bogoljubow's 3 . . . B–N5+ as a safe equalizing method which preserves the characteristics of the Nimzo-Indian.

| 4 P–K3 | B–N2 |
| 5 B–Q3(154) | |

154
B

The beginning of the recommended method. White is going to castle K-side and then, in most variations, fianchetto his QB and thus have his two bishops raking adjacent diagonals in the direction of the black king, when Black castles. How White follows up depends upon how Black deploys his centre pawns.

If Black holds back his centre pawns and sets up a restricted centre with pawns at Q3 and K3, White will, after completing his development, advance in the centre himself by P–K4, and

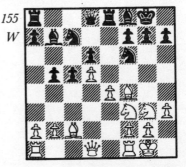

155
W

perhaps P–Q5 or N–K1 and P–KB4. Diagram 155 (from the game Mattison-Colle, Karsbad 1929) illustrates the resulting type of position, in which White is securely entrenched in the centre and has fine attacking prospects.

Another dubious plan for Black is to play his KN to K5, with the intention of supporting it by . . . P–KB4 and by his fianchettoed QB. The trouble with this is that the knight cannot be maintained at its advance post, and after the inevitable exchange of minor pieces, White can exploit the weaknesses on the K-file that result from Black's impetuosity.

Masters nowadays prefer to play for equality in a restrained fashion, developing their KB at K2 in conjunction with the advance . . . P–Q4 or . . . P–QB4 (or in some cases both) and then exchanging pawns. Black then hopes that White's 'hanging pawns' at QB4 and Q4 will prove weak in the sequel. An illustration of the type of position which may result is provided by diagram 156 (from Barcza-Golombek, Saltsjöbaden 1952).

156
B

If White plays passively here, Black can develop heavy pressure on the hanging pawns, e.g. by . . . N–QR4 and . . . B–R3. On the other hand, if White is allowed time to organize his attack,

he can open up the position and give his bishops splendid opportunities by the advance P–Q5. Golombek actually played 1 . . . Q–B2 but after 2 P–Q5 P×P 3 N×P Q–N1 4 Q–Q2 N×N 5 P×N N–N5 6 B–K4 his king was exposed to the raking fire of the bishops. Diagram 157 (from Shauwecker-Parma, Bath 1973) shows, on the other hand, a favourable position for Black. White has exchanged too many pieces and allowed his QBP and KP to become serious liabilities.

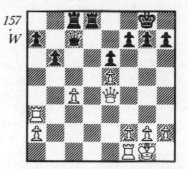

157
W

We are now in a position to consider specific variations based on these possible plans. From diagram 154:

5 . . . B–N5+ – Variation 1
5 . . . N–K5? – Variation 2
5 . . . P–B4 – Variation 3
5 . . . B–K2 – Variation 4

5 . . . P–Q4 6 0–0 will transpose to either C or D.

Variation 1

    5 . . .   B–N5+
    6 QN–Q2!

White does not play 6 N–B3, since Black would obviously like this transposition to the Nimzo-Indian, nor 6 B–Q2, when White's attacking prospects are much diminished by the exchange of bishops. After the text move, . . . B×N+ would give White the two bishops and these can be used for attacking purposes.

6 ...   P–Q3

Thus Black commits himself to the 'small-centre' plan. 6 ... 0–0 7 0–0 P–Q4 is possible, but in that case Black has to meet 8 P–QR3 (He hoped for *8 P–QN3 QN–Q2 9 B–N2 N–K5!=*) by 8 ... B–K2 transposing to line D, but with White having the extra move P–QR3.

7 0–0   QN–Q2
8 P–K4   B×N

9 N×B P–K4 10 P–Q5 N–B4 11 B–B2 P–QR4 12 P–B4 (This is correct strategy, opening up the position for the two bishops.) 12 ... P×P 13 R×P 0–0 14 P–QN3 N4–Q2? (He had to try *14 ... N3–Q2 15 B–N2 N–K4* followed by *... P–KB3* with a 'hedgehog' position. Now he loses control of the ... QR1 / ... KR8 diagonal.) 15 B–N2 N–K4 16 N–B3! R–K1 17 N–Q4 B–B1 (To prevent *18 N–B5*, but allowing something even worse.) 18 N–B6 N×N 19 P×N Q–K2 20 Q–B3 K–R1 21 R×N Black resigned: Barden-Minty, Cheltenham 1953. Observe the deadly part played in this game by the black-squared bishop, freed from the opposition of the corresponding enemy piece.

Variation 2

5 ...   N–K5?
6 0–0   P–KB4

This is the only consistent move, in view of:
a) 6 ... B–Q3 7 QN–Q2 P–KB4 8 Q–B2! Fridstein-Volkevich, Moscow 1968.
b) 6 ... B–K2 7 QN–Q2 N×N 8 B×N P–QB4 9 B–B3 B–KB3 10 P–K4 N–R3 11 P–K5 Najdorf-Wotulo, Manila 1973.

7 KN–Q2!

Another good plan is 7 QN–Q2 B–K2 8 Q–B2 P–Q4 9 N–K5! as in Kottnauer-Benkner, Lucerne 1952–3.

7 ...   B–K2

Wild queen moves have also been tried:
a) 7 ... Q–R5 8 N–QB3 B–Q3 9 P–B4 N×N 10 P×N 0–0 11 Q–K2 N–B3 12 R–N1 R–B3 13 P–B5! B–KB1 14 P–K4 with decisive opening of the centre; Ilivitsky-Bivshev, 20th USSR Ch 1952.
b) 7 ... Q–N4 8 P–B4 Q–N3 9 N×N B×N 10 B×B P×B 11 N–B3 B–N5 12 N–N5 K–Q1 13 P–QR3! B–K2 14 Q–B2 and Black's development is difficult; Ketslakh-Bivshev, Leningrad 1962.

8 N–QB3   N×N.B6
9 P×N   0–0

10 P–K4 P–B4 (If *10 ... P×P 11 N×P* threatening *Q–R5* and an attack.) 11 KP×P! KP×P 12 P–Q5! P–Q3 13 Q–B2 B–B1 14 N–B3 N–R3 15 R–K1! N–B2 16 B–B4 Black is permanently weak on K3; Simagin-Goldenov, 20th USSR Ch 1952.

Variation 3

5 ...   P–B4(*158*)

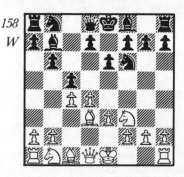

6 0–0   B–K2

6 ... P×P 7 P×P B–K2 8 QN–Q2 0–0 9 P–QN3 P–Q4 10 B–N2 N–B3 11

R–B1 R–B1 12 Q–K2 was played in Averkin-Belyavsky, 41st USSR Ch 1973; White stood rather better. White can also consider developing his QN at Q2 in the text variation.

 7 N–B3   P×P

Black has to play with great precision, in view of:

a) 7 . . . 0–0 8 P–Q5! P×P 9 P×P P–Q3 (or *9 . . . N×P 10 N×N B×N 11 B×P+ K×B 12 Q×B N–B3 13 R–Q1*) 10 P–K4 P–QR4 11 P–QR4 QN–Q2 12 N–Q2! with a central breakthrough looming; Moiseyev-Ilivitsky, 20th USSR Ch 1952.

b) 7 . . . P–Q4 8 BP×P! KP×P 9 B–N5+ (or *9 Q–R4+*) 9 . . . K–B1 (relatively best) 10 P–QN3 P–QR3 11 B–K2 N–B3 12 B–N2 R–QB1 13 N–K5! (Kotov-Botvinnik, 13th USSR Ch 1944); Black cannot get his KR into play, and he has problems with his QP.

 8 P×P   P–Q4

8 . . . 0–0 may also be possible, depending upon how you feel about the complications after 9 P–Q5!? P–KR3 (*9 . . . B–N5? 10 N–K4!*) 10 N–Q4 B–B4. The difference between the text move and the previous note is that Black can now meet 9 P×P by 9 . . . N×P! (since White has no KP to advance) and if 10 B–N5+ B–B3! 11 Q–R4 Q–Q2!= (12 N–K5? N×N).

 9 P–QN3   0–0
 10 B–N2   N–B3
 11 Q–K2   R–B1

It is important for Black to avoid 11 . . . P×P 12 P×P R–B1 13 KR–Q1 R–K1 14 QR–B1, reaching diagram 156. 14 . . . N–QN5 would then be rather better than Golombek's move, but after 15 B–N1 B×N 16 P×B Q–Q3 17 N–K4 Q–B5 18 K–R1 (Bisquier-McCormick, Omaha 1949) White's two bishops are more significant than

his disrupted K-side (compare the next illustrative game).

 12 QR–B1   R–K1

12 . . . N–QN5 13 B–N1 P×P 14 P×P B–R3 15 N–K4! gives White a strong attack: 15 . . . N5–Q4 16 N×N+ N×N 17 N–K5 B–N2 18 KR–Q1 R–K1 19 R–B3! B–N2 20 B–B2 Q–B2 21 R–KR3! followed by P–Q5; Langeweg-Bobotsov, Beverwijk 1966.

 13 KR–Q1   B–Q3

This line, suggested by the Russian analyst Voronkov, is one of the critical lines, but it has not been tried yet in master play. The main point is that Black threatens 14 . . . N–QN5 15 B–N1? B–B5 winning the exchange, whereas if Black had exchanged pawns at move 11, White would meet . . . B–Q3 by N–K4, e.g. 15 . . . N×N 16 Q×N P–B4 17 Q–K3! and Black has yet to find a satisfactory way of freeing his game. But with the black pawn still at d5, White cannot force this line; if you do not like the idea of playing a move like 14 P–QR3, you could employ Keres's set-up instead: 11 R–B1 R–B1 12 R–K1 and if 12 . . . N–QN5 13 B–N1 Anyway, it is clear that Black has many ways of going wrong in the first dozen moves, while White has possible alternatives in the lines based on QN–Q2.

Variation 4

 5 . . .   B–K2
 6 N–B3   P–Q4
 7 0–0   0–0(*159*)

This is less committal. Although positions similar to Variation 3 can arise, Black at least need not fear lines based on B–QN5+.

 8 Q–K2

8 P–N3 P–B4 9 B–N2 BP×P leads to Variation 3.

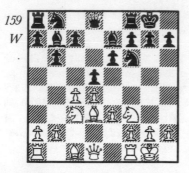

159
W

8 ...   P–B4

Black might do better to try 8 ...
N–K5!?, or 8 ... QN–Q2 (so as
eventually to recapture on QB4 with
the knight).

9 QP×P

With this move, White strikes out in a
new direction.

9 ...   QP×P

Another critical line is 9 ... NP×P!?
(9 ... B×P!? even) e.g. 10 R–Q1
Q–N3! 11 P×P P×P 12 P–QN3!
QN–Q2 13 B–N2 KR–K1! with
possibly an edge to White since here it is
Black who has hanging pawns; 11th
Candidates' match game Korchnoi-
Mecking, 1974.

10 B×BP   B×P
11 P–K4!   QN–Q2

11 ... KN–Q2 would be safer. Now
we follow the game Petrosian–Karpov,
41st USSR Ch 1973:

12 P–K5!   B×N
13 P×B   N–R4
14 R–Q1   Q–K2
15 P–B4   P–N3
16 P–B5!   KP×P
17 P–K6!

Black cannot avoid getting a lost
ending now. He tried 17 ... N2–B3 18
P×P+ K–N2 19 Q×Q B×Q 20 N–N5!
QR–B1 21 B–N3 P–QR3 22 N–Q4
R×P but after 23 B–K3! N–N5 24 B×R
(24 B–K6!?) 24 ... K×B 25 QR–B1 the

former World Champion's remorseless
technique did not fail. The final phase is
worth studying as an example of the
correct exploitation of the advantage of
the exchange for a pawn: 25 ... R–B4
26 K–N2 N4–B3 27 B–Q2 R–Q4 28
B–K1 P–QR4 29 N–B3 R×R 30 R×R
N–K5 31 N–Q2 N–Q3 32 P–N3 N–K4
33 N–N1 K–K3 34 N–B3 N4–B2 35
P–B3 B–Q1 36 B–B2 N–B1 37 N–N5
N1–Q3 38 N–Q4+ K–Q2 39 B–N3
B–K2 40 K–B1 B–B3 41 N–N5 B–K2 42
P–KR4 K–K3 43 N–Q4+ K–Q2 44
K–N2 B–B3 45 N–N5 B–K2 46 P–R4
This brings the tentative phase to an
end. White's adjournment analysis has
convinced him that if Black marks time
with 46 ... K–K3 47 N–Q4+ K–Q2
then 48 P–R5 followed by P×P will
begin to open a way for the rook into
Black's position. So Karpov tried 46 ...
P–R3 but Petrosian continued 47
P–R5! P×P 48 B–B2 B–Q1 49 N–Q4
P–B5 50 N–K2 K–B3 51 N×P P–R5 52
N–N6 N–N2 53 P–B4 B–B3 54
R–QB1+ N–B4 55 K–R3 N–Q3 56
B×N! P×B 57 N×P P–R4 58 N–B3
K–Q4 59 R–Q1+ B–Q5 60 N–Q2
K–K3 61 K–N3 N–B4+ 62 K–B3
P–R5 63 N–B4 B–B6 64 K–N4 B–N5 65
R–Q3! Black resigned. The rook
dominated the ending with the
minimum of movement! At the end,
Black is in zugzwang: 65 ... B–K8 66
N–K3! or 65 ... K–B3 66 R–Q5
winning the KRP.

The Bogoljubow Variation
1 P–Q4   N–KB3
2 P–QB4   P–K3
3 N–KB3   B–N5+

We recommend this as the safest
answer to 3 N–KB3. The Bogoljubow
has the great advantage that there are

few tactical traps contained in it, which makes it very suitable for adoption by players who have· neither time nor inclination to gain a wide acquaintance with lines requiring exact knowledge of the order of moves. If Black keeps his strategical aims well in the foreground of his play in the Bogoljubow, White will find it almost impossible to surprise him.

    4 B–Q2

4 QN–Q2 avoids the bishop exchange, but threatens nothing. Black's simplest reply is 4 . . . 0–0 (4 . . . *P–B4?!* 5 *P–QR3!* or *4* . . . *P–Q4 5 Q–R4+*) 5 P–K3 P–Q4 6 P–QR3 B–K2 (*6* . . . *B×N+ 7 Q×B P–QN3* is possible.) when:

a) 7 B–Q3 P–B4! 8 0–0 P–QN3 9 BP×P KP×P 10 P–QN3 B–R3! 11 B×B N×B 12 Q–K2 N–B2! 13 B–N2 N–K3 14 N–K5 R–B1 and Black stands well; Drimer-Gipslis, Romania–Latvia 1967.

b) 7 P–QN4 P–QN3 8 B–N2 (*8 P–B5 P×P 9 NP×P N–K5!* or *9 QP×P N–K5 10 B–N2 P–B4!=*) 8 . . . P–B4 9 QP×P NP×P 10 P–N5 P–QR3 11 P×P B×P 12 Q–B2 N–B3 13 B–Q3 is a line suggested by the East German master Malich. However, it is not compulsory for Black to play . . . P–B4; he could develop his QB instead.

    4 . . .   Q–K2

This is more elastic than 4 . . . B×B+ which can follow later on. Bronstein experimented with 4 . . . P–QR4!?, but the weakening of Black's QN4 does not seem justified if White avoids 5 B×B?!

    5 P–KN3

This is better than:

a) 5 P–K3 P–Q4 or 5 . . . P–QN3 or 5 . . . B×B+, all equalizing.

b) 5 N–B3 P–QN3 and Black has a good variation of the Nimzo-Indian, because of his grip on K5, e.g. 6 P–K3 B×N 7

B×B N–K5 Marshall-Capablanca, Berlin 1928.

    5 . . .   N–B3(*160*)

This move is generally considered best, but other ideas are:

a) 5 . . . P–QN3 6 N–B3 B–N2 7 B–N2 0–0 8 0–0 P–Q3 9 P–QR3 B×N 10 B×B B–K5 11 P–QN4 QN–Q2 12 Q–N3 P–QR3 with complicated play; A. Zaitsev-Petrosian, Moscow 1969.

b) 5 . . . 0–0 6 B–N2 B×B+ 7 Q×B (*7 QN×B!?*) 7 . . . P–Q3 8 N–B3! P–K4 9 0–0-Pachman; White has more space and can eventually prepare active play in the centre or on the K-side

160
W

    6 B–N2

In the 4th Korchnoi-Petrosian Candidates' match game 1971, White surprised his opponent with 6 N–B3!? and after 6 . . . B×N? 7 B×B N–K5 8 R–B1 0–0 9 B–N2 P–Q3 10 P–Q5 N–Q1 11 P×P P×P 12 0–0 Black had to choose between exchanging pieces (allowing the threat of P–B5) or allowing White to keep the two bishops. However, as Holmov pointed out, 6 . . . 0–0 is better as there is no need to exchange until White takes a move out to play P–QR3.

    6 . . .   B×B+

    7 QN×B

Not 7 Q×B N–K5 8 Q–B2 Q–N5+ Böök-Keres, Stockholm 1944; Black stood well.

7 ...   P–Q3
8 0–0   P–QR4

This restrains White on the Q-side. In a closed position like this, there need be no hurry about castling–it cannot be prevented eventually. Now White can play:

9 *P–K4* – Variation 1
9 *Q–B2* – Variation 2

Variation 1

9 P–K4   P–K4
10 P–Q5   N–QN1
11 N–K1   QN–Q2

Another good line is 11 ... P–KR4!? 12 P–KR4 B–N5 13 P–B3 B–Q2 when White has to abandon his usual idea of attacking the enemy king by P–KB4–5. The continuation of the game Bondarevsky-Furman, 16th USSR Ch 1948, was 14 N–Q3 N–R3 15 Q–K2 0–0 16 Q–K3 KR–K1 17 K–R2 P–KN3 18 B–R3 K–N2 19 B×B N×B 20 P–N3 N–N5! 21 N–K1 P–QB3! and Black had good winning chances.

12 N–Q3   P–QN3
13 P–QN3   N–B4
14 Q–B2   P–KR4

Black, having blocked the centre and the Q-side, begins operations on the K-side. Now, as in the previous note, Black does not castle (because of 15 P–KB4 P×P 16 P×P threatening P–K5) but instead threatens ... P–KR5, a typical motif, forcing a weakening of the white king's field. White can prefer a different kind of weakness by 15 P–KR4 but after 15 ... N–N5 Black's knight is well-placed for observing any White activity, and he has a completely satisfactory game; Nedeljović-Petrosian, Belgrade 1954.

Variation 2

9 Q–B2

Now we follow a game Morcken-Pirc, Amsterdam 1954. The text move begins a manoeuvre which does not interfere with Black's plans, and is not so forceful as 9 P–K4.

9 ...   0–0
10 Q–B3   B–Q2

11 KR–Q1 KR–K1 12 P–N3 (This was the last moment for *12 P–K4*, and if *12 ... P–K4 13 P–Q5*.) 12 ... P–K4 (Now if *13 P–Q5 N–Q5 14 N×N P×N 15 Q×QP Q×P* the scope of Black's pieces is enhanced.) 13 P×P P×P 14 N–B1 B–N5 15 Q–N2 P–K5 16 N–Q4 Q–K4 17 P–B3 QR–Q1! (A neat zwischenzug which gains material. White's reply is forced, for if *18 P–K3 P×P* and the knight is pinned.) 18 P×B N×N 19 K–R1 N×KNP (Black has won a pawn and retains his positional advantage. The interest from now on lies in the powerful way in which Pirc uses the excellent outposts for his knights in combination with mating threats by his heavy pieces.) 20 P–K3 N–B6 21 Q–K2 Q–B3 22 P–KR3 P–B3 (The first of a number of neat tactical points: if 23 P×N Q–R3+.) 23 QR–N1 Q–R3 24 R–R1 P–KB4 25 QR–B1 N5–K4 26 R–R1 P–KN4 27 QR–N1 P–N5 28 P–KR4 Q–N2 29 Q–QB2 N–Q6 30 P–R3 Q–B6! 31 R.Q1–QB1 (*31 Q×Q N–B7* mate) 31 ... P–B4 32 R–R1 R–Q3 33 B×N Q×Q 34 R×Q NP×B 35 K–N1 N–K4 36 R–N1 N–N5 37 R.B2–B1 R.K1–Q1 38 P–N4 RP×P 39 P×P P×P 40 R×P R–Q8 41 R–B3 R×N+ White resigned.

11 THE KING'S INDIAN DEFENCE

(from White's viewpoint)

Strange as it may seem, we do not recommend this famous defence for club play or weekend tournaments. To practise it, one needs not only a style of play which revels in complicated positions, but also one which can adapt itself to cool defence, difficult positional warfare, and strategical movements on opposite wings, all of which are encompassed by this opening. Further, the King's Indian addict needs a thorough knowledge of the order of moves and the many slightly differing transpositional lines in the commonly-played system where White fianchettos his KB and occupies the centre.

Dangers arising from inadequate knowledge of a particular variation are not confined to one side only, so we advise the club player confronted with the King's Indian to avoid the well-known fianchetto, Sämisch and Classical variations, and instead play either for all-out attack with the Four Pawns Attack or choose the flexible Averbakh Variation.

1 P–Q4	N–KB3
2 P–QB4	P–KN3
3 N–QB3	B–N2
4 P–K4	P–Q3

White should now choose between:
5 P–B4!? – Four Pawns
5 B–K2 – Averbakh

The Four Pawns Attack
5 P–B4!?
This move gives White an impressive wall of pawns, but puts him behind on development. It can still be played as a speculative attacking line, which we shall illustrate by one game: Szabo-Zuckerman, Las Vegas 1973.

5 ...	0–0
6 N–B3	P–B4

Black must strike a blow against the white centre without delay. 6 . . . P–K4 is less effective, as after 7 BP×P! P×P 8 P–Q5! P–B4 9 B–N5! the blockading manoeuvre ... N–K1–Q3 has been prevented. Vladimirov-Nezhmetdinov, USSR 1954, continued 9 . . . P–KR3 10 B–R4 P–KN4 *(10 . . . Q–N3 11 Q–Q2 N–R4 12 B–B2!)* 11 B–N3 N×KP 12 N×N P–B4 13 B–Q3! favouring White.

7 P–Q5	P–K3
8 B–K2	P×P
9 BP×P*(161)*	

The best practical chance at club level, although 9 KP×P (aiming for an eventual attack with P–KB5) or the wild 9 P–K5?! also come into consideration.

9 ...	R–K1

Also important:
a) 9 . . . P–QN4!? 10 B×P *(10 P–K5!? is unclear.)* 10 ... N×KP 11 N×N Q–R4+ 12 K–B2 Q×B 13 N×QP leads to lines in which Black should recover

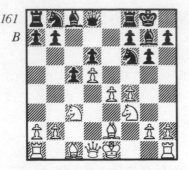

161
B

his pawn, but with a somewhat inferior pawn structure.

b) 9 ... N–R3 10 P–K5! with a strong centre for White.

c) 9 ... B–N5 10 0–0 QN–Q2 11 P–KR3 B×N 12 B×B R–K1 13 P–KN4 P–KR3 14 P–KR4 and Black has little counterplay; Peev-Bohosian, Bulgarian Ch 1971. However, the Scottish master Pritchett prefers 12 ... P–QR3! 13 P–QR4 R–N1 14 P–R5 N–K1!? or 14 ... P–QN4.

10 P–K5!

Only this advance is in the spirit of the Four Pawns.

   10 ...   P×P

10 ... KN–Q2 11 P×P P–QR3 12 P–QR4 N–KB3 13 0–0 B–N5 14 N–K5 is quite good for White.

   11 P×P   N–N5

   12 0–0!

Alekhine's 12 B–N5 has fallen out of favour, because of 12 ... Q–N3! 13 0–0 N×KP 14 N×N (*14 P–Q6!? is a new idea.*) 14 ... B×N 15 B–QB4 Q–N5! (*15 ... Q×P? 16 P–Q6 B–B4? 17 R×B! P×R 18 B×P+*) 16 Q–B3 B–B4 when 17 P–KN4 loses to 17 ... Q×P!

   12 ...   N×KP

   13 B–KB4

White counts on his strong passed pawn and lead in development to give him an attack worth the pawn.

   13 ...   QN–Q2

If 13 ... Q–N3 14 K–R1 and 14 ... Q×P?! fails to 15 N–QR4 Q–N5 16 B–Q2 Q–N5 17 N×N Q–Q5 18 N×KBP! Q×R 19 N–R6+ with a strong attack; Toth-Popov, Budapest 1965.

   14 P–Q6   N×N+

15 B×N N–K4 (He seeks relief in exchanges; if *15 ... P–QR3 16 N–Q5!*) 16 N–N5 (Leading to complications which White had to calculate precisely.) 16 ... B–B4 17 N–B7 N×B+ 18 Q×N B×P 19 N×KR B×R 20 N–B7 B–Q5+ 21 B–K3! (to expose weaknesses near Black's king) 21 ... R–B1 22 B×B P×B 23 Q–B4 (protecting the valuable QP) 23 ... B–K3 (desperation) 24 N×B P×N 25 Q–B7+ K–R1 26 P–Q7 R–R1 27 Q×KP K–N2 28 R–B7+ K–R3 29 Q–R3+ K–N4 30 P–N3 P–KR4 31 Q–R4+ K–R3 .31 Q–B4+ Black resigned.

The Averbakh Variation

   5 B–K2   0–0

   6 B–N5(*165*)

White's last two moves introduce the variation named after the Soviet grandmaster Yuri Averbakh. Black has to play very carefully to avoid suffering either a strong attack on his king (see diagram 162 or a bad ending (diagram 163). Diagram 164 shows the kind of position he should seek.

Averbakh-Panno, Buenos Aires 1954 (*162*).

Black unwisely closed the centre, leaving White free to launch a pawn storm that led eventually to the decisive opening of the KR-file. The game went 10 P–KN4! N–K1 11 P–R4 P–B4 12 P–R5 P–B5 13 P–N5! R–B2 14 B–N4 Q–Q1 15 B×B Q×B 16 N–B3 B–B1 17 K–K2! R–N2 18 R–R4 N–Q2 19 P×P

162
W

P×P 20 Q–R1 B–K2 21 R–R8+ K–B2
22 Q–R6 N–B1 23 R–R1 R–QN1 24
B×P! Q–B2 (*24 ... P×B 25 R–R4*) 25
Q–R2 N–Q2 26 Q–R3 N–B1 27
R×N+! K×R 28 Q–K6 R–N1 29
N–R4 B–Q1 30 N×P+ K–N2 31 N×P
Black resigned.

Polugayevsky-Uhlmann, Amsterdam 1970

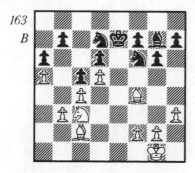

163
B

This type of minor piece ending in
which White has the two bishops is
nearly always winnable. The game
continued 24 ... P–R4 25 B–Q2 N–K1
26 P–N3 B–Q5 27 K–N2 N–N2 28
P–B4 N–B4 29 N–Q1 N–R3 30 K–B3
P–B4 31 B–Q3 K–Q1 32 N–K3 K–K2
33 N–B2 B–N7 34 K–K3 N–B3 35
N–K1 B–Q5+ 36 K–B3 B–N7 37 N–N2
N–Q2 38 N–R4 K–B3 39 K–K3 N–B2
40 B–B2 B–R8 41 K–K2 B–N7 42
B–K1 B–R8 43 P–KN4! RP×P 44 P×P
P×P 45 N×P K–N2 46 N–R4 K–B1 47

B–B5 N–B3 48 B–B8 N–Q1 49 N–B5
N–R4 50 B–Q2 B–Q5 51 N×B Black
resigned.

Uhlmann-Adorjan, Amsterdam
1971

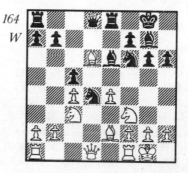

164
W

This is a satisfactory position for
Black, as in return for the pawn his well-
posted pieces give him a strong
initiative. White's safest line now is
probably 13 N×N P×N 14 Q×P N×P!
15 Q×N Q×B 16 Q–B3! but after 16 . . . .
Q–N5 Black's chances are definitely not
worse.

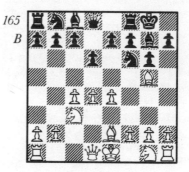

165
B

How should Black meet the
Averbakh? From diagram 165:

6 ... QN–Q2 – Variation 1
6 ... P–KR3 – Variation 2
6 ... P–B4 – Variation 3

One of the first ideas behind
Averbakh's set-up is that Black's
natural King's Indian move 6 ...

P–K4 is a blunder here, because of 7 P×P P×P 8 Q×Q R×Q 9 N–Q5 and White wins at least a pawn.

Variation 1

6 ...   QN–Q2

To force the advance willy-nilly.

7 ·Q–Q2   P–K4
8 N–B3

Olafsson's plan 8 P–Q5 N–B4 9 B–B3!? may also be good. After 9 ... P–QR4 White can try 10 R–Q1 (to forestall ... P–B3) or 10 P–KR4 P–B3 11 KN–K2 hoping for 11 ... P–N4? 12 QP×P! P×P 13 N–Q5 N–K3 14 N2–B3 R–R3 15 P–B7! N×BP 16 P–R5 Olafsson–Savon, Moscow 1971.

8 ...   P–B3

8 .. P×P 9 N×P N–B4 10 P–B3 P–KR3 11 B–K3! KN–Q2 12 0–0–0 leaves White in firm control.

9 0–0   P×P
10 N×P   N–B4
11 Q–B4!

Not 11 P–B3?? N3×P! and White resigned. Holm–Geller, Lugano 1968.

11 ...   Q–K2
12 QR–Q1   N4×P?!

Somewhat better is 12 ... Q–K4 13 B–B3 but White still stands well – Boleslavsky.

13 N×N   Q×N
14 Q×P!   N–Q2
15 B–B3   Q–K4
16 B–B4

White dominates the central lines; Polugayevsky-Geller, Amsterdam 1970.

Variation 2

6 ...   P–KR3
7 B–K3

One of the points of White's fifth move is that ... N–N5 is impossible, so that a subsequent Q–Q2 will gain a tempo by attacking the KRP.

7 ...   P–B4

7 ... P–K4 8 P–Q5 QN–Q2 is complicated, but most masters prefer White. 9 Q–Q2 K–R2!? or 9 ... P–KR4 (Uhlmann-Gligorić, Leningrad 1973) may be all right for Black, but Polugayevsky's 9 ·P–KR3 and Keene's 9 P–KN4 are superior attacking continuations.

8 P–Q5

8 P×P Q–R4 9 B–Q2! Q×BP 10 N–B3 N–B3 11 P–KR3! N–Q5 12 N×N Q×N is like a Maroczy Bind line of the Sicilian; Uhlmann-Gligorić, Amsterdam 1971, showed chances to be about equal.

8 ...   P–K3
9 Q–Q2

Uhlmann has experimented with 9 P×P B×P 10 Q–Q2 K–R2! 11 P–KR3! (not 11 0–0–0 N–B3!). After 11 ... N–B3 12 N–B3 Q–K2 13 0–0 QR–Q1! (Donner-Gligorić, Amsterdam 1971) the game is unclear.

9 ...   P×P
10 KP×P   K–R2(166)

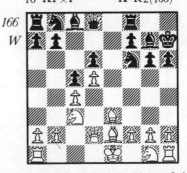

166
W

One of the critical positions of the Averbakh.

11 P–KR3

This is practically the only move seen in master chess. However, on the principle that naive aggression often works well in fast time-limit games, the reader might prefer 11 P–KR4!? as played in Harding-Basman, British Universities' Team Ch 1968. White does not fear 11 . . . N–N5, because he gains valuable time for attack by 12 B×N B×B 13 P–B3 B–Q2 14 P–R5.

11 . . .   R–K1

Or 11 . . . N–R3 12 B–Q3! (*12 N–B3 B–B4 13 B–Q3 Q–Q2! =*) 12 . . . R–K1 13 KN–K2 N–B2 14 0–0 when 14 . . . P–QN4 15 N×P N×N 16 P×N N×P 17 B×NP+ P×B 18 Q×N R–QN1 19 N–B4 favoured White in Polugayevsky-Jansa. Siegen 1970.

12 B–Q3   P–QN4!?

Black seems to get a sufficient initiative for the pawn:

a) 13 P×P P–R3 14 KN–K2 P×P 15 B×QNP N–K5 16 Q–B2 B–B4 17 B–Q3 Q–R5 (Gerusel-Westerinen, Berlin 1971) and now 18 0–0 is essential.

b) 13 N×P N–K5 14 B×N (*14 Q–B2 N–N6!*) 14 . . . R×B 15 R–B1 P–R3 16 N–R3   B–Q5   (or   16 . . . Q–N4) – Westerinen

Variation 3

6 . . .   P–B4
7 P–Q5 (*167*)

167
B

7 . . .   P–K3

Or:

a) 7 . . . . P–N4?! 8 P×P P–QR3 9 P–QR4! – Boleslavsky

b) 7 . . . P–QR3 8 P–QR4 Q–R4 (*8 . . . P–K3 9 N–B3 P×P 10 KP×P*) 9 B–Q2 P–K3 (*9 . . . P–K4?* reaches diagram 162.) 10 N–B3 P×P 11 KP×P Q–B2 12 0–0 B–N5 13 P–R3 B×N 14 B×B QN–Q2 and Black has a passive position. It may be defensible, if he can avoid drifting into endings like diagram 163, but experience has shown White's practical chances to be good.

c) 7 . . . P–KR3 8 B–K3! see Variation 2. Not 8 B–B4!? P–K3! 9 P×P B×P 10 B×QP R–K1 11 N–B3 N–B3 12 0–0 N–Q5! arriving at diagram 164.

8 Q–Q2!

By preventing . . . P–KR3, White maintains the useful pin on the knight.

8 . . .   P×P
9 KP×P   R–K1
10 N–B3   B–N5

One of Black's problems in this kind of position is that it is hardly possible to avoid giving up the bishop pair – this piece just has nothing else to do! But after 11 0–0 QN–Q2 12 P–KR3 B×N 13 B×B P–QR3 (*13 . . . Q–N3 14 Q–B2! P–QR3 15 B–Q2!*) 14 P–QR4 Q–K2 (*14 . . . Q–B2 15 QR–K1 P–KR4!* is relatively best.) 15 QR–K1 Q–B1 16 B–Q1 R×R? (*16 . . . P–R3 17 B–B4 N–R2* is better.) 17 R×R R–K1 18 R×R Q×R 19 B–B2 N–N3 20 P–QN3 QN–Q2 21 B–B4 Q–K2 22 Q–K2! K–B1 23 Q×Q+ K×Q 24 P–R5 diagram 163 has arisen.

Perhaps the most important development in the theory of the QP openings in the last twenty years has been the rise of those forms of King's Indian Defence in which Black combines the fianchetto of his KB not with the advance . . . P–K4, but with . . . P–QB4. The first of these to gain popularity was the Yugoslav Variation against the P–KN3 King's Indian. The success of this led people to try 6 . . . P–B4 also in lines where the white KB is developed at K2, and the most popular forms today are those based on 2 . . . P–QB4. In each case, Black intends to work for play on the QN-file, and on the black squares commanded by his KB, once White has been induced to play P–Q5. Diagrams 168 and 169 show positions in which Black's counterplay is getting well under way, while the next two show what to avoid.

Favourable Positions for Black
Kashdan-Gligorić, Hollywood 1952

168
W

Black's mobile Q-side pawns and K-file pressure are obvious advantages. After 17 B–B2?, he broke through with 17 . . . N×NP! 18 Q×N P–N5 19 N–Q1 N×KP and soon won.

Bondarevsky-Trọianescu, Sczawno-Zdroj 1950

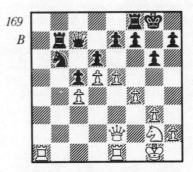

169
B

A typical Benoni endgame – the base of Black's pawn chain is easily defended, whilst White's (the pawn at QB4) is vulnerable; moreover, White's king is the more exposed. Black took advantage of these factors to win as follows: 26 . . . R–R2 27 P×P P×P 28 P–B5 R×R 29 R×R Q–Q1 30 R–R6 R–K1 31 Q–B1 Q–B2 32 P–R4 Q–N2 33 R–R3 N–Q2 34 P×P RP×P 35 P–R5 P×P 36 R–KB3 N–K4 37 R–B5 Q–N7 38 K–R2 R–R1 39 R–N5+ K–B1 40 Q–B5 R–R7 41 Q–B8+ K–K2 42 Q–B7+ N–Q2 White resigned.

Good Positions for White
Grunfeld-Mattison, Debrecen 1925

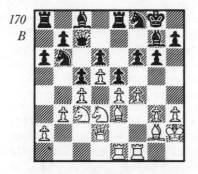

170
B

Black has made no attempt to achieve counterplay either by ... P–QN4 or by ... P–KB4. Consequently, White has the initiative and fine attacking prospects along the KB-file.

O'Kelly-O'Riordan, Dublin 1954

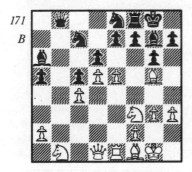

171
B

White has solidified the Q-side, and has shut out the dangerous black KB.
Now we consider in detail:
Yugoslav Variation
Yugoslav against P–K4 and B–K2
Modern Benoni Lines
Miscellaneous Lines

Yugoslav Variation

1 P–Q4	N–KB3
2 P–QB4	P–KN3
3 N–KB3	B–N2

4 P–KN3	0–0
5 B–N2	P–Q3
6 0–0	

Reshevsky introduced a line with delayed castling, but it achieved nothing special: 6 N–B3 P–B4 7 P–Q5 N–R3 8 N–Q2 N–B2 9 Q–B2 (compare the Blocked Variation) 9 ... R–N1 10 P–QN3 P–K3 11 P×P (*11 B–N2 P×P 12 P×P P–QN4 13 0–0 R–K1*) 11 ... B×P 12 B–N2 P–Q4 (justification for the 10th move) 13 P×P KN×P 14 N×N B×B 15 Q×B N×N 16 0–0 Q–B3= Stahlberg-Furman, Bucharest 1954.

6 ...   P–B4(*172*)

Introducing the Yugoslav Variation–so-called because its main ideas were worked out by Yugoslav players in the 1950s.

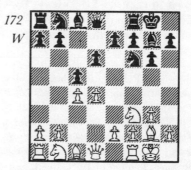

172
W

Now:
7 N–B3 N–B3 8 P–Q5 – Panno
7 P–Q5 – Blocked
7 P×P – Exchange

Yugoslav Panno

7 N–B3   N–B3

This move, inducing White to advance the QP, was one of the main Yugoslav contributions. Formerly it had been thought that Black had to exchange pawns and remain cramped.

8 P–Q5   N–QR4

The counter-attack against the QBP

is an important theme of Black's play in modern lines of the King's Indian. It recurs in the Panno Variation (6 . . . N–B3 instead of 6 . . . P–B4) into which the Yugoslav may transpose.

9 N–Q2

9 Q–Q3 seems logical (to hold up . . . P–QN4), but the queen is rather exposed. Black continues best with 9 . . . P–QR3 when:

a) 10 P–QR4 R–N1 11 N–Q2 B–Q2 12 R–R2 N–N5 13 P–N3 and Black achieves 13 . . . P–QN4 after all; Fairhurst-Barden, Paignton 1952.

b) 10 P–K4 N–Q2 (*10 . . . P–QN4 11 P–K5!? gives White an attack.*) 11 R–N1 P–QN4 12 P×P P×P 13 N×P B–QR3 14 P–QR4 P–B5 15 Q–B2 B×N 16 P×B R–N1 17 B–Q2 R×P 18 B×N Q×B 19 Q×P R×NP 20 R×R B×R Evans-Rossolimo, Milwaukee 1953; multiple exchanges have led to a drawn position.

9 . . .   P–QR3

9 . . . P–K4!? is relatively less analysed. A sample line is 10 P–K4!? (*10 P×Pep!?* – Keene – may be best.) 10 . . . N–K1 (*10 . . . N–N5?! 11 P–KR3 or 11 P–N3*) 11 P–N3 P–QR3 12 B–N2 R–N1 13 Q–B2 P–B4= Smejkal-Hübner, Leningrad 1973. Black, with . . . P–QN4 still in reserve, has adequate counterplay.

10 Q–B2

If 10 P–K4, Black quietly prepares his Q-side advance by 10 . . . B–Q2 e.g. 11 Q–K2 R–N1 12 P–QR4 Q–B2 13 P–R3 P–QN4 Palmason-Barcza, Prague 1954.

10 . . .   R–N1

Others:

a) 10 . . . P–K3 11 P–K4 (*11 P×P B×P 12 P–N3 P–Q4*) 11 . . . P×P 12 BP×P? (*12 KP×P is critical.*) 12 . . . P–QN4 13 R–K1 R–K1 14 N–B1 R–R2 15 P–B3 R2–K2 16 B–K3 (*16 N–K3 P–B5 17 B–Q2 N–N2*) 16 . . . N–B5 reaching diagram 168.

b) 10 . . . B–Q2 11 P–QN3 P–QN4 12 B–N2 and it is doubtful whether the plan, of building up on the QN-file, to which Black is committed will really achieve anything, while White has a long-term idea of breaking through in the centre:

b1) 12 . . . Q–N3 13 N–Q1 KR–N1 14 P–K4 P×P 15 P×P Q–Q1 16 B–QB3 N–K1 17 N–N2 R–R2 18 N–Q3 P–K3 19 B×B N×B 20 P–K5! winning in 40 moves; Keene-Calvo, Lugano 1968.

b2) Somewhat better is 12 . . . R–N1 13 QR–N1 Q–B2 14 P–KR3 R–N2 15 KR–B1 R1–N1 16 P×P P×P 17 P–K4 (Gereben-Johansson, Amsterdam 1954) with the sort of position where victory usually goes to the player with the greater middle-game talent, since the two players' opposing advantages cannot easily be cancelled out by exchanges.

11 P–N3   P–QN4
12 B–N2

A difficult position in which, although some theoreticians hold that White may get a slight positional advantage, practical chances (especially at club level) are certainly not worse for Black. Two examples:

a) 12 . . . P×P 13 P×P B–R3 14 P–K3? (White must try *14 N3–N1!* or *14 P–B4.*) 14 . . . B–B4 15 P–K4 (*15 Q–B1 B–Q6*) 15 . . . B×N 16 N–Q1 B–Q2 17 B×N P×B 18 Q×B N×P winning a pawn and the game; Taimanov-Smekjal, Leningrad 1973.

b) 12 . . . P–K3 13 P×KP (better to keep the tension) 13 . . . BP×P 14 P×P P×P 15 N3–K4 B–N2!= thanks to Black's active pieces; Donner-Penrose, Holland–England 1966.

Blocked Variation

7 P–Q5	N–R3
8 N–B3	N–B2(*173*)

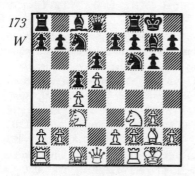

In the diagrammed position, White has tried several moves:

9 P–K4 – Variation 1
9 P–KR3 – Variation 2
9 N–Q2 – Variation 3
9 P–QR4 – Variation 4

9 B–B4? P–QR3 10 P–QR4 R–N1 11 P–R5 P–QN4 12 P×Pep R×P 13 P–N3 B–B4 14 N–R4 B–Q2 15 R–R3 Q–N1 and Black has heavy pressure: Donner-Toran, Barcelona 1952.

Variation 1

9 P–K4

Hoping to break through with P–K5 soon.

    9 ...   R–N1

The order of moves might seem of small importance here, but the text is more accurate than 9 ... P–QR3 to which White does not reply 10 P–QR4 R–N1 (transposing to the column), but 10 R–K1 R–N1 11 P–KR3 (to prevent ... N–KN5) 11 ... P–QN4 12 P–K5:
a) 12 ... N–Q2 13 P×P P×P 14 B–N5 N–B3 15 N–K4 P×P 16 KN–Q2 and besides regaining the pawn, White places both knights on dominating squares.
b) 12 ... N–K1 13 P–N3 NP×P 14

NP×P P–QR4 15 R–N1 B–R3 16 B–B1 led to diagram 171; White's position is the more solid.

    10 P–QR4

If 10 R–K1 P–QN4.

    10 ...   P–QR3
    11 P–R5

If White does not make ready for capturing en passant, his opponent obtains still stronger pressure on the QN-file, e.g. 11 Q–K2 P–N3 12 P–K5 N–K1 13 B–B4 P–QN4 14 RP×P RP×P 15 BP×P B–Q2 16 KR–K1 N×NP 17 N×N B×N Filip-Radulescu, Bucharest 1953. Not only has Black the typical pressure with rook and bishop against ... QN7, but also he can eventually transfer his remaining knight to the formidable square ... Q5.

    11 ...   P–QN4
    12 P×Pep   R×P

13 R–K1 (Keene prefers *13 R–R3*.) 13 ... R–N5 14 P–K5 N–N5 15 P×P P×P= Vaitonis-Geller, Saltsjobaden 1952; Black has excellent counterplay on the black squares.

Variation 2

9 P–KR3	P–QR3

Or 9 ... R–N1 10 P–QR4 P–N3! 11 P–K4 P–QR3 (Najdorf-Petrosian, Santa Monica 1966) when Najdorf should have played 12 N–Q2!

10 P–QR4	R–N1
11 P–R5	N–Q2!

The older move 11 ... P–QN4 is suspect on account of 12 P×Pep R×P 13 N–Q2! P–K3 14 N–N3 P×P 15 P×P B–Q2 16 N–R5! Averbakh-Boleslavsky, 23rd USSR Ch 1956.

12 B–Q2	P–QN4
13 P×Pep	N×NP
14 P–N3	P–K3
15 P×P	N×KP=

e.g. 16 N–K1 (or *16 R–B1 P–Q4*) 16

... P–QR4 17 R–R3 B–Q2 18 N–Q5 N×N 19 B×N Q–B3 = Furman–Korchnoi, 22nd USSR Ch 1955.

Variation 3

9 N–Q2(*174*)

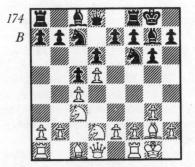

174
B

9... R–N1!?

Or 9 ... P–QR3 10 P–QR4 when:
a) 10 ... R–N1 11 P–R5 P–QN4 12 P×Pep R×P 13 N–N3! transferring the knight to QR5 – van Scheltinga.
b) 10 ... P–N3! 11 Q–B2 B–Q2 12 R–Q1 P–QN4 13 RP×P RP×P 14 R×R Q×R 15 P×P N×NP 16 N×N B×N 17 N–B4 B×N 18 Q×B R–N1 with a quick draw; Dunkelblum-Schmid, Venice 1953.

10 P–QR4 P–N3
11 R–K1

Others:
a) 11 Q–B2 P–QR3 12 N–N3 P–K3 = – Boleslavsky
b) 11 N–N5 is critical, e.g. 11 ... R–N2 (*11 ... P–QR3 12 N–R7 and 13 N–B6*) 12 R–N1 P–QR3 13 N–QB3 P–QN4 14 N–N3:
b1) 14 ... B–Q2? 15 N×BP! P×N 16 P–Q6 R–N3 17 P×N Q×P 18 B–B4 Geller-Bertok, Leningrad 1957.
b2) 14 ... P×BP! 15 N–R5 R–N5 16 N–B6 Q–Q2 17 N×R P×N 18 N–R2 P–QR4 is a promising exchange

sacrifice; Black has chances on the Q-side and against the white QP – analysis.

11 ... P–QR3
12 P–K4 B–N5

12 ... P–QN4 was playable at once, but Black wants to drive White's queen to a square where his second idea of ... P–K4 will have more effect. We are following Donner-Ivkov, Opatija 1953.

13 Q–B2 B–Q2
14 B–B1

To hold up ... P–QN4; but since this is quite ineffective, a much better idea was 14 N–N3 to reply to 14 ... P–QN4 by 15 RP×P P×P 16 N–R5.

14 ... P–K4

Excellent: if White does not take en passant, the typical K-side attack begins by ... N–R4 and ... P–KB4, strengthened by White's denuding his own king of defenders.

15 P×Pep QN×P
16 P–R3

Not only was ... N–Q5 threatened, but if 16 N–B3 N–N5 followed by ... N–K4.

16 ... N–Q5
17 Q–Q1 N–K1
18 N–B3 N×N+

19 Q×N N–B2 20 Q–Q1 N–K3 21 N–K2 B–B3 22 B–N2 Q–Q2 (intending ... QR–Q1 and ... Q–N2) 23 N–B3 KR–K1 24 Q–Q3 N–Q5 25 B–K3 P–QN4! 26 BP×P P×P 27 P×P B×P 28 N×B Q×N 29 Q×Q R×Q 30 B×N B×B 31 R–K2 B×NP 32 R–R6 B–K4 33 B–B1 R–N8 Despite the bishops of opposite colours, the pawn which Black has gained as a result of his superior opening strategy is decisive. Donner-Ivkov continued 34 K–N2 P–N4 35 R2–R2 R–B8 36 R6–R4 B–Q5 37 R–R8 R×R 38 R×R+ K–N2 39 R–R2 K–B3 40 B–Q3 K–K4 41 R–R7 P–B5

42 R–K7+ K–B3 43 R–B7 B–B4 44
P–K5+ K×P 45 B×RP P–B6 46
R–K7+ K–Q5 47 R–K2 P–Q4 48
P–R4 P×P 49 P×P K–B5 White
resigned.

Variation 4
9 P–QR4
Probably best: White will restrict
Black's Q-side activities and then try for
a central advance.
    9 ...   R–N1
Usually played, but Black can also
consider 9 ... P–QR3 10 P–R5 R–N1
11 N–K1 N–Q2 e.g. 12 Q–B2 P–QN4 13
P×Pep N×NP 14 N–QR4 P–K3 15
N×N R×N 16 P×P N×P 17 P–K3
Q–K2 = Marović-Möhring, Zinnowitz
1966.

    10 B–B4
For 10 N–Q2 see Variation 3. With
the fashionable text move, White
attempts to hinder ... P–K3 and ...
P–K4 by pressure against the black QP.
    10 ...   P–QR3
    Others:
a) 10 ... N–R4 11 B–Q2 P–N3 12 P–K4
and Black's KN is decentralized.
b) 10 ... P–N3 11 P–K4 P–QR3 (*11 ...
B–N5 12 P–R3! –* Keene) 12 P–K5
N3–K1! 13 R–K1 P–QN4 14 RP×P
RP×P 15 P–N3 NP×P 16 NP×P
R–N5! 17 B–KB1 B–N5 18 R–R3 P–R3
19 N–R2 R–N3 Vukić-Bogdanović,
Sarajevo 1971; Black can just equalize.
    11 P–R5   P–QN4
    12 P×Pep   R×P(*175*)
This sort of position is typical of
Benoni systems. Positional players tend
to prefer White, because of his solid
centre and more integrated pawn-
structure. But combinative players can
point to Black's control of the QN-file,
his potential pressure on the ... QR1 /
... KR8 diagonal and the vulnera-

bility of the white QBP. Here are a
couple of possible continuations:

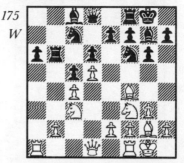

175
W

a) 13 R–R2 R–K1 14 P–N3 P–K4 15
P×Pep N×P 16 N–QR4 N×B 17 N×R
Q×N 18 P×N N–K5 19 Q–Q3
(Korchnoi-Gligoric, Buenos Aires
1960) 19 ... B–B4 20 N–R4 N–B6 21
N×B N×R 22 N×B K×N = – analysis
by Boleslavsky; Black must not be
afraid of unbalanced material
situations in his fight for active
counterplay.
b) 13 P–N3 B–B4 14 N–K1 Q–Q2 15
R–R3 B–R6 16 N–Q3 B×B 17 K×B
N–R4 18 B–Q2 P–K3 19 P–K4 P×P 20
KP×P = Vukić-Tringov, Sarajevo
1967.

Exchange Variation
    7 P×P   P×P
    8 N–B3
Najdorf had some success with the
strange-looking move 8 N–K5 until the
correct reply was found: 8 ... KN–Q2!
9 N×N Q×N! 10 N–B3 N–B3 11 Q–Q5
Q×Q 12 P×Q N–N5 Ivkov-Gligorić,
Yugoslav Ch 1955.
    8 ...   N–B3(*176*)
Symmetrical opening variations are
often in White's favour. But here, if
Black is careful, he should equalize
comfortably, so the Exchange Variation against the Yugoslav is rarely seen
nowadays.

176
W

9 B–K3

9 B–B4 is also tricky:

a) 9 ... N–Q5 10 B–K5! since Black does not want to exchange his KB.

b) 9 ... N–KR4 10 B–K3:

b1) 10 ... Q–R4 11 Q–B1! N–Q5 12 R–K1 B–K3 13 B–Q2 and White has the edge: Ivkov-Tal, Havana 1963. Note that 13 ... B×P? loses to 14 N–Q5.

b2) 10 ... N–Q5 11 Q–Q2 B–N5 12 KR–Q1 B×N 13 B×B N×B+ 14 P×N Q×Q 15 R×Q B×N 16 P×B P–N3 = Geller-Gligorić, Stockholm 1962.

9 ...   B–K3

Black does best to maintain the symmetry at this point. 9 ... Q–R4 used to be played, but 10 B–Q2! then not only contains threats to the queen but also prepares for Q–B1 and B–R6, e.g. 10 ... B–K3 (*10 ... B–B4 11 Q–B1*) 11 P–N3 (Boleslavsky suggests *11 N–QR4!* immediately.) 11 ... Q–Q1 12 Q–B1 N–KN5 13 P–KR3 N5–K4 14 N–KN5! Friedman-Barden, Twickenham 1956.

10 B×P

Others get nowhere:

a) 10 R–B1 B×P 11 B×P Q–R4 12 B–K3 KR–Q1 13 B–Q2 Q–R3 with a clear initiative for Black; Zita-Ragozin, Prague 1956.

b) 10 Q–R4 N–Q5! 11 B×N P×B 12

N–QN5 B–Q2 13 Q–N3 N–K5 and even if White wins the QP it will not benefit him: 14 QR–Q1 N–B4 (Ragozin played *14 ... B×N* followed by ... *N–Q3.*) 15 Q–R3 B×N 16 Q×N B–QB3 17 N×P B×B 18 K×B R–B1 19 Q×RP Q–B2 20 N–B3 B×P 21 QR–N1 R–R1 Ilivitsky-Szabo, Budapest 1955.

10 ...   Q–R4

The symmetry can no longer be maintained. After 10 ... B×P? White plays 11 N–Q4 (or *11 Q–R4 B–QR3 12 KR–Q1*) 11 ... N×N 12 B×N B–QR3 13 P–QN4!

11 B–QR3   KR–Q1

Or the line given by Boleslavsky: 11 ... B×P 12 N–Q4 N×N 13 Q×N QR–B1 14 Q–B4 (Spassky-Tal, 29th USSR Ch 1961) 14 ... N–R4! e.g. 15 Q–K3 B×N 16 Q×B Q×Q 17 P×Q B×KP 18 KR–K1 B–R3 19 B×KP KR–K1 =.

12 N–Q2!   N–KN5

Another Boleslavsky suggestion; now the game is getting very complicated and the better tactician should come out on top, after for example the line given by Keene: 13 N–Q5 N5–K4 14 P–B4 N×P 15 N×N Q–N4 16 N4–K3 B–Q5 when Black seems to be recovering all his material, and leaving White with weaknesses.

Yugoslav v. Classical

The Yugoslav System has not been tried out so often against the Classical King's Indian set-up, where White develops his bishop at K2, but it is playable:

1 P–Q4	N–KB3
2 P–QB4	P–KN3
3 N–QB3	B–N2
4 P–K4	P–Q3
5 N–B3	0–0

5 ... P–B4 should transpose, as

White won't play 6 P×P Q–R4 7 P×P? N×P etc.

6 B–K2   P–B4(*177*)

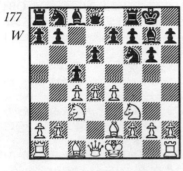

177
W

7 0–0

7 P–Q5 is helpful to Black, who can reply either 7 ... N–R3 or 7 ... P–K3 – in either case transposing below unless White meets 7 ... P–K3 by 8 P×P?! P×P 9 0–0 N–B3 10 P–KR3 Q–K2= Newman-Barden, Hastings 1953.

7 ...   N–B3

7 ... P×P leads to positions of the Maroczy Bind type, while 7 ... N–R3!? 8 R–K1 P×P 9 N×P N–B4 10 B–B1 P–QR4 11 P–B3 B–K3 (Rajagopal-Harding, Wijk aan Zee 1972) is also just about playable.

8 P–Q5   N–QR4

9 B–B4

Against 9 P–KR3 Black counter-attacks strongly by 9 ... P–QR3 10 B–K3 R–N1 11 Q–B2 B–Q2 12 P–QR4 N–K1 13 B–Q3 Q–B1 14 K–R2 P–B4 Morry-Barden, Birmingham 1952.

9 ...   N–R4

10 B–K3   P–K4

11 P×Pep   B×P

12 Q–R4 P–QR3 13 QR–Q1 N×BP 14 B×N P–QN4 with sharp play and equal chances; Maderna-Geller, Argentina USSR 1954.

Modern Benoni Lines

1 P–Q4   N–KB3

2 P–QB4   P–QB4

Originally a way of reaching the Yugoslav Variation (avoiding the Exchange line) this move is now commonly played with quite different ideas in mind.

3 P–Q5(*178*)

Others:

a) 3 P×P P–K3 followed by 4 ... B×P with easy equality.

b) 3 N–KB3 P×P 4 N×P is a harmless form of the English Opening. Black meets it best by 4 ... P–K3 5 P–KN3 (*5 N–QB3 B–N5! 6 N4–N5 P–Q4!*) 5 ... P–Q4 6 B–N2 P–K4 7 N–KB3 P–Q5 8 0–0 N–B3 9 P–K3 B–K2 10 P×P= Ilivitsky-Keres, 16th USSR Ch 1948.

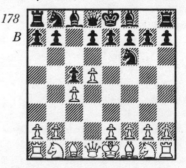

178
B

Now:

3 ... P–Q3 – Hromadka

3 ... P–K3 – Tal

3 ... P–QN4!? – Benko

Hromadka System

3 ...   P–Q3

This (or 3 ... P–KN3 first) was the oldest form of the Modern Benoni.

4 N–QB3   P–KN3

5 P–K4

5 P–KN3 leads to the Yugoslav Variation.

5 ...   B–N2

6 B–K2

White can also transpose to the Four Pawns Attack (chapter 11, p. 143) by 6 P–B4!? 0–0 7 N–B3 P–K3 8 B–K2.

| 6 ... | 0–0 |
| 7 B–B4 | |

Following an old recommendation by Pachman. 7 B–N5 transposes to the Averbakh (Variation 3) but that has less point now that Black has already played ... P–B4.

| 7 ... | N–R3! |

Pachman analysed 7 ... QN–Q2 8 N–B3 P–QR3 9 0–0 Q–B2 10 P–KR3:

a) 10 ... N–K4? 11 N×N P×N 12 B–K3 N–K1 13 N–R4 P–N3 14 P–QN4 and White stands well.

b) 10 ... R–N1 11 Q–Q2! (*11 P–QR4 N–K4*) 11 ... R–Q1 12 QR–K1 N–K4 13 N×N P×N 14 B–R6 with an edge to White.

| 8 N–B3 | N–B2 |
| 9 0–0 | |

9 Q–Q2 might be more precise. Then if 9 ... N–R4, 10 B–R6.

| 9 ... | P–QR3 |

Keene suggested 9 ... N–R4 10 B–K3 P–K4 as a reasonable alternative. Now we follow Hecht-Filipowicz, Bath 1973:

10 P–QR4	B–N5
11 P–R5	R–N1
12 N–K1	B×B
13 Q×B	P–QN4=

14 P×Pep R×P 15 N–Q3 P–K3!? 16 KR–N1 P×P 17 KP×P R–K1 18 Q–B2 N–K5 19 N×N R×N 20 B–N3 Q–K2 and Black's weak pawns at QR3 and Q3 counter-balance White's weak QNP and QBP; moreover White can easily contest Black's apparent control of the K-file. The game ended 21 K–B1 R–Q5 22 R–K1 Q–Q2 23 R.R1–Q1 P–QR4 24 R–K2 N–R3 25 R1–K1 B–B3 Draw agreed.

Tal's Method

| 3. ... | P–K3 |

Black aims for some extra freedom, based on the half-open K-file, at the risk that White may be able to use his QB4 for a knight. The main ideas in this system were discussed in chapter 1 (pages 14–16).

4 N–QB3	P×P
5 P×P	P–Q3
6 N–B3	

For lines with 6 P–K4, see chapter 1.

| 6 ... | P–KN3 |
| 7 P–KN3 | |

Or 7 N–Q2 B–N2 8 N–B4 0–0 9 B–B4 (*9 B–N5!?*) when Donner-Planinc, Wijk aan Zee 1973, went 9 ... P–N3!? 10 B×P (*10 N×QP N–R4!* with interesting complications again) 10 ... R–K1 11 B–N3 N–K5 12 N×N R×N 13 P–K3 P–QN4 14 N–Q6 R–QN5. Black had a strong attack, White's king being stuck in the centre and his pieces discoordinated.

If 7 B–N5, the best plan is 7 ... P–KR3 8 B–R4 P–KN4 9 B–N3 N–R4 e.g. 10 P–K3 N×B 11 RP×N B–N2 12 Q–B2 N–Q2 13 B–Q3 (Tal-Tatai, Las Palmas 1975) 13 ... Q–K2.

7 ...	B–N2
8 B–N2	0–0
9 0–0(*179*)	

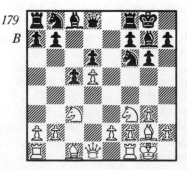

179
B

Black has tried several plans here. We shall look at just two:

9 ... *N-R3* – Variation 1

9 ... *P-QR3* – Variation 2

9 ... Q-K2!? has been experimented with.

9 .... R-K1, in order to hold up P-K4, turns out to be a waste of time after 10 N-Q2 QN-Q2 11 P-KR3 P-N3 12 R-K1 B-QR3 13 P-QR4 P-KR4 14 N-N5! Donner-Milic, Beverwijk 1955. This position illustrates forcibly the dangers of the Modern Benoni: if Black now captures at QN5, he has a very weak backward QRP, but otherwise White brings tremendous pressure to bear on the QP, by N-B4 and B-B4.

Variation 1

9 ...   N-R3

10 P-KR3

Korchnoi's move, denying Black's pieces access to ... KN5 as a prelude to central operations. But in view of Planinc's plan in the illustrative game that follows, White should perhaps try some other move:

a) 10 P-K4 N-B2 11 P-QR4 P-N3 (or *11 ... B-N5=*) 12 B-B4 N-R4 13 B-N5 P-B3 14 B-K3 P-B4 with complications difficult to assess; Zak-Nezhmetdinov, USSR 1951.

b) 10 N-Q2 N-B2 11 N-B4! is critical, e.g.:

b1) 11 ... R-N1 12 P-QR4 (or *12 B-B4 N3-K1 13 N-K4* with an edge – Boleslavsky) 12 ... P-QR3 13 B-B4 N2-K1 14 P-R5 Q-B2 15 Q-Q2 B-Q2 16 B-R6 B-N4 17 N-R3 B-Q2 18 N-B4 B-N4 19 N-N6 Szabo-Malich, Marianske Lazne 1959. Black failed to find Q-side counterplay, and was eventually over-run on the K-side.

b2) 11 ... N3-K1 12 P-QR4 P-N3 or 12 ... R-N1 should be tried.

10 ...   B-Q2!

Renouncing the 'automatic' 10 ... N-B2 since after 11 P-K4 N-Q2 12 R-K1 White has a solid position and central superiority.

11 P-K4   Q-B1

12 K-R2   R-K1

13 R-K1   P-B5

Black has promising counterplay. Marovic-Planinc, Amsterdam 1973, went on 14 P-K5 P×P 15 N×P B-B4 16 B-N5 N-QN5 17 R-QB1 N-Q2 18 N×N Q×N 19 R×R+ R×R 20 Q-Q2 N-Q6 21 R-Q1 P-N4 22 P-KN4 P-N5 23 N-K2 B-K5 24 B×B R×B 25 P-B3 R-K1 26 P-N3 Q×QP 27 P×P Q×KBP 28 N-N1 B-K4+ White resigned.

Variation 2

9 ...   P-QR3

10 P-QR4   QN-Q2

11 N-Q2(*180*)

An alternative plan is 11 B-B4 Q-B2 12 Q-Q2 R-K1 13 KR-B1 P-B5 14 B-R6 (Smyslov-Tolush, Leningrad 1951). In this case White abandons his idea of occupying QB4, and hopes instead that by exchanging the enemy KB and occupying the QB file his KR vis-à-vis the black queen, he will be able to undermine Black's Q-side advance (e.g. by P-QN3). This idea has not been tried sufficiently for a judgement to be made on its value.

11 ...   R-N1

11 ... R-K1 turns out, as usual, to be a loss of time;

a) Donner-Pachman, Hastings 1954–55, continued 12 R-K1 R-N1 13 N-B4 N-K4 (Pachman later preferred *13 ... N-N3*.) 14 N-R3 R-K2 15 P-KR3 N-K1 16 P-B4 N-Q2 17 K-R2

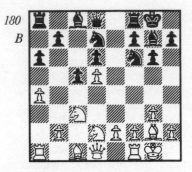

180
B

P–B4 18 P–K4 P×P 19 N–B4 and White had a powerful grip.

b) 12 P–R5 P–QN4 13 P×Pep N×NP 14 N–N3 N–B5 15 R–R4 N–N3 16 R–R2 N–B5 17 Q–Q3 (impossible with Black's rook on QN1) 17 ... N–K4 (*17 ... R–N1! 18 Q×N R–N5* is better.) 18 Q–B2 N–B5 19 N–Q1 N–N3 20 N–K3! and Black can no longer prevent the powerful N–R5.

    12 N–B4!   N–K1

Not 12 ... N–N3 13 N×P Q×N 14 B–B4 winning the exchange.

    13 P–R5   N–K4
    14 N–N6   N–B2
    15 N–K4

Others:

a) 15 P–B4 is less solid, e.g. 15 ... N–N5 16 N–B4 R–K1 17 N–K4 N–N4 18 P–KR3 B–B4! with active play for Black; Donner–Keres, Hastings 1954–55.

b) Boleslavsky recommends 15 Q–N3!, chiefly to prevent ... N–N4; this needs further examination.

    15 ...   B–B4
    16 B–N5   P–B3
    17 B–Q2   B×N

18 B×B P–B4 19 B–N2 N–Q2 20 N–B4 N–K4 Smyslov–Pachman, Amsterdam 1954. White could now find nothing better than 21 N–N6 N–Q2 with a draw by repetition of position.

The Benko Gambit

    3 ...   P–QN4!?

This is the Benko (or Volga) Gambit, about which a lot has been written in the last few years. The gambit appears to have passed its peak of popularity, but it is still playable by those who enjoy steady positional pressure (down the open Q-side files and long black diagonal after 4 P×P P–QR3 etc.) and do not mind being a pawn down.

Unfortunately for Black, White does not have to accept the gambit. We recommend club players to meet it by 4 P–QR4, which avoids most of the prepared analysis and forces Black either to close the position by 4. . . P–N5 (leaving White with play in the centre and on the K-side) or, by taking one of the pawns, to yield White some scope for manoeuvring on the Q-side. Black may be able to equalize the position, but he will not get the sort of game he wants. A sample line is 4 P–QR4 P×BP!? 5 N–QB3 P–Q3 6 P–K4 B–R3 7 N–B3 P–N3 8 N–Q2 B–KN2 9 B×P.

Miscellaneous

Two miscellaneous Benoni systems remain for brief consideration.

The Old Benoni

    1 P–Q4   P–QB4
    2 P–Q5

2 P–K4!? is the Sicilian, Morra Gambit.

    2 ...   P–Q3
    3 P–K4   P–KN3
    4 N–QB3   B–N2

a) White can get a good game by 5 P–KN3 N–KB3 6 B–N2 0–0 7 KN–K2 as in Kjellander–Schmid, 2nd World Corres Ch 1956–9.

b) 5 N–B3 N–B3 6 B–K2 leads to a more heavyweight game:

bl) After 6 ... N–R3 7 0–0 N–B2 8 P–QR4 P–QR3 9 N–Q2 B–Q2 (*9 ... P–N3* is somewhat better.) 10 N–B4! P–QN4 11 P–K5! White won in style in Botvinnik-Schmid, Leipzig 1960.

b2) 6 ... 0–0 7 0–0 N–R3 8 N–Q2 (or *8 B–KB4 N–B2 9 P–QR4 N–R4 10 B–K3 P–K3=*) 8 ... N–B2 9 P–QR4 P–K3! 10 N–B4 N3–K1 11 B–K3 P–N3 12 Q–Q2 B–QR3 13 B–R6 P×P 14 B×B K×B 15 P×P B×N 16 B×B Q–R5 = Nedeljkovic-Fuderer, Yugoslav Ch 1953

The Blumenfeld Counter-Gambit
After 1 P–Q4 N–KB3 2 P–QB4 P–K3 3 N–KB3 P–QB4 (instead of the Queen's Indian) 4 P–Q5 (*4 P–K3 P–Q4* is a form of Tarrasch Queen's Gambit.), Black can play Tal's line by 4 ... P×P 5 P×P P–Q3 or play:

4 ...   P–QN4!?

This has still not been refuted. Accepting the gambit gives Black a powerful centre after 5 QP×P BP×P 6 P×P P–Q4, so the critical line runs 5 B–N5! KP×P 6 P×QP P–KR3 (*6 ... P–Q3!? 7 P–K4 P–QR3 8 P–QR4! B–K2 9 B×N!*) 7 B×N Q×B 8 Q–B2 P–Q3 9 P–K4 P–R3 10 P–QR4! P–N5 11 KN–Q2 B–K2 12 N–B4 QN–Q2 13 QN–Q2 0–0 14 B–Q3 (Lipnitsky-Tolush, 18th USSR Ch 1950) when Black should play 14 ... N–K4 with a tense position and chances for both sides.

13 OTHER DEFENCES TO 1 P–Q4

(from White's viewpoint)

The Dutch Defence

   1 P–Q4   P–KB4

This defence has found favour from time to time with leading masters, such as Botvinnik, Larsen and Korchnoi, and indeed if White replies carelessly, even against a club opponent, Black's attacking chances are prolific. As your opponent will be expecting either the positional 2 P–KN3 or Staunton's 2 P–K4, both of which require you to know lots of analysis, we recommend you to try:

   2 N–QB3

White fights for control of the central squares Q5 and K4.

   2 . . .   P–Q4

Against 2 . . . N–KB3 White furthers his plan with 3 B–N5. Then:

a) A drastic example of what can happen is Polugayevsky-Franco, Havana 1966: 3 . . . N–K5 4 N×N P×N 5 P–KB3! P–Q4 6 P–K3 B–B4 7 P×P B×P 8 N–K2 P–KR3? (more weaknesses) 9 B–KB4 N–B3 10 N–B3 B–N3 11 B–Q3 B–B2 12 0–0 P–K4?! (struggling for air) 13 P×P Q–Q2 14 P–K6! Q×P (or *14 . . . B×P 15 Q–R5+ K–Q1 16 QR–Q1* with a decisive attack) 15 N–N5 Black resigned.

b) 3 . . . P–Q4 can be met by 4 B×N (or 4 *P–B3* below) 4 . . . KP×B (*4 . . . NP×B? 5 P–K4*) 5 P–K3 P–B3 6 B–Q3 with chances for both sides; not 6 . . . Q–N3?! 7 R–N1! N–R3? because of 8 Q–B3 P–KN3 9 P–QR3 B–K2 10

P–KR4 B–K3 11 P–QN4 0–0–0 12 KN–K2 Perez-Prins, Madrid 1959.

   3 P–B3

White could also try with 3 B–N5 or 3 N–B3 to get a positional advantage based on the 'hole' at K5.

   3 . . .   N–KB3

Every move relates to the critical squares, Instead 3 . . . P–K3? or 3 . . . P–B4 would be met by 4 P–K4, while 3 . . . N–QB3 4 P–K4 QP×P 5 P–Q5 also allows White a dangerous initiative.

   4 B–N5

Gambit-lovers can try 4 P–K4!? BP×P (or *4 . . QP×P 5 B–QB4!?*) 5 P×P P×P 6 B–KN5 with good chances.

   4 . . .   N–B3

Black will have weaknesses on the K-file after 4 . . . P–K3 5 P–K4 B–K2 6 P×BP, but perhaps he can find a way through the complications that arise from 4 . . . P–B4!? 5 P–K4!?

After the text move, Bronstein-Slepukhov, Moscow 1948, continued 5 Q–Q2 P–K3 6 P–K4!? QP×P 7 0–0–0 B–N5 8 P–QR3 B–R4 (*8 . . . B–K2* may be better.) 9 B–QB4 0–0 10 KN–K2 P×P 11 P×P K–R1 12 Q–K1 Q–K1 13 Q–N3 and in return for his pawn White controls the centre and has attacking chances on the KN-file.

The Grünfeld Defence

   1 P–Q4   N–KB3
   2 P–QB4   P–KN3
   3 N–QB3   P–Q4

This defence reacts violently against the player who tries to over-run it. An example is the game Canal-Gligorić, Dubrovnik 1950, which continued 4 B–N5 N–K5 5 P×P N×B 6 P–KR4 N–K5 7 N×N Q×P 8 N–QB3 Q–QR4 9 P–K3 B–N2 10 B–B4 P–QB4 11 Q–B3 0–0 12 N–K2 P×P 13 P×P N–B3 14 P–R5 N×P 15 N×N B×N 16 P×P RP×P 17 0–0–0 Q–KN4+ 18 R–Q2 B–KB4 19 N–Q5 QR–B1 20 N×P+ Q×N 21 R×B Q–N4+ White resigned. If the queen interposes, 22 . . . Q×Q+ followed by 23 . . . P–QN4 wins a piece.

Against the Grünfeld, White has numerous playable alternatives at his fourth move, but Black will be prepared for the well-known forcing lines based on 4 P×P N×P 5 P–K4 or on 4 B–B4. Therefore, we recommend that you keep the game in positional channels with the little-known line:

  4 P×P   N×P
  5 Q–N3 N–N3

There is no reasonable alternative, as 5 . . . B–K3? loses the QNP, 5 . . . N–KB3 would block the KB, and 5 . . . P–B3 6 P–K4 leaves White with the lion's share of the centre.

  6 N–B3   B–N2
  7 B–B4   B–K3

7 . . . B×P? loses to 8 0–0–0 threatening 9 P–K3.

  8 Q–B2   N–B3
  9 P–K4! (*181*)

This move is very embarrassing for Black's minor pieces, whereas 9 P–K3 N–N5 10 Q–Q1 0–0 11 B–K2 P–QB4 (Padevsky-Hort, Monte Carlo 1968) gives Black good play.

  9 . . .   N–N5

White's QP is taboo:
a) 9 . . . N×P? 10 N×N B×N 11 N–N5!
b) 9 . . . B×QP? 10 N–QN5 R–QB1 11 R–Q1.

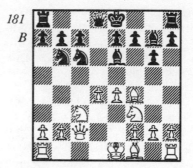

181
B

c) 9 . . . 0–0? 10 P–Q5 N–N5 11 Q–N3.
  10 Q–Q1

It will not be easy for Black to organise play against the pawn centre, e.g. 10 . . . P–QB3 11 P–KR3 or 10 . . . B–N5 (*10 Q–N1*, to avoid the pin, is also good.):
a) 11 B–K2 0–0! (*11 . . . B×N* etc. is too risky with the king in the centre.) 12 0–0!? B×N 13 B×B B×P 14 N–N5 B×NP 15 QR–N1 Q×Q 16 KR×Q N–R5! and Black stands well
b) 11 Q–N3! when:
b1) 11 . . . N–R3 12 N–K5 B×N 13 P×B or 13 B×B P–KB3 with interesting complications.
b2) 11 . . . N–B3 12 B–QN5! (*12 N–N5? B×N*) 12 . . . B×N 13 P×B and if 13 . . . B×P (*13 . . . Q×P 14 R–Q1*) White has 14 R–Q1 0–0 15 B×N P×B 16 B–K5 P–QB4 17 N–N5 with good chances–analysis.

The Old Indian Defence

  1 P–Q4   N–KB3
  2 P–QB4 P–Q3

This can be a way of entering the King's Indian Defence, or can lead to independent set-ups with the black bishop played to K2.

  3 N–QB3 P–K4

Larsen tried 3 . . . B–B4!? a few times. A good line for White is 4 P–KN3 P–K4

5 B–N2 P–B3 6 P–K4 B–N5 7 P–B3 B–K3 8 P–Q5 P×P 9 BP×P B–Q2 10 B–K3 N–R3 11 KN–K2 B–K2 12 0–0 0–0 13 Q–Q2 Krogius-Vasyukov, 32nd USSR Ch 1964–5.

4 N–B3	QN–Q2

If 4 . . . P–K5 5 N–Q2 B–B4 6 P–K3 (Pachman suggested 6 P–KN4!) 6 . . . P–B3 7 B–K2 P–Q4 8 Q–N3 Q–Q2 9 P×P P×P 10 P–B4! P×Pep 11 N×P B–Q3 12 N–K5! B×N 13 P×B and Black's QP is very weak; Smyslov-Bronstein, 17th USSR Ch 1949.

5 B–N5	B–K2

Not 5 . . . P–KN3 6 P×P P×P 7 N×P N×N 8 Q×Q+ K×Q 9 B×N+–a trap worth knowing.

6 P–K3	0–0
7 B–K2	P–B3

If 7 . . . N–K1 8 B×B Q×B 9 0–0 P–QB3 10 P–QN4 P–K5 11 N–Q2 KN–B3 12 Q–B2 R–K1 13 QR–K1 N–B1 14 P–B3 P×P 15 B×P N–K3 16 N–K4 (Fuderer-Phillips, Hastings 1954–55) and White is already en route to one of his fundamental objectives in this line, the posting of a knight on Q6.

8 0–0	R–K1

8 . . . N–K1 9 B×B Q×B 10 Q–B2 P–KB4 11 P–QN4 P–KN4 (Filip-Barcza, Budapest 1954) is sharp, but still in White's favour.

9 Q–B2	Q–B2
10 P–KR3	

a) 10 . . . N–B1 11 B–R4 N–N3 12 B–N3 B–B1 13 P×P P×P 14 P–QR3 B–Q2 15 P–N4 with a slight but definite initiative for White; Flohr-Lilienthal, Budapest 1950.

b) 10 . . . B–B1 11 KR–Q1 P–KN3 12 QR–N1 P–QR4 13 P–QR3 B–N2 14 P–QN4 RP×P 15 RP×P N–B1 (Nievergelt-Schmid, Amsterdam 1954) and now White should have played 16 P–B5! P×QP 17 P×P.Q6 Q×P 18 N×P

N–K3 19 N–B5 with better-coordinated pieces.

The Budapest Defence

1 P–Q4	N–KB3
2 P–QB4	P–K4

This is sometimes tried by combinative players hoping to catch the opponent off-balance, but if White meets the gambit correctly it is unsound.

3 P×P	N–N5

3 . . . N–K5? (in order to cause trouble by . . . B–N5+) is simply refuted by 4 P–QR3:

a) 4 . . . N–QB3 5 N–KB3 B–B4 6 P–K3 threatening both 7 Q–Q5 and 7 P–QN4;

b) 4 . . . P–Q3 5 Q–B2 B–B4 6 N–QB3 N×P 7 Q×B N×R 8 P–K6 P×P 9 Q×P+ Q–K2 10 Q–N4 eventually winning two pieces for a rook.

4 N–KB3	

White should be content with a small positional advantage, since 4 B–B4 P–KN4! leads to lively complications, not unfavourable to Black.

4 . . .	B–B4
5 P–K3	N–QB3
6 B–K2	N5×P.K4

7 N–B3 P–Q3 8 0–0 0–0 9 P–QN3 B–B4 10 B–N2 R–K1 11 N–QR4 (Foltys-Bakonyi, Budapest 1948) White obtains the two bishops, and then his pressure on the KR1/QR8 diagonal ensures him a lasting positional advantage.

The Modern Defence

1 P–Q4	P–KN3

This is quite a popular response nowadays. Black hopes for lines like 2 P–QB4 B–N2 3 N–QB3 P–Q3 4 P–K4

P–K4, or 4 . . . N–Q2, or 4 . . . N–QB3 in which he plays a kind of King's Indian Defence in which the advance of his KBP is not obstructed by his KN.

We recommend White to play 2 P–K4, and study the material given on the Modern and Pirc Defences in chapter six.

The English Opening (1 P–QB4)
There are several possible transpositions here into Queen's Gambit and QP openings. We give the most common:
a) 1 P–QB4 P–QB3 2 P–Q4 P–Q4 = Slav Defence;
b) 1 P–QB4 P–K3 2 N–QB3 N–KB3 3 P–Q4 P–Q4 = Queen's Gambit Declined;
c) 1 P–QB4 P–K3 2 N–QB3 N–KB3 3 P–Q4 B–N5 = Nimzo-Indian Defence;
d) 1 P–QB4 N–KB3 2 N–QB3 P–KN3 3 P–K4 P–Q3 4 P–Q4 B–N2 = King's Indian Defence (avoiding the Grünfeld);
e) 1 P–QB4 N–KB3 2 P–Q4 P–K3 3 P–KN3 and now:
e1) 3 . . . P–Q4 4 B–N2 leads into the Catalan, a modern positional opening. The player of the Catalan does not like to be disturbed from the safe and sound development which he expects with it, and accordingly we recommend all types of players who meet it to answer:
e2) 3 . . . P–B4 and if 4 P–Q5 P×P 5 P×P P–QN4, which introduces a sharp early struggle for the initiative with which the Catalan player may be unfamiliar, and which he certainly will not particularly welcome;
f) 1 P–QB4 N–KB3 2 N–QB3 P–Q4 3 P×P N×P is an attempt by Black to transpose into the Grünfeld Defence by 4 P–Q4 P–KN3 etc. A more original treatment is 4 P–KN3 P–KN3 5 B–N2

e.g. 5 . . . N×N 6 NP×N B–N2 7 R–N1 N–Q2 8 N–B3 0–0 9 0–0 P–K4 (9 . . . N–N3 10 N–Q4!) 10 P–Q4! P–QB3 11 P–K4 Q–R4 (11 . . . P–N3 12 B–N5!) 12 Q–B2 P×P 13 P×P with advantage to White; Botvinnik-Symslov, 16th match game 1958.

Black can also turn the game into symmetrical channels with 1 . . . P–QB4, a move which rightly has a reputation for drawishness, or go into a reversed Sicilian by 1 . . . P–K4. A popular line in modern master chess goes 1 P–QB4 P–K4 2 N–QB3 N–KB3 3 N–B3 (or 3 P–KN3 B–N5) 3 . . . N–B3 4 P–KN3 B–N5 e.g. 5 B–N2 (5 N–Q5 P–K5 is complicated.) 5 . . . 0–0 6 0–0 P–K5 7 N–KN5 B×N 8 P×B R–K1 9 P–Q3 P×P = Ree-Benko, Wijk aan Zee 1972.

Queen's Pawn Games
A few other openings with 1 P–Q4 are worth noting.
    1 P–Q4   N–KB3
2 B–N5 – Trompowski
2 N–QB3 – Veresov
2 N–KB3 – Colle
2 P–K3 – Stonewall

Trompowski
2 B–N5 had a slight vogue in 1973–5. However, Hort showed a good line for Black: 2 . . . P–B4 3 P–Q5 N–K5 4 B–R4? (4 B–B4 Q–N3 5 B–B1! = is necessary) 4 . . . Q–N3 5 Q–B1 P–N4 6 B–N3 B–N2 7 P–B3 Q–KR3! Now Black threatens 7 . . . N×B, having

prevented the natural recapture with the RP. Thereafter, Black dominates the black squares.

Richter-Veresov Attack
2 N–QB3 is more dangerous. Black can play for a French Defence with 2 . . . P–K3, or meet 2 . . . P–Q4 3 B–N5 by 3 . . . P–B4 4 B×N (*4 P–K3 N–B3 5 N–B3 B–N5=*) 4 . . . KP×B 5 P×P (*5 P–K3 and 5 P–K4!?* may be better) 5 . . . P–Q5 6 N–K4 B–B4 7 N–N3 B1×P! (since 8 N×B? loses to 8 . . . Q–R4+ 9 Q–Q2 B–N5).

Colle System
2 N–KB3 P–Q4 3 P–K3 P–B4 4 QN–Q2 QN–Q2 5 P–B3 P–K3 6 B–Q3 is a quiet system with which the Belgian master Colle scored many successes in the 1920s. The most convincing way for Black to equalize is simple development by 6 . . . B–Q3 7 0–0 0–0 e.g.:
a) 8 R–K1 Q–N3 9 P–QN3 P–K4 10 P–K4 BP×P 11 BP×P QP×P 12 QN×P N×N.
b) 8 P–K4 BP×P 9 BP×P P×P 10 N×P N×N 11 B×N Q–N3 12 B–Q3 N–B3 13 Q–K2 B–Q2 14 KR–Q1 B–B3=– analysis by Pachman.

The Stonewall
2 P–K3 P–Q4 3 B–Q3 P–B4 4 P–QB3 inaugurates the Stonewall System, in which White intends to solidify the centre by P–KB4 and then build up a K-side attack based on a knight at K5. In club chess this idea often achieves successes because Black replies with routine moves which do nothing to cut across White's plans. However, there are a number of good defensive systems, of which we note two:
a) 4 . . . QN–Q2 5 P–KB4 P–KN3. A K-fianchetto, nullifying the pressure on KR7, is all the more powerful since here White cannot hope to exchange the black-squared bishops. After 6 N–B3 B–N2 7 0–0 0–0 8 N–K5 Q–B2 White's advanced knight can soon be driven off by . . . N–K1 and . . . P–B3, and in the long run the lack of opportunities for the white QB should tell against him.
b) 4 . . . N–B3 5 P–KB4 (*5 N–B3 B–N5 6 QN–Q2 P–K4*) 5 . . . B–N5 6 N–B3 P–K3 7 0–0 B–Q3 8 Q–K1 B×N!, preventing N–K5, is the other plan. Then if 9 R×B Q–B2 10 N–Q2 0–0–0 followed by . . . P–KR4, . . . QR–N1 and . . . P–KN4, Black's attack is the more dangerous.

Reti's Opening (1 N–KB3)
Like the English, the Reti is a subtle modern opening in which the fight for central control is carried on by indirect means. It is rarely seen outside master chess, for its successful execution depends upon deep positional judgement. At club level, the chief value of 1 N–KB3 lies in its transpositional possibilities; White is usually aiming for a King's Indian with reversed colours and an extra move in hand (compare page 83: King's Indian Attack against the French).

For the player who has not the time to study the large number of possibilities after 1 N–KB3, we recommend a King's Indian formation, only delaying a move of the QP until White has committed himself to P–Q4 (when Black can easily transpose into the Yugoslav System) or to P–Q3, when it is safe to copy White's moves for a while. For example, 1 N–KB3 N–KB3 (*1 . . . P–KN3* can throw some players off their stride!) 2 P–KN3 P–KN3 3 B–N2 B–N2 4 0–0 0–0 5 P–Q3 P–Q4 (or *5 . . . P–Q3 6 P–K4 P–K4* etc.) 6 QN–Q2 P–B4 7 P–K4 N–B3 8 R–K1 P–K3 9

P–B3 P–QR4 10 P–K5 (or *10 P–QR4 P–N3* with a good game) 10 ... N–KN5 11 P–Q4 P×P 12 P×P P–B3! (destroying the white spearhead at once) 13 B–R3 N–R3 14 P×P Q×P 15 Q–K2 N–B4 16 B×N Q×B 17 K–N2 B×P! and Black is lost; Dely–Sandor, Hungarian Ch 1953.

Larsen's Opening (1 P–QN3)

1 P–QN3 is still occasionally played, but it should give White less chance of undermining Black's centre than the Reti. After 1 ... P–K4 (*1 ... P–QB4* is also good.) 2 B–N2 (*2 P–QB4* gives Black no problems.) 2 ... N–QB3 3 P–K3 P–Q4 4 B–N5 B–Q3 5 P–QB4 P×P, Larsen's gambit line 6 N–B3 is refuted by 6 ... P×P 7 Q×P (or *7 N×P Q–N4!*) 7 ... Q–K2 as in Sully-Botterill, Welsh Ch 1973, while quieter continuations are inconsistent with White's need to fight for K5.

Bird's Opening (1 P–KB4)

1 P–KB4 can be met in two quite different ways. Firstly, a game illustrating the positional treatment, based primarily on fianchettoing Black's KB: Oette-O'Kelly, Stuttgart 1955. 1 P–KB4 N–KB3 2 N–KB3 P–KN3 3 P–QN3 B–N2 4 B–N2 P–Q4 5 P–K3 0–0 6 P–Q3 P–N3 7 Q–K2

B–N2 8 P–N3 P–QR4! 9 QN–Q2 P–R5 10 B–N2 P×P 11 RP×P R×R+ 12 B×R QN–Q2 13 0–0 Q–R1 14 N–K5 Q–R7 15 N.Q2–B3 N–B4 16 B–B3? N×NP 17 Q–B2 P–Q5 18 N×QP B×B 19 K×B N×N 20 B×N P–B4 21 B–B3 N–Q4 22 B–Q2 Q×P 23 R–B1 Q–N6 24 P–K4 N–B3 25 Q–K1 R–R1 26 R–N1 Q–K3 27 N–B4 N–Q2 28 B–B3 R–R7+ 29 K–N1 Q–R6 30 R–N2 B×B White resigned.

The combinative treatment lies in From's Gambit, which is more dangerous than its reputation: 1 P–KB4 P–K4!? 2 P×P (*2 P–K4* is the King's Gambit.) 2 ... P–Q3 3 P×P B×P 4 N–KB3 with two methods:

a) 4 ... P–KN4 5 P–Q4 (*5 P–KN3* is sounder.) 5 ... P–N5 6 N–N5 (*6 N–K5! Q–B3!=*) is sometimes given as a refutation, but Black can play 6 ... P–KB4 7 P–K4 P–KR3 8 P–K5 B–K2 9 N–R3 P×N 10 Q–R5+ K–B1 11 B–QB4 R–R2! 12 Q–N6 B–N5+! with favourable complications; Zeh-Rothgen, corres 1961–2.

b) Black gets good positional compensation for the pawn by 4 ... N–KB3, e.g. 5 P–KN3 N–B3 6 B–N2 B–N5 7 P–Q3 Q–Q2 8 N–B3 0–0–0 9 0–0 P–KR4 with chances for both sides. The better tactician usually wins in the From.

INDEX OF COMPLETE GAMES

(First named player has White)

INDEX OF OPENINGS AND VARIATIONS